China's Camel Country

Culture, Place, and Nature

Studies in Anthropology and Environment

K. SIVARAMAKRISHNAN, SERIES EDITOR

Centered in anthropology, the Culture, Place, and Nature series encompasses new interdisciplinary social science research on environmental issues, focusing on the intersection of culture, ecology, and politics in global, national, and local contexts. Contributors to the series view environmental knowledge and issues from the multiple and often conflicting perspectives of various cultural systems.

Thomas White

China's Camel Country

Livestock and Nation-Building at a Pastoral Frontier

University of Washington Press Seattle

This book will be made open access within three years of publication thanks to Path to Open, a program developed to bring about equitable access and impact for the entire scholarly community, including authors, researchers, libraries, and university presses around the world. Learn more at https://about.jstor.org/path-to-open/.

Design by Mindy Basinger Hill
Composed in Garamond Premier Pro
Photographs by the author unless otherwise noted
Maps by Evangeline McGlynn

UNIVERSITY OF WASHINGTON PRESS uwapress.uw.edu

LIBRARY OF CONGRESS CATALOGING-IN-PUBLICATION DATA

Names: White, Thomas (Anthropologist), author. | Sivaramakrishnan, K., 1957– writer of foreword.
Title: China's camel country : livestock and nation-building at a pastoral frontier / Thomas White.
Other titles: Culture, place, and nature.
Description: Seattle : University of Washington Press, 2024. | Series: Culture, place, and nature | Includes bibliographical references and index.
Identifiers: LCCN 2023050768 | ISBN 9780295752426 (hardcover) |
ISBN 9780295752433 (paperback) | ISBN 9780295752440 (ebook)
Subjects: LCSH: Pastoral systems—China—Alxa Zuoqi (Qi) | Camels—Social aspects—China—Alxa Zuoqi (Qi) | Camel industry—China—Alxa Zuoqi (Qi) | Politics and culture—China—Alxa Zuoqi (Qi) | Herders—China—Alxa Zuoqi (Qi)—Social conditions—21st century. | Mongols—China—Alxa Zuoqi (Qi)—Social conditions—21st century. | Mongols—China—Alxa Zuoqi (Qi)—Ethnic identity. | Environmental policy—China. | China—Cultural policy. | Alxa Zuoqi (China : Qi)—Social conditions—21st century.
Classification: LCC SF55.C6 W48 2023 | DDC 636.2/9509517—dc23/eng/20240412
LC record available at https://lccn.loc.gov/2023050768

For Ronja and Emil

Contents

Foreword

K. Sivaramakrishnan

AS CAMEL POPULATIONS first declined, then revived, and pastoralists found ways to elude their sedentarization by the Chinese state, these processes intersected with government response to desertification in the northern and western parts of China. Saving grasslands became intertwined with camel keeping in the twenty-first century. Through an engaging analysis of these developments in the last three decades in particular, Thomas White offers an account of the fate of pastoralism, particularly camel culture, in western China. He writes about a region known as Alasha League in western Inner Mongolia, verging on the great Gobi Desert, which has been home to Mongolian pastoralists. They traded in and by camels and sent their products through Mongolia into the steppes of Central Asia and Russia. Thomas White depicts the response of camel keepers to first a decline in Bactrian camels and their habitats in the late twentieth century and later a revival of the camel culture through conservation efforts initiated by the Chinese government in the twenty-first century. He offers a sophisticated view from the western edges of China on the environmental history dominated so much by accounts from the arable zones south and east of Inner Mongolia.[1]

This perspective is a significant contribution. As Kenneth Pomeranz has written in a recent review of the work of David Bello and Jonathan Schlesinger, Chinese environmental history focused topically on agriculture and water. Work on regions beyond the river valleys—mountain and steppe, or along the coast—brought other commodities, forests, and animals and their keepers more integrally into modern Chinese environmental history.[2] The environmental anthropology of China has been a little more wide-ranging in terms of topics and regions. It has recently included works on the arid zone, ethnic minorities, and urban issues, among other things.[3] There has also been a welcome focus in some recent work on the environment and development of the borderlands of China from Tibet to Manchuria.[4]

Thomas White is advancing this work with fresh questions of how an ecological civilization is being imagined in China. As he shows, the Alasha region of Inner Mongolia, where his research is situated, has been visited by forces of commodity extraction and global integration over the last hundred years. It has also become the target of conservation activity in the last few decades. Such activity, as Thomas White goes on to show, results in protection activity directed at landscapes and pastoralists as cultural heritage and for ecosystem services. At the same time larger forces of accelerated economic development unleashed in China since the 1980s had caused a precipitate decline in camel populations in Alasha by the 2000s.

China had also introduced patterns of sedentarization of herders and demarcation of their lands that were detrimental to the survival of pastoralists. Their ability to construct graduated land rights for pasture and other uses through their mobility was constrained. Camel pastures were enclosed and privatized, though not always restricting their freedom to roam. They, pastoralists and their camels, were also targeted for conservation. From the Alasha region such efforts appeared to be a continuation of projects of assimilation that had an older history in China's relations with ethnic minorities. What, however, Thomas White reveals is that conservation also provided local intellectuals and social elites with a language and set of policy priorities through which to resist incorporation and coercion in certain situations.

Thomas White not only questions the extent to which the Chinese state was effective in imposing an environmental vision on Inner Mongolia and its herders. He also identifies the nomination of the Bactrian camel as endangered genetic resource and efforts to preserve it as a source of opportunities to defend local lifeways and deflect some of the absorptive pressure cast on ethnic minorities in China. The endurance of pastoralism, in fact, is a story of adaptation that includes some migrant Han Chinese also becoming pastoralists. At the same time the celebration of camel culture, and the Bactrian camel, fuels efforts to turn the "discourse of frontiers" into a resource for challenging the stigmatization of both the camel and its keepers by turning their primitivity into a biological treasure.[5]

Thomas White, through his situated ethnography, works with local leaders and scientists as they forge alternate visions to what the Chinese government proposes for both development and conservation in the region. Along the way the Bactrian camel becomes cultural and ecological heritage, shapes the making of collective identity and frontier ideologies, and participates in the economy as worker and food.

Thomas White is theoretically wide-ranging, yet admirably clear in his argumentation. In this book he makes an original contribution to the study of pastoralism, environmental questions in China, and animal studies. Food studies, organic farming, and the anthropology of science also get illuminated in later chapters on meat and dairy production. Thomas White takes interspecies or more than human anthropology into exciting new directions by combining it with an analysis of regional political economy.[6] In this way the book connects classical studies of pastoralism in Africa, and Asia, with new orientations in the anthropological study of the environment, nonhuman life, conservation, and agropastoral societies situated at the edges of nation-states.

There is growing interest in finding alternatives to dominant models of economic development that have hastened the planet into the Anthropocene. People wishing to learn from the culture and landscape of Inner Mongolian camel keepers and their struggles to preserve identity, livelihood, and territory—among other native societies in remote parts of the globe adapting to rapid environmental and social change—will come to this work not only from China or East Asia but from around the world.

Notes

1. See Mark Elvin, *The Retreat of the Elephants: An Environmental History of China* (New Haven, CT: Yale University Press, 2006); Robert Marks, *China: Its Environment and History* (Lanham, MD: Rowman and Littlefield, 2011). A useful review may be found in Sabine Dabringhaus, "Perspectives on the Environmental History of China," *Journal of Chinese History* 2 (2018): 281–90.

2. See Kenneth Pomeranz, "*Across Forest, Steppe, and Mountain: Environment, Identity, and Empire in Qing China's Borderlands* by David A. Bello, and *A World Trimmed with Fur: Wild Things, Pristine Places, and the Natural Fringes of Qing Rule* by Jonathan Schlesinger (review)," *Harvard Journal of Asiatic Studies* 79, nos. 1–2 (2019): 275–85. Forest history has now emerged more robustly in China studies. See Ian Miller, *Fir and Empire: The Transformation of Forests in Early Modern China* (Seattle: University of Washington Press, 2020); and Meng Zheng, *Timber and Forestry in Qing China: Sustaining the Market* (Seattle: University of Washington Press, 2021).

3. Many of these contributions are new PhD dissertations. One recent work on the sand drifting from the west into urban centers like Beijing, which brings camel herders to the attention of the Chinese metropole, as Thomas White notes,

is Jerry Zee, *Continent in Dust Experiments in a Chinese Weather System* (Oakland: University of California Press, 2022). But his book has little to say about places like Inner Mongolia and their residents.

4. See, for instance, Jarmila Ptackova, *Exile from the Grasslands: Tibetan Herders and Chinese Development Projects* (Seattle: University of Washington Press, 2020); Emily Yeh, *Taming Tibet: Landscape Transformation and the Gift of Chinese Development* (Ithaca, NY: Cornell University Press, 2013); and Norman Smith, ed., *Empire and Environment in the Making of Manchuria* (Vancouver: University of British Columbia Press, 2017).

5. The term *discourse of frontiers* is used, in many ways anticipating a lot of the discussion around frontiers and resource frontiers in anthropology a couple of decades later, in K. Sivaramakrishnan, *Modern Forests: Statemaking and Environmental Change in Colonial Eastern India* (Stanford, CA: Stanford University Press, 1999). Also see, for more recent and influential discussions of frontiers in human geography and anthropology, Jason Cons and Michael Eilenberg, eds., *Frontier Assemblages: The Emergent Politics of Resource Frontiers in Asia* (Hoboken, NJ: Wiley, 2019).

6. I refer here to Heather Swanson, *Spawning Modern Fish: Transnational Comparison in the Making of Japanese Salmon* (Seattle: University of Washington Press, 2022).

Acknowledgments

THIS BOOK PROJECT has been many years in the making, and along the way I have benefited significantly from the help and support of numerous people. I would like to thank the families who hosted me in Alasha, and all the friends I made there, who appear pseudonymously in this book. I am particularly grateful to the couple I call Batbagana and Sarna for welcoming me into their home and for their generosity with their time and knowledge, and their patience with me, at a time of uncertainty and anxiety for herders in Alasha. Altanuul, who sadly passed away before this book was finished, helped me develop this into an ethnographic project by introducing me to people in Khöövör.

Friends and colleagues in Hohhot provided invaluable support during and after my fieldwork. Particular thanks are due to Professor Nasan Bayar for hosting me at Inner Mongolia University, for his calm assistance as I navigated the complexities of fieldwork in China, and for his pathbreaking scholarship. Tsetsen cheerfully helped navigate various administrative hurdles. I was also fortunate to benefit from the knowledge and experience of Professors Altanbulag and Baohua, and the friendship of many people, especially Daichin, Düüren, Javkhlan, Sargai, Sümbürkhüü, Uyakhan, and Ulaana. Thanks to William White and Ronan Popert for their hospitality at the China University of Geosciences in Beijing whenever I passed through the city.

The book could never have been written were it not for my *bagsh*, Caroline Humphrey. Her guidance, support, institution-building, and vast knowledge of region and discipline are exemplary. Another model of scholarship and mentorship is Uradyn Bulag, who gave unstintingly of his time and expertise, reading multiple drafts of chapters and providing thorough, rigorous comments. Any outstanding errors or omissions are on my head.

I am grateful to Stevan Harrell, who went above and beyond the call of blind peer reviewing duty in reading several drafts, commenting meticulously and generously on what he read, and responding to my numerous email queries following his gracious removal of the cloak of anonymity.

The book was incubated in the unique environment of the Mongolia and Inner Asia Studies Unit (MIASU) at the University of Cambridge. I am very grateful for the material and intellectual support it has provided me over the years. My research on a pastoral region of Inner Mongolia followed in the footsteps of its director, David Sneath, and he has been a constant source of guidance and support during my time at Cambridge. James Laidlaw also provided valuable advice during the early stages of this project. I have benefited from the presence of other long-standing members of the MIASU community, including Hildegard Diemberger, Libby Peachey, Robbie Barnett, and Sayana Namsaraeva, as well as Uranchimeg Ujeed and Hürelbaatar Ujeed, who provided vital assistance as I started my fieldwork in Inner Mongolia more than ten years ago. On numerous occasions over the years Franck Billé has been of great help, despite being on the shores of a distant sea. Ed Pulford read and commented with characteristic astuteness on a draft of the book. I am also grateful for the company and insights of other MIASU peers and friends, Teo Benussi, Joseph Bristley, Joe Ellis, Liz Fox, and Beth Turk. Thanks are also due to Chloe Gayer-Anderson and Anna Clayton for all their help. Others whom I got to know in the Department of Social Anthropology and the wider university also shaped my thinking in many ways, often by kindly reading and commenting on things I had written: Maan Barua, Josh Booth, Emilie Glazer, Nayanika Mathur, Patrick McKearney, David Nally, Emma Pask, Joe Philp, Branwyn Poleykett, Qiruona, Jonas Tinius, Michael Vine, and Max Watson.

I would like to thank my former PI at the University of Fribourg, Agnieszka Joniak-Lüthi, for being an excellent boss, mentor, and friend, and for curating scholarly camaraderie among an extended group of scholars in Switzerland and beyond: Darren Byler, Jessica di Carlo, Hassan Karrar, Lena Kaufmann, Judd Kinzley, Verena La Mela, Till Mostowlansky, Galen Murton, Tim Oakes, Nadine Plachta, Björn Reichhardt, Alessandro Rippa, Eric Schluessel, Rune Steenberg, Emilia Sulek, Zarina Urmanbetova, and Max Woodworth. My thinking about China and its borderlands has benefited from exchanges with all of these people.

I am grateful to Mareile Flitsch for her support and for inviting me to present some of this work at the University of Zürich. Another chapter was presented at the Food Studies Center at SOAS, University of London. Thanks are due to participants there, and especially the organizer, Jakob Klein, for helpful comments. Natasha Fijn, Morten Pedersen, Emily Yeh, and Jerry Zee kindly read and commented on early versions of some of these chapters.

At the University of Washington Press, Lorri Hagman guided this project almost to completion, and I am grateful for her patience, as well as her meticulous editing and advice. I count myself fortunate to have worked with Caitlin Tyler-Richards, as well as K. Sivaramakrishnan and Marcella Landri. Thanks to Eve McGlynn for bearing with me cartographically.

Parts of chapter 4 were published in 2021 in an article that appeared in the *Journal of the Royal Anthropological Institute*. The research on which this book is based was supported by funding from King's College Cambridge and the University of Cambridge. While working on the first draft, I was fortunate to be employed at the University of Fribourg, Switzerland, on a project funded by the Swiss National Science Foundation. I subsequently received a research fellowship from MIASU, which allowed me to continue work on the book. While finalizing the manuscript, I was supported by a grant from the UK's Economic and Social Research Council (ES/W005433/1).

Thanks are due to my siblings, Elisabeth, Cecilia, and William, and my parents, Hugh and Carolinne, for their long-standing support. Finally, this book project has been a feat of endurance on the part of my family, so I am deeply indebted to Suki for her understanding of what I was up to, but also to Ronja and Emil for being delightfully unaware.

xv

Acknowledgments

Abbreviations

ACS	Alasha Camel Society
CPPCC	Chinese People's Political Consultative Conference
BRI	Belt and Road Initiative
ICH	intangible cultural heritage
IMAR	Inner Mongolia Autonomous Region
MPR	Mongolian People's Republic
PES	payments for ecosystem services
PRC	People's Republic of China
RLRG	Removing Livestock and Restoring Grassland
TPA	Targeted Poverty Alleviation

Note on Transliteration

MY TRANSLITERATION of Mongolian terms is based on the Khalkha dialect and the Cyrillic script, because this is closer to the Alasha dialect than the standard dialect of Inner Mongolian. In the case of certain proper names (e.g., Ulanhu), I have adopted the more conventional transliteration.

My transliteration of Chinese follows the standard pinyin system.

Chinese words are indicated with a *C*; Mongolian words are indicated with an *M*.

China's Camel Country

Introduction
Reimagining Pastoralism
at China's Margins

IN AUGUST 2021, a well-known Chinese actor was killed when the car she was traveling in collided with two camels in a remote part of western Inner Mongolia. As the Chinese internet processed the story, the unusual manner of her death meant that celebrity gossip was interspersed with discussion of the particularities of animal husbandry in this border region of Alasha. Popular online news sources reported that Alasha was China's Camel Country (C. Zhongguo Luotuo zhi Xiang) and mentioned the state policies that had been adopted to protect the local Alasha Bactrian camel breed. They noted that camels had to be herded in a free range (C. *san yang*) manner and admired the "smart herding system" (C. *zhineng fangmu xitong*) some herders now employed, which involved the use of satellite technology to check the location of their animals with mobile phones.[1] The fault, most comments seemed to agree, lay with the speeding driver rather than the local herders.

Containing around two-thirds of China's domestic camel population, in 2012 Alasha was formally granted the title of China's Camel Country by the national Ministry of Agriculture (C. Nongye Bu), an occasion marked by a large festival (M. *naadam*) in the small city of Bayanhot. As local Mongol herders in ethnic costume paraded their camels in front of a large stage, officials gave speeches that told of the recovery of the camel population in Alasha and the success of conservation measures adopted in recent years.[2] Camel Country does not fit neatly with established narratives about the fate of pastoralists in China. In recent years scholars and commentators in the West have held up herders as tragic exemplars of the deleterious effects of the Chinese state's authoritarian brand of environmentalism and developmentalism. "China fences in its nomads, and an ancient life withers," declared the *New York Times* in 2015 (Jacobs 2015). Western journalists who traveled to Alasha in the early 2000s brought back stories of resettled herders who still "mourn[ed] their old way of life" (O'Toole 2006). But as the coverage of the car crash made clear, extensive forms of animal husbandry are still found in some parts of China and are being reimagined in the light of novel discourses and technologies. The case of Camel Country requires us to think beyond teleological tropes of pastoralist vanishing and to develop new ways of conceptualizing the complex politics and practices of pastoralism at China's margins.[3]

At the turn of the millennium, camel herding in Alasha appeared to conform to declensionist understandings. In the most populous part of the region, Alasha Left Banner, there were only 30,356 camels left by 2003, down from 190,073 in 1981. Local and national media spoke of the impending extinction of the Alasha Bactrian camel. Once a vital form of transportation across the arid expanses of China's west, by the 1980s these "ships of the desert" were used on only a few local routes in Alasha, mainly to transport salt. Increasingly obsolete as pack animals, the value of camel products such as hair and meat paled into insignificance when compared with the commodity that had transformed western Inner Mongolia at the end of twentieth century: cashmere.[4]

China began to open up its socialist economy to global capital at the end of the 1970s, and in 1980 the Japanese conglomerate Mitsui entered into a joint venture in Inner Mongolia, establishing a cashmere factory in the neighboring region of Yeke Juu, today's Ordos (Bulag 2004b; Waldron et al. 2014). As rural Alasha became part of this global value chain, many herders sold off camels to focus on herding goats. With profits from the sale of cashmere, richer herders swapped their adobe homes for comfortable brick houses on the grasslands.

However, the sandstorms that occurred with increasing frequency throughout the 1990s led to anxiety across Northeast Asia about the ecological costs of this economic boom in the form of grassland degradation. In Alasha, people joked sardonically that the first time Beijingers heard of their remote region was when they discovered on the streets of the capital copies of the *Alasha Daily News* that had been blown there by a sandstorm. As concerned Chinese officials, scientists, and photographers, as well as Japanese NGO workers and Western journalists, arrived in Alasha, it gained the unwanted sobriquet of "the cradle of the dust storm" (Pingjun Ding 2008).

Under Beijing's dust-heavy skies, the scapegoating began. Chinese media

MAP 1. Location of Alasha and Inner Mongolia within China

talked of the need to slaughter goats to protect Beijing (C. *shadiao shanyang baowei Beijing*), and in 2000 Premier Zhu Rongji ordered over 300,000 goats to be culled (Rennie 2000). Their voracious grazing habits were seen to be more destructive than other livestock and their numbers were deemed far in excess of the carrying capacity of the pastures.[5] Official discourse on grassland degradation was shaped by powerful globally circulating narratives of desertification that have been deployed across pastoral regions of the world to dispossess marginalized herders (Davis 2016). These negative understandings were also inflected by China's deeply rooted stigmatization of minority pastoralists as backward and wasteful (Williams 2002).

However, the threatened extinction of Alasha's camels appeared to strike a chord in China and beyond, as the ecological crisis of China's arid western regions was rendered as rivers of camel tears. In 2001, a Japanese TV company traveled with a Chinese environmental activist to Alasha to film a program titled *The Weeping Camel*.[6] The following year, this activist, Lu Tongjing, organized a photography exhibition at Beijing's Museum of Natural History, *The Weeping Camel and the Ecological Crisis of Desertification*, which featured images of scrawny camels, apparently on the verge of starvation (Cui 2002). Alasha's domestic camels thus joined a select menagerie of charismatic wild megafauna, such as the Tibetan antelope, whose endangerment conveyed to the Chinese public the urgency of the environmental problems that have accompanied rapid economic development (Yeh 2014b).

Various explanations for endangerment circulated through China's media. Some focused on market forces and the profit motive, which induced herders to sell off their camels and switch to goats. The characteristic image here was that of mass slaughter. In 2002 one local official gave the following testimony: "Last year, after acquiring a slaughterhouse here in Alasha, one large company alone slaughtered 6,500 camels; once, when they were slaughtering camels, I was there watching. It was a massacre. Even baby camels were being slaughtered, and the camels who were waiting to be killed stood there weeping" (Jiang et al. 2002). Other reports concentrated on the ongoing drought and the worsening condition of the grasslands (Cui 2002). These were sometimes accompanied by images of starving camels and moving, if biologically questionable, descriptions of their inability to locate food, having been blinded by sandstorms (Li Yanchun 2004). In national publications aimed at teenagers, Alasha's camels were recruited to nationalist narratives, with the Japanese blamed for encouraging environmentally destructive cashmere production in China (Li Yanchun 2004).

According to herders in Alasha, however, state policies were also to blame. By the late 1990s, much of Alasha's rangeland had been contracted out to individual households, in line with a policy of privatization implemented in agricultural regions from the early 1980s, as China moved toward a socialist market economy (C. *shehuizhuyi shichang jingji*). Given the large spatial requirements of camels, this policy had a particularly deleterious effect on camel husbandry, since herders were accustomed to allowing these animals to roam freely over collectively owned land. While enclosure was supposed to combat the degradation of the grasslands by preventing the tragedy of the commons (Hardin 1968), critics argued that it had the opposite effect, since in many places herders were no longer able to adopt strategies of mobility to relieve stocking pressure and respond to localized drought (Humphrey and Sneath 1999).

In 2000 the Chinese state initiated the Open Up the West (C. Xibu Da Kaifa) development strategy. This nation-building project targeted the spatially uneven economic development that had come to characterize the era of Reform and Opening Up (C. Gaige Kaifang). Beginning in the late 1970s, these reforms had initially privileged eastern and coastal areas, and rebalancing was deemed necessary to bind the country's poorer western regions closer to the center (Goodman 2002). Reforms were accompanied by a range of policies that addressed the environmental problems of the country's west. The rapid economic development ushered in by the introduction of market reforms in the late 1970s had led to severe ecological problems in these regions: devastating floods on the Yangzi River in 1998, for example, blamed on intensive logging in its upper reaches, had left thousands dead and millions homeless (Lang 2002). As with the sandstorms, these floods created an acute awareness of the ecological effects of China's west on the densely populated heartlands of China proper. The upcoming 2008 Beijing Olympics also created a sense of urgency.

At the turn of the millennium the state implemented a suite of destocking policies under the rubric of Removing Livestock and Restoring Grassland (RLRG; C. Tuimu Huancao). While goats had been singled out for blame, other livestock, including camels, were also initially severely affected. Stories circulated about whole herds of camels being slaughtered, as local officials zealously and indiscriminately applied the destocking policies. In some parts of Alasha, herders were resettled away from the grasslands and had to find new employment, part of a policy of ecological migration (C. *shengtai yimin*) adopted across China (Ptackova 2020). The new settlement of Luanjingtan, created in the south of Alasha in 1993, was pioneering in this respect.

In Inner Mongolia, this vigorous state environmentalism coincided with a mining boom, as the region's mineral resources were funneled eastward to fuel China's breakneck economic growth (Woodworth 2017). For many Mongols, the destocking policies, and the urbanization with which they were correlated, were merely a pretext for opening up Mongol land to mining interests, continuing the ethnicized processes of dispossession that in the nineteenth and twentieth centuries had been characterized by Han Chinese agrarian expansion (Bulag 2004b; Yi Wang 2021). Given the deep association of pastoralism with Mongol identity (Khan 1996), and the Han Chinese character of Inner Mongolia's urban areas, these policies seemed to presage the ultimate assimilation of the Mongols.[7]

In this context Mongol elites in Alasha looked to the conservation of the camel as a means of defending pastoralist land use. Their partial successes in this respect and the resulting shifts in understandings of pastoralism and culture are the subject of this book. By the time I began fieldwork in 2012, many herders in Alasha had moved away from the grasslands, especially in the south of the region; others were anticipating having to sell a large proportion of their sheep and goats to comply with stocking limits, but some herders were being encouraged to herd camels by conservation policies that indirectly buttressed local forms of mobility and attitudes toward land that were supposed to have been replaced by the privatization of tenure.

In Alasha, camel husbandry was now celebrated as local heritage and as an ecologically sound mode of grassland management but also for its economic potential, in light of developments in science and technology. Pastoralism was thus not simply a vanishing form of land use subject to increasing restriction by the state (see also Tan 2018). Instead, Mongol elites in Alasha, their allies among Han Chinese intellectuals, and Mongol scientists based in the regional capital of Hohhot sought to reimagine pastoralism, in various and contested ways, in the light of state policies and discourses of heritage, conservation, and biotechnology, and to define its place, its past, and its future in China. Herders in turn participated in and negotiated this reimagining. The creation of Camel Country has important implications for how we understand the politics of China's state environmentalism and nation-building, and the centrality of the country's peripheries in these processes.

The Politics of State Environmentalism

In 2018 the concept of ecological civilization (C. *shengtai wenming*) was written into China's constitution, consolidating the country's state-led approach to environmental crises. This term, with origins in late Soviet ecological thought (Foster 2017), has been enthusiastically promoted by Xi Jinping, who became general secretary of the Chinese Communist Party (CCP) in 2012. It signals an ambition for China to assume a role of global environmental leadership by drawing on the deep affinity for nature that, it is claimed, characterizes traditional Chinese culture (Pan Yue 2006; Gare 2012). Some observers have welcomed the Chinese state's apparent enthusiasm for environmental governance, particularly as it stood in stark contrast to the Trump administration. From the perspective of ecological Marxism, for example, John Bellamy Foster (2017, 453) has written that "with all of its environmental contradictions China has forcefully raised the issue of forging an 'ecological civilization' as a project—something that is still lacking among the leading capitalist powers within the hegemonic core of the world economy." Among political scientists, China has come to be understood as a prime example of authoritarian environmentalism, meaning "a non-participatory approach to public policy-making in the face of severe environmental challenges" (Gilley 2012). Some have suggested that the intensification of global environmental challenges may mean that it is to authoritarian environmentalism, rather than more democratic forms, that humanity increasingly looks for its survival (Beeson 2010).

Scholarship in political ecology, however, highlights how projects of social reordering can lie behind the environmentalist rhetoric of states (McElwhee 2012). China's state environmentalism has been criticized as a technocratic project of socioenvironmental engineering that privileges urbanization, re-producing inequalities between urban and rural people (Rodenbiker 2021). Ecological civilization must also be analyzed from China's ethnic margins. Some scholars have recently argued that it is fundamentally connected to the state's nation-building project and its desire to secure control over the peoples of China's peripheries following several decades of ethnic unrest (Li and Shapiro 2020; Salimjan 2021).

But it is important to recognize that this "coercive environmentalism," as Yifei Li and Judith Shapiro phrase it, does not always work as intended. Policies can be contradictory, and the degree and manner of implementation often depend on local conditions (Kolås 2014). In pastoral regions, herders have sometimes been able to circumvent restrictions on herding, for exam-ple by leaving livestock in the care of relatives rather than selling them (Yeh 2013a, 1179) or by grazing livestock at night to avoid detection (Fu 2016).[8] In addition to employing these weapons of the weak (Scott 1985), local groups of herders have petitioned various scales of government, as well as organizing protests (Long 2017; Xinxin Wang and Kevin Lo 2022).

However, it is not only herders who have pushed back against these pol-icies. Minority cultural elites based in Beijing and in the capitals of au-tonomous regions have used song, film, and literature to contest the state environmentalist discourse that places blame for environmental degradation on herders (Baranovitch 2016a). In Alasha, another kind of minority elite has also criticized this discourse. These elites are normally employed as state officials or retired from such jobs. Despite this bureaucratic employment, many of them are closely connected to pastoral regions through kinship ties or by virtue of having worked in the countryside earlier in their career. While urban/rural distinctions can be important in Alasha, the minority elites discussed in this book should not be thought of as having merely a romantic attachment to the pastoralist way of life (cf. Khan 1996).

The Chinese state, dominated at its upper echelons by Han Chinese, nevertheless includes a significant proportion of minority cadres at regional and local levels of the autonomous regions. These cadres are not simply stooges for the Han majority (Harrell 2007). In several parts of China, for example, minority cadres have actively opposed the production and circula-tion of derogatory representations of minorities by Han Chinese (Gladney 1994; Bulag 2008). While they are inevitably constrained by the parameters of political discourse in China, in some instances they are able to "re-cook political language" to advocate for their communities (Barnett and Diemberger 2008, 2). Minority cadres occupy the role of broker, representing the state to their communities and their communities to the state; such a role can often be a conflicted one, with minority cadres placed in a double bind (Harrell 2007; Bulag 2002b).

Even after retirement, minority cadres can remain important local figures. While they are no longer tasked with implementing state policy, many seek to promote the interests of their community, particularly through support for cultural activities (Harrell 2007). They can thus become what are known as folk scholars or amateur scholars (C. *minjian xuezhe*), a term that refers to the lack of a post at a state institution. However, even though they no longer occupy positions within the state, these retired cadres remain steeped in its discourses, familiar with its structures, and connected socially to its current personnel. I use the term *penumbra of the state* to conceptualize their ambiguous status.

In 2005 a small group of retired and serving Mongol officials based in Bayanhot founded the Alasha Inner Mongolia Society for the Conservation of Camels, Ecology, and the Environment (C. Neimenggu Alashan Baohu Luotuo, Baohu Shengtai Huanjing Xiehui), which was registered initially with the Alasha League Environmental Protection Bureau (C. Huanbao Ju). In official terms, the Alasha Camel Society (ACS), as I refer to it, is a "popular organization" (C. *minjian zuzhi*), sometimes translated as NGO, though in China it is common for such organizations to be much more closely entangled with the state than Western notions of civil society suggest (Hansen 2008). While other commentators have suggested that the ACS is a community organization (Köhler-Rollefson 2008), it is better understood as existing in the penumbra of the state.

The story of one of its founding members, Danzan, is instructive here.[9] He was in his eighties when I got to know him in 2013 and had served as a secretary to the last prince of Alasha for several years before 1949, when the People's Republic of China was established. Danzan was given a job in the new government and eventually became head of the Alasha League Bureau of Agriculture and Animal Husbandry (C. Nongmu Ju) before retiring in 1995. When I met him for the first time, he gave a long, angry account of the wrongheadedness of the RLRG policy. "I'm a member of the Communist Party [C. *dangyuan*]," he said, "but this policy does not suit pastoral regions!" The blame for desertification had been wrongly placed on livestock. Instead, he said, the problem was the result of the end of "nomadic culture" (M.

nüüdeliin soyol), which had been brought about by the allocation of pastures to individual households. This had led to the degradation of pastureland and had "destroyed the unity" (C. *pohuai tuanjie*) of the Mongols.

In the years immediately following its establishment, members of the ACS advocated for camel husbandry by issuing reports and policy proposals, as well as traveling to Beijing to meet officials from the national Ministry of Agriculture. Some of these proposals were published on official websites, at a time when the Chinese state was allowing the internet to act in limited ways as an opinion forum. The ACS thus made use of the expanded scope for consultation that had emerged in reform-era China, particularly under the leadership of Hu Jintao (2002–12), when the CCP sought to maintain its power and preempt demands for democratization by introducing certain governance reforms and consulting more widely outside the party (Tsang 2009; Teets 2013).

In recent decades, an international pastoralist rights movement has emerged, enabling pastoralists in several countries to forge strategic connections with the global indigenous peoples' movement and its struggles for land rights (Upton 2014; Bassi 2017). However, the Chinese state argues that indigenous rights have no relevance in China, because they imply the presence of external colonizers (Elliott 2015); instead, China scales diversity by recognizing fifty-six nationalities (C. *minzu*), some of which (such as the Mongols) have been granted putative rights of autonomy for certain territories, though the kinds of collective rights associated with indigeneity elsewhere are not present.[10] In recent decades anthropologists have described how ideas of indigeneity, or their analogues, have gained purchase in some parts of China (Sturgeon 2007; Hathaway 2010; Luo 2018). However, the presence of transnational NGOs in Alasha has been limited compared to the biodiversity hot spot of Yunnan, and the struggles of pastoralists here have not been articulated with reference to globally circulating rights-based discourses.

Instead, the ACS bolstered its reports and policy proposals by forging connections with Han Chinese grassland scientists critical of the RLRG policies, as well as with UNESCO initiatives such as Man and the Biosphere, the Chinese National Committee for which included a long feature on camels and an editorial from an ACS member in a special issue of its magazine dedicated to Alasha (Chinese National Committee for Man and the Biosphere 2008). In yoking together the protection of camels with the protection of ecology and the environment, the original name of the ACS was itself an implicit refutation of the idea that camels were responsible for the degradation of the grasslands. Baigal, another ACS member, explained that their aim was "to protect the environment, and camels are also a part of the ecology."

The ACS arranged for a Han Chinese ecologist, Liu Shurun, to visit Alasha. In a popular book (2012), he criticizes a 2006 "proposal regarding the improvement of the ecological and environmental situation in Alasha League" issued by several senior officials in Alasha. Liu strongly objects to the proposal's claim that Mongolian pastoralism is "primitive and backward" (C. *yuanshi luohou*) and that the best way of improving the ecology of Alasha would be to move all the herders off the fragile grasslands and raise livestock on fodder in pens. In response to claims in the official proposal that camels "cause the greatest harm to grassland flora," Liu Shurun (2012, 434) argues that "the traditional herding of camels has protected the pastures of Alasha" (C. *chuantong de luotuo fangmu baohu le Alashan de caochang*).

In the 1990s, Mongol herders in the east of the region were apparently suspicious of grassland science and Han Chinese scientists (Williams 2000). Their suspicion is echoed in much political ecology, which critiques the relationship between science and state power (e.g., Nadasdy 2003; Blakie and Muldavin 2004). However, as anthropologists Knut Nustad and Heather Swanson (2022, 934) have recently pointed out, "Ecological science is not a simple handmaiden of state knowledge regimes." And if members of the ACS and others involved in advocating for pastoralism in Alasha appeared to have become environmental subjects (Agrawal 2005; Yeh 2009), learning to think and speak in the official language of ecology and conservation, they deployed this discourse in defense of a form of land use that has been stigmatized by state environmentalism.

Livestock Endangerment and the Rescaling of Culture

How did it become possible to conceive of the defense of pastoralism in Alasha in terms of animal conservation? By the beginning of the twenty-first century, the camels that remained in the region played a minor role in a pastoral economy structured around the sale of cashmere. However, their rapidly declining numbers meant that they could become a powerful metonym of the disappearance of the Mongolian pastoral way of life, in a characteristically late-modern alignment of natural and cultural endangerment that was occurring in many parts of the world (Sodikoff 2012).

As China's economic and political power grew rapidly at the end of the twentieth century, this "endangerment sensibility" (Vidal and Dias 2016) came to have particular resonances at the country's peripheries. In Hong Kong, for example, concerns over the endangerment of certain locally unique species were entangled with anxieties surrounding the handover of Hong Kong to China and perceived threats to the city's cultural specificity (Choy 2011). In Inner Mongolia, writers and artists were able to draw parallels in their work between the extinction of charismatic wild animals, such as wolves, and the cultural extinction of the Mongols. Such animals provided safe metaphors, allowing oblique criticism of politically sensitive issues such as Han Chinese settler colonization (Baranovitch 2021).

But endangerment in Inner Mongolia could also be metonymical, involving some of the domestic animals constitutive of Mongolian pastoralism. Endangerment was generative (Sodikoff 2012), enabling a form of politics in this sensitive border region. In the early twenty-first century, an ethnic Mongol scientist at Inner Mongolia Agricultural University initiated efforts to protect several breeds of Mongolian horse. Mobilizing around the endangerment of the horse and establishing connections with Beijing-based NGOs enabled local Mongols in Kheshigten Banner in the east of the region to argue in 2010 against grazing ban policies. "If the grasslands are to be restored," they wrote to the local government, "we have no choice but to protect horses and implement a modern nomadic system" (Zhou Wei 2010). As with the camel in Alasha, horse numbers in other parts of Inner Mongolia had declined precipitously, partly as a result of their obsolescence as a means of transportation but also due to grazing bans and grassland enclosure, which was incompatible with their wide-ranging grazing habits. Like the camel, the horse could thus stand for a particular way of engaging extensively with the land that is regarded as characteristically Mongolian (Williams 2002) and ecologically sound.

Across much of Alasha, ecological conditions do not allow herders to keep horses. Instead, extensive forms of animal husbandry are here associated particularly with the wide-ranging camel, whose physiology, appetites, and behavior are particularly ill suited to the stall-rearing vision of modernized animal husbandry promoted by the state across much of Inner Mongolia (Tracy 2013). Scholars in geography and anthropology have recently emphasized the significance of the liveliness and materiality that nonhuman animals bring to human projects (Barua 2016; Govindrajan 2018). Seen in this light, camels are not simply empty vessels into which symbolic meaning is poured; instead their materiality affords an association with nomadic forms of land use, and their mobility has consequences for relations among humans at various scales.

A distinctive form of biopolitics had thus emerged in Inner Mongolia in the early twenty-first century. As animal endangerment was a politically safe problem, advocating for the protection of certain breeds of livestock made it possible to argue for the value of Mongolian pastoralist land use. Scholarly literature on conservation biopolitics tends to be in a critical vein, emphasizing how certain forms of life (including human) are diminished and marginalized, even as others are singled out for protection (Biermann and Anderson 2017). But in a context where the articulation of an indigenous identity (Tania Li 2000) and attendant notions of rights over land was not possible, this livestock biopolitics represented a strategic local adaptation to political constraints, one that was not without minor successes. By presenting sensitive questions of land use in the language of livestock conservation, as well as local cultural heritage, these advocates were engaging in a form of issue framing, a common tactic among those in China who seek to influence policy (Mertha 2009).

In 2008 the ACS arranged a meeting with officials from the central Ministry of Agriculture in Beijing. They took with them a DVD featuring emotive footage of camels being slaughtered in large numbers in Alasha Right Banner as a result of the stocking limits. According to Baigal, they told the officials that policies regarding camels were contradictory: on the one hand, camels were supposed to be protected as a fine breed (C. *youliang chuzhong*), but at the same time they were subject to the RLRG policy, which left many herders no choice but to dispose of them en masse. In large part as a result of this lobbying, I was told, camels were exempted from the stocking limits in Ejine and Alasha Right Banners, and each household in Left Banner was allowed to herd sixty camels, though even this limit did not appear to be strictly enforced. In addition, four Alasha Bactrian camel genetic resource conservation zones (C. *Alashan Shuangfengtuo pinzhong yichuan ziyuan baohu qu*) were established in different parts of Alasha Left Banner for the in situ conservation of this breed.[11] The Alasha Bactrian camel thus became a biopolitical exception to the state's destocking policies.[12]

In early twenty-first-century China, the endangerment sensibility manifested itself in an "intangible cultural heritage fever" (C. *feiyi re*; Blumenfield and Silverman 2013; Maags and Svensson 2018). Conservation of the Alasha Bactrian camel was accompanied by the formal listing of "the camel husbandry practices of the Mongol nationality" (C. *Mengguzu yangtuo xisu*) as part of Alasha's contribution to China's national list of intangible cultural heritage. Such listing was probably also influenced by heritage competition with Mongolia, where forms of camel culture have been developed in Gobi regions in recent years, as a result of similar concerns over the dwindling numbers of camels (Thrift 2016).[13] While some scholars argue that heritage in China works as an important tool of governance (Oakes 2012; Rippa 2020), recent scholarship in various contexts shows that it is not merely a top-down, state-directed phenomenon but can afford agency to marginalized communities (Peutz 2018; Herzfeld 2021). As in pastoral areas in other parts of the world (Cormack 2016; Leblon 2016; Bindi 2022), discourses of heritage in Alasha provided a way of asserting the value of pastoralism.

The idea that certain kinds of livestock are not simply material resources but instead central to the cultures of particular peoples has a long history in anthropology and related disciplines. From cattle among the East African Nuer (Herskovits 1926; Evans-Pritchard 1940), reindeer for the Siberian Eveny (Vitebsky 2005), to the sheep of the Navajo (Weisiger 2011) such animals are seen to be implicated in multiple aspects of social life from kinship to cosmology. In the Mongolian cultural region, multispecies pastoralism tends to be the cultural ideal, and herders often talk of the desirability of having all of the "five muzzles" or "five kinds" (M. *tavan khoshuu mal*)—sheep, goats, cattle, camels, and horses—even though this is often not achieved (White and Fijn 2020). Of the five, the horse is generally held in highest regard (Meserve 2000), and for some scholars it is the key domesticate in Mongolian herding society, which is characterized by a complex interactive mutuality between human and horse (Fijn 2011, 152).

However, for scholars working predominantly in European contexts, the linking of livestock and people needs to be deconstructed and shown to be a means through which nations are made and imagined (Tamminen 2019; Svendsen 2021). Such historicizing insights have also been brought to bear in the case of certain wild animals, such as the giant panda, which emerged as a Chinese national icon only in the latter part of the twentieth century (Songster 2018). But the case of Siberian Russia perhaps provides the most helpful point of comparison: in the Sakha Republic, ideas of the key domesticate have shifted in response to broader political and social changes, from the reindeer during the Soviet period to the horse following the collapse of the Soviet Union and, more recently, to an endangered native breed of cattle (Stammler-Gossman 2010; Tarasova 2020).

In Alasha, the camel's cultural prominence in the early twenty-first century must be placed in historical perspective and contextualized in relation not only to globalized discourses and affects of endangerment but also to political-economic and nation-building processes in China. Such processes introduced new layers of complexity into the relationship between livestock and human collectivity. The conservation of camels in Alasha thus provides a window onto significant shifts during the Xi Jinping era in the way China's borderlands are incorporated into nation-building projects.

The designation of Alasha as China's Camel Country, for example, was characteristic of an emphasis on local branding and regional specialization during the reform era (Oakes 1999). But as intellectuals elaborated a locally distinctive Alasha camel culture (C. *Alashan luotuo wenhua*; M. *Alasha temeen soyol*), they also increasingly adopted discourses that downplayed differences of ethnicity in favor of a conception of Alasha as a frontier region characterized by hybridity. This reflected important shifts in the nation-building project within the PRC. With the system of nationality classification introduced in the 1950s (Mullaney 2011), the state institutionalized ethnic difference even as it aimed for national integration. The continued presence of "backward" minority nationalities at the frontiers allowed the center to portray itself as the vanguard of modernity, a legacy of Chinese imperialism in an age of nation-building (Fiskesjö 2006). However, in the Xi era, the Chinese state has increasingly come to see minority nationalities as Frankenstein's monsters (Bulag 2021), created by the state through its nationality classification program only to later turn on their creator. While the People's Republic of China was long defined as a "unitary multinational state" (C. *tongyi de duo minzu guojia*), in 2018 a reference to the "Chinese nation" (C. *Zhonghua minzu*) was included in the constitution (Bulag 2021). Building this nation has become a priority for Xi Jinping.

This assimilatory intensification has received its most brutal manifestation in the carceral regime of Xinjiang and the repression of many Uyghur religious and cultural practices (Byler 2021), but in Inner Mongolia, after the fieldwork for this book was conducted, it was also strikingly evident in the 2020 downgrading of the status of Mongolian language in Mongolian schools (Atwood 2020). Subsequent propaganda texts in Inner Mongolia sought to promote the idea of a superordinate Chinese culture (M. *Dundiin soyol*) over those of different nationalities (Baioud 2023).

Some commentators thus talk of cultural erasure (e.g., Ruser et al. 2020) in minority regions of China, but the case of Camel Country shows that nation-building is also manifest in more subtle *cultural rescaling* such that the defense of Mongolian pastoralism increasingly had to be couched in a discourse of a *local* Alasha camel culture, since discourses of locality were more politically acceptable than those of nationality. Nation-building proceeded not simply through standardization and similarity (cf. Kipnis 2012) but also through the rescaling of difference away from nationality and toward depoliticized locality, understood as a space of cultural exchange and hybridization. The defense of pastoralism, a central pillar of Mongol identity and autonomy in Inner Mongolia, thus unavoidably participated in this broader project of nation-building through rescaling. Conservation begat new scales of culture.

Livestock biopolitics directed at the national conservation of endangered local breeds was characteristic of this rescaling from nationality to locality. But the camel, with its history as an infrastructure of long-distance trade and cultural exchange, also has symbolic affordances for other kinds of rescaling. The creation of Camel Country must be understood in relation to the Silk Road imaginary that is part of China's Belt and Road Initiative (BRI), the vision for transcontinental infrastructural investment and connectivity launched by Xi in Kazakhstan in 2013. There is by now a burgeoning literature on BRI imaginaries (e.g., Grant 2018; Rippa 2020); this book shows how they have been taken up in a remote borderland of China and deployed in the defense of a stigmatized form of land use. The meanings of pastoralism and its associations with remoteness have in turn been transformed in light of the BRI. This was part of another cultural rescaling in the Xi era, as China was increasingly understood as not simply a territorially bound nation-state but also a civilizational state that had projected its benign influence through expansive historical trade networks, which were now being echoed in the form of the BRI (Grant 2016).

The rescaling of culture, however, was not a completed project. It continued to coexist awkwardly in Alasha with the long-established figure of the Mongol herder (M. *Mongol malchin*) and attendant notions of a nationality-scaled Mongolian culture (M. *Mongol soyol*), creating tensions for those involved in the conservation of camels and camel heritage. Importantly, contested ideas of culture and conservation were not simply the preserve of urban intellectuals but were instead implicated in the everyday practice of actually existing pastoralism in rural Alasha and the conflicts that emerged on formally enclosed but unfenced pastureland. Here, herders grappled with the selective nature of livestock biopolitics, as apparent official support for endangered camels coexisted with the unmaking of pastoral livelihoods based on the herding of "excessive" goats and sheep.

Making Frontier Livestock

We live in an age of globally expanding commodity frontiers (Moore 2000; Beckert et al. 2021). This idea highlights the social and ecological transformations of rural peripheries across the globe by the extraction and commodification of resources that have fueled processes of urbanization and industrialization, often at great spatial distance. Today one important manifestation of this expansion can be seen in the form of livestock frontiers (Schneider and Coghe 2021). Across the world, new areas of land are being opened up to livestock production and the production of animal feeds, while animals are being commodified in new ways. Much of this is a result of increasing consumption of meat (Weis 2013), but Inner Mongolia has also been transformed in recent decades by the rapid growth in appetite for dairy products in China (Tracey 2013; Mak 2021a), as well as global demand for cashmere.

The expansion of livestock frontiers has been characterized by the commodification of a limited number of species and breeds of domestic animal and a concomitant decline in the biodiversity of livestock. In Alasha, this was exemplified by the simultaneous boom in cashmere production and endangerment of the region's camels. Increasingly obsolescent as a means of transportation, these animals' hair continued to be sold, but prices had steadily decreased.[14] By the turn of the millennium, the official *Alasha Left Banner Gazetteer* reported that the camel was being affected negatively by the "mood of the market" (C. *shichang xingqing*), and thus "protecting and rescuing" (C. *baohu he zhengjiu*) the Alasha Bactrian camel was a matter of extreme urgency (ALBG 2000, 290–91).

The global discourse of livestock conservation emerged from twentieth-century anxieties produced by the standardization of animal bodies in the interests of increased productivity. Even as it pursued genetic homogenization to maximize profits, livestock production needed a reserve pool of diverse genetic material from which to draw, in order to allow future improvement through cross-breeding and adaptation of livestock to changing consumer demands as well as transformed environments (Tamminen 2019). The very possibility of continued improvement of livestock came to be seen as conditional upon the conservation of genetic resources.

However, in Alasha the economic logic of camel conservation was slightly different. Here the threat to the Alasha Bactrian camel did not come from careless hybridization with other breeds in the interests of increasing productivity, which was seen to be eroding China's livestock genetic resources in other contexts (Yuan 2014). Conservation was not about ensuring that certain livestock products currently produced would still be able to be produced in the future; instead it involved imagining new uses for this animal now that it was obsolete in what had for centuries been its main economic function. Through its 2006 listing as a national-level livestock genetic resource protected breed (C. *guojiaji chuqin yichuan ziyuan baohu pinzhong*; Ministry of Agriculture 2006), the Alasha Bactrian camel now embodied a particular understanding of the relationship between nonhuman life and economic value, and of the state's responsibility for managing this: while it might lack market value in the present, it needed to be conserved to cater to market demand in the future. But to ensure the support of the *local* state, the task for those involved in camel conservation was to elaborate what forms this demand might take, and thus what kind of resource this animal might be—in other words, to perform the camel's potential as a resource. This work preceded the actual production and marketing of camel products and was part of a broader local political project to defend camel husbandry by articulating its value.

Recent literature in anthropology and geography has sought to move beyond the analysis of resource claiming that has long preoccupied social scientists in order to attend to resource-making (Ferry and Limbert 2008; Richardson and Weszkalnys 2014; Kama 2020). Seen in this light, resources are not simply out there in nature; instead, heterogeneous materials and forms of life have to be constructed as resources worthy of exploitation through a constellation of practices and knowledges. While studies of resource-making have hitherto focused largely on fossil fuels, this perspective is also illuminating when it comes to unconventional livestock commodities. In the case of the Alasha Bactrian camel, this resource-making depended on the work of local livestock technicians and ethnic Mongol scientists based at universities in Hohhot, the capital of Inner Mongolia.

Science and technology (C. *keji*) have a central place in the Chinese state's vision of national rejuvenation in the reform era, from their status as the first of Deng Xiaoping's Four Modernizations (C. Si Ge Xiandaihua) to the recent Made in China 2025 industrial strategy. While the Chinese state places great faith in the capacity of science and technology to solve social and environmental problems, anthropologists have shown how such faith is often misplaced and instead generates new, unforeseen problems, such as pollution and toxic food (Greenhalgh 2020). The legitimation of Chinese sovereignty over minority regions often relies on claims that the benevolent Chinese state has brought the fruits of scientific progress to these "backward" regions (Williams 2000; Yeh 2013b). Much recent scholarly and media attention outside China, however, has focused on the country's apparent "malevolent technological turn" (Franceschini and Loubere 2022, 21), particularly the application of new surveillance technologies to manage populations, most egregiously in the case of Muslims in Xinjiang (Byler 2021).

However, it is also important to recognize that science and technology development in China is not simply imposed from above by a technocratic and authoritarian state; instead, the state relies on globally circulating ideas of grassroots innovation and the celebration of entrepreneurial makers of technology (Lindtner 2020), as part of its emphasis on indigenous innovation (C. *zizhu chuangxin*). This desire to move away from foreign technology transfer can be seen across the country in the development of local technological solutions to particular problems—for example, the use of insects to manage organic waste in the city of Guangzhou (Amy Zhang 2020). While existing anthropological literature has examined this drive for innovation in the context of this southern Chinese metropolis, its effects have also been felt in remote Alasha. Here local technological innovations, including satellite tracking devices for free-range camels, automatic watering troughs triggered by microchips in ears, and milking machines that cater to the irregular udders of these animals, channeled the state's emphasis on innovation toward a technopolitical defense of extensive pastoralism in the context of grassland enclosure and grazing bans.

The making of camels as resources depended on the biophysical properties of these animals and on the novel understandings of these properties emerging from the ecological and life sciences. In European contexts, these have allowed certain livestock to be valued in new ways: as a source of biomatter to treat human neonates, for example (Svendsen and Koch 2013) or as ecological engineers, whose grazing and defecation are prized for their alleged role in ecological restoration (Lorimer and Driessen 2016). While these instances have been analyzed in relation to expanded modes of biopolitics that seek to secure human life by managing nonhuman life, it is important to attend to their distinctive modulations beyond the Global North (Turnbull and Barua 2023). In the case of the Alasha Bactrian camel, novel livestock resource-making must also be understood in relation to the particular ethnic and spatial politics of China's peripheries.

Rather than treating the camel as an obsolete animal threatened by modernity, those in the penumbra of the state had begun to insist that this animal's body was "full of treasures." I was told, for example, that the camel still had many "genetic secrets" (C. *yichuan mimi*) that had not been discovered. In the early twentieth century the promise of mineral resources and concern with securing national territory drew Chinese geologists to frontier regions such as Inner Mongolia (Shen 2013); now, with biotech central to the Chinese state's vision of national rejuvenation (Wahlberg 2012) and with genomes rather than territories still to be mapped, the camel's body came to be figured as an exciting terra incognita.

Resource-making is fundamentally related to conceptions of time (Ferry and Limbert 2008). If the camel lacked value in the present, it was nevertheless important to think long term. Alasha's status as a "climate frontier" (Paprocki 2019) loomed large here. In the words of one Mongol livestock technician, "It's possible that when climate change reaches a certain stage, the only things that will be able to survive will be camels and humans, because camels can survive in the most hostile of environments, and humans will be able to drink their milk and eat their meat. They will be the final partners of humanity" (C. *renlei zuihou de huoban*).

But other futures enabled by the camel were more optimistic. Camel antibodies apparently held out promise for new cancer treatments. The genes that enabled camels to regulate body temperature in accordance with extremes of ambient temperature were also something that "no other species of livestock possess." Such genetic material constituted precious resources for bioengineering and would be "especially useful to the future development of biotechnology" (Batuchulu and Siqinbielige 2017, 75). Here we can see how the "breathless futurology" of biotechnology produces a particular kind of anticipation (Harrington et al. 2006, 3; Adams et al. 2009). A hopeful "resource affect" (Weszkalnys 2016) conveying promises of local wealth but also human progress came to be attached to the Alasha Bactrian camel and was transmitted via various media, including new social media platforms, as well as TV and radio. Local Mongolian-language radio shows, for example, talked of camels as "treasures of the future" (M. *ireedüigiin erden*).

Biotech imaginaries transform understandings of value, such that living matter once thought obscure and worthless becomes a subject of intense interest (Landecker 2010). This is evident in the resignifying of the primitivity of the camel. Some Han Chinese officials have used the notion that the Alasha Bactrian camel is a primitive (C. *yuanshi*) breed to criticize emphasis on the camel, since this primitivity was seen to correlate with low productivity. This was part of a broader denigration of the primitive, nomadic (C. *yuanshi youmu*) nature of animal husbandry in Alasha that was still evident in official texts around the turn of the millennium (ALBG 2000, 286). Texts from the early 1990s collocate the Alasha Bactrian camel's "low productive ability" and the "coarse" (C. *cufang*) mode of husbandry with its status as an "ancient" (C. *gulao*) local breed (Alashan Meng Luotuo Kexue Yuanjiusuo

1991). Modernizing states in China have often equated the primitivity of the cultures of minorities with the unimproved or underdomesticated nature of the animals they kept (Christmas 2017; Frank 2018).

However, in the twenty-first century, proposals produced by advocates for pastoralism in Alasha began to embrace this primitivity, whose connotations had shifted: "The Alasha Bactrian Camel is an ancient, primitive breed" (C. *gulao de yuanshi pinzhong*), announces one official planning document proudly, before going on to refer to the distinctive genetic makeup of the camel and the promise it holds for biotechnology (Batuchulu and Siqinbielige 2017, 75). With the biologization of the frontier, primitivity was not a stage to be superseded but an unspoiled condition full of potential.

A similar shift can be seen in the valorization in Alasha of the wildness of the camel, which now came to be seen in the positive light of ecosystem services and organic food. While scholars have used metaphors of domestication to refer to frontier statecraft in China and beyond (e.g., Yeh 2013b; Klinger 2017, 85), recent Chinese literary works such as *Wolf Totem* (C. Lang tuteng; Jiang 2004) demonstrate that the taming of frontier wildness is no longer always to be desired; instead wildness can provide resources for national reinvigoration (Bulag 2010; Bayar 2014a). Indeed, across China's peripheries, tropes such as wildness and remoteness once associated negatively with backwardness have recently come to be revalorized as healthy and unspoiled (Klein 2020). This is exemplified by the recent popularity in China of *yuanshengtai*, literally meaning "original ecological" with connotations of "pristine," "authentic," and "primitive" (Yu Luo 2018).

As in the case of pastoral frontiers elsewhere in the world (Regassa, Hezekiel, and Korf 2019), Alasha has been imagined as a form of "terra nullius." In recent years several industrial zones have been established in rural parts of Alasha, far from Bayanhot. A local official in northeast Alasha, where one such zone had been recently established, told me that polluting industries were being relocated from China's eastern cities, where citizens' "environmental consciousness" (C. *huanbao yishi*) was more developed, to these remote parts of Alasha whose few inhabitants "did not understand about pollution." Beneath the rhetoric of development that accompanied the Open Up the West strategy, then, it was possible to discern what anthropologist Traci Voyles calls "wastelanding." Writing in the context of uranium mining in Navajo lands, Voyles (2015, 10) refers to the "racial and spatial politics that render certain bodies and landscapes pollutable."

In 2014, however, herders in the south of Alasha made contact with journalists in Beijing and informed them that factories in an industrial zone deep in the desert were illegally dumping untreated waste. The photos that emerged, showing pipes belching out noxious black liquid amid the dunes, caused a national scandal (Jie Chen 2015). Xi Jinping ordered an investigation, and several local officials were sacked. Those involved in the promotion of camel husbandry in Alasha were optimistic that this would herald a shift in local government policy. "Development based on industry won't work now," one member of the ACS told me, stressing the potential of the camel as resource instead. Alasha's remoteness would be harnessed to a new frontier imaginary.

Ultimately, the most successful resource-making project in early twenty-first-century Camel Country imagined camels as a source of milk, promoted as a health food. This involved the work of Mongol scientists who published research in Chinese into the medicinal properties of camel milk and appeared on national television to promote the consumption of this unconventional commodity. In collaboration with international scientists, they promised innovations in camel breeding that would allow these animals to produce more milk and thus make camel dairying economically viable. In other words, Alasha's "semiwild" camels would have to be submitted to new processes of taming and selective breeding. However, these processes involved networks of transnational expertise, framed as part of the BRI, in which ethnic Mongol scientists played a pioneering role, thereby inverting long-standing tropes of backward minorities and remote peripheries.

This vision of technoscience-assisted camel dairying convinced a local government in Alasha, in collaboration with a southern Chinese businessman and ethnic Mongol scientists, to reorient its rural economy around the production of camel milk. This kind of partnership between state and capital has been noted by other scholars working on agrarian change in China (e.g Schneider 2017; Qiangqiang Luo et al. 2017). In Alasha, the expansion of the livestock frontier does not simply represent a local instantiation of a singular logic of dairy capitalism (Narayanan 2021), but must instead be analyzed in complex relation to the politics of culture and land use in this pastoral borderland, which had come to center on conservation of this animal. Engagement with the market in China's peripheries can be intricately bound up with cultural politics and projects of the revalorization of stigmatized people and places (Yeh 2022).

Importantly, however, these conceptions of camels as resources were not shared by all Mongols in Alasha. In light of a well-established literature on contested processes of commodification in pastoralist societies (e.g., Ferguson 1985; Kabzung and Yeh 2016), this book analyzes some of the tensions that emerged as minority elites sought to incorporate camel husbandry more fully into the market economy by performing camel potential. But these tensions did not simply reflect residual traditional pastoralist attitudes or an indigenous ontology that could be neatly counterposed to the state (Nadasdy 2007; de la Cadena 2010); instead, they were unintentionally fostered by the state itself through its promotion of certain forms of heritage and its discourses of conservation.

Study Area and Research Methods

In administrative terms, Alasha is a league (C. *meng*; M. *aimag*), a unit specific to Inner Mongolia that is equivalent to the prefecture (C. *zhou* or *diqu*) in other minority regions of China, or the prefecture-level city (C. *diji shi*) in China proper. The number of leagues in Inner Mongolia has decreased in recent years, as the state pursued a strategy of fiat urbanization, scaling up leagues to the status of municipality (C. *shi*; M. *hot*). The parts of Inner Mongolia that remain leagues are those seen to be most typically Mongolian (rural, pastoralist; Bulag 2002a). As a league, Alasha is marked as comparatively backward but also a site of authentic pastoral life.

Alasha League is divided into three banners (C. *qi*; M. *khoshuu*). Alasha Left Banner, where I conducted my research, is the most easterly and most populous, and contains the capital, Bayanhot (map 2). In 2014 the banner had an official population of 143,347, 66 percent of which were Han Chinese, while Mongols constituted 27 percent. To the west of Left Banner lie the more sparsely populated Alasha Right Banner and Ejine Banner. It emerged early on in my research that I would not be allowed to travel to Ejine Banner, which contains the launch site for China's satellite program and is thus highly sensitive. In 1958 one-third of the population of the banner was relocated to make way for this site (Klinger 2017, 94). While other parts of Alasha were not off limits in the same way, there is a significant military presence across the region. In recent years, some herders in Alasha have protested against missile tests close to their homes (Qiao Long 2016).

As I was a lone white male traveling in this remote region, some wondered whether I was a spy or a journalist. When I grew a short beard, other suspicions emerged: was I distributing subversive Islamic literature to the local Muslim population to foment unrest? My affiliation with a university in Hohhot, the capital of Inner Mongolia, and the sheaves of red-stamped documents that came with it, apparently reassured the security services on the one occasion I was (politely) interrogated in a hotel room.

KM ▬▬▬▬▬ 150
MI ▬▬▬▬▬

N

MONGOLIA

Ejine
Banner

Alasha League

Bayannuur

Yellow River

GANSU

Alasha Right
Banner

Badain
Jaran

Khöövör

Ordos

Bayanhot

Alasha Left
Banner

=-=- National Boundary
— Province / Autonomous Region
‑‑‑‑ League / Municipality
‑‑‑‑‑ Banner

QINGHAI

NINGXIA

SHAANXI

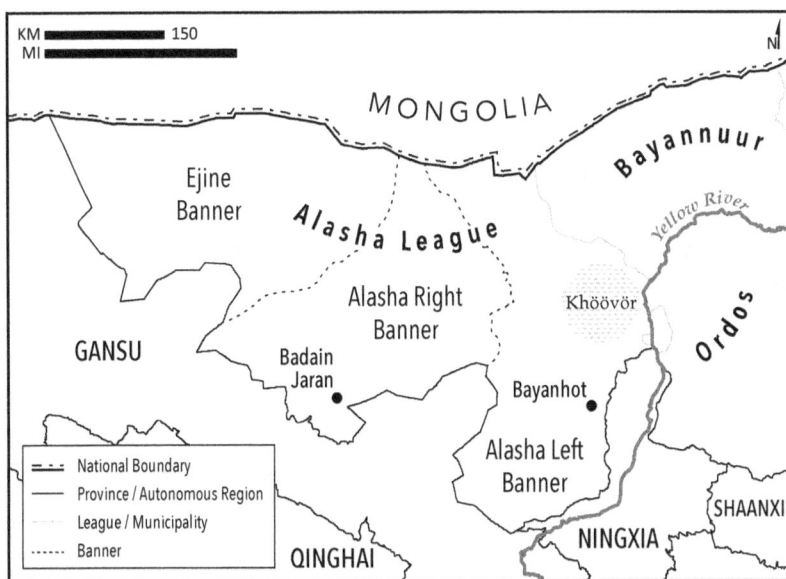

MAP 2. Alasha League and surrounding areas

Through the recommendation of a retired Mongol official in Bayanhot, I spent much of my fieldwork living with a herding family in the northeast of Alasha Left Banner, in a region to which I refer by its historical name of Khöövör.[15] This part of Alasha is known for its ethnic and religious diversity and as the home of around two thousand Muslim Mongols, said to be the descendants of Central Asian traders who partly assimilated with the local (Buddhist) Mongol population while retaining their religion. Khöövör lies at the frontier of pastoralism and agriculture: most of the land is arid grassland, but at its eastern edges irrigation channels bring water from the Yellow River, supporting a significant population of Han Chinese farmers. The mountains in the north of Khöövör were home to dozens of small-scale mines, and in 2009 a railway was built across the region that ran to the Mongolian border to provide transportation for coal imports from that country.

In the same year, plans for the construction of an industrial park (C. chanye yuanqu) in Khöövör were announced. By the time of my fieldwork, it was still being built, and locals were unsure what it would mean for the future viability of herding. Farther south, on the edges of the desert, a project to divert floodwater away from the Yellow River was underway. While I conducted fieldwork, there were rumors that this was in fact a project to irrigate the desert and allow thousands of impoverished peasants from Sichuan to be

23

Introduction

resettled, echoing stories circulating online among Inner Mongols in other parts of the region (Lipes 2013). Though it was Khöövör's ethnic and religious diversity that had initially sparked my interest in the region, it became clear that the region also provided a vantage point on the politics of land use in China's ethnic borderlands.

Khöövör is today subdivided into several *gatsaa*, including the one I refer to pseudonymously as Bayantal, where I lived. The *gatsaa*, an administrative unit unique to Inner Mongolia, is equivalent to the administrative village (C. *xingzheng cun*) in the rest of China. However, it should be noted that the *gatsaa* in Alasha has none of the concentrated settlement implied by the English term *village*. This is not because herders conform to the stereotype of yurt-dwelling nomads moving with their herds; in fact, it has been several decades since herders in this part of Alasha moved between pastures according to the seasons. Instead, as in much of Alasha, solid brick houses are scattered about the arid grassland, often separated by several kilometers.

The village was once the paradigmatic "field" of ethnographic fieldwork, the small-scale location where anthropologists studied small-scale societies, living among "human communities of face-to-face interaction" (Gupta and Ferguson 1997, 15). Toward the end of the twentieth century, this model came under increasing criticism, particularly from proponents of multi-sited ethnography who emphasized the need to adapt ethnographic methodology to study the circulation of objects, identities, and meanings (Marcus 1995). Even where their research was not explicitly multi-sited, anthropologists increasingly abandoned the rural in favor of studies of urban elites and scientific experts, to take two examples relevant to my own study.

If anthropology now often prefers to study diffuse networks rather than emplaced sites (Sorge and Padwe 2015), in my case it was precisely by spending a protracted period of time in a single site that I came to appreciate the diffuse networks of which the members of my household were part. Batbagana, my host, was in his sixties and was a retired party secretary of the *gatsaa*. In a way that was characteristic of those in the penumbra of the state, his networks included minority elites and cultural officials in Khöövör and in Bayanhot. They also extended to journalists and documentary makers from Hohhot, but also as far away as Hong Kong. On several occasions while I lived in Bayantal, television crews arrived to document practices of pastoralist heritage (fig. 1).

At the same time, Batbagana was on good terms with several other herders in Bayantal who helped each other out with various camel herding tasks and

FIG. 1. A herder is filmed by a television crew as he conducts a ritual to bring about the flourishing of his livestock.

sometimes traveled together to distant parts of Alasha to take part in camel racing events, which gave me the opportunity to expand my network of informants. Camels were vectors of social relations both within the *gatsaa* and far beyond its boundaries. Asking questions about camels took me to neighboring households but also to the region's administrative headquarters in the small Khöövör Town, as well as to the homes of retired officials in Bayanhot and scientific conferences in distant parts of Alasha. I would normally stay for a few days each month in Bayanhot, and during this time I developed a group of friends who provided an urban Mongol perspective on the issues in which I was interested. In the countryside my research was conducted predominantly in Mongolian, but in the city my informants would frequently code-switch, using Chinese to discuss aspects of government policy, for example. Such code-switching is common in contemporary Inner Mongolia (Baioud and Khuanuud 2022).

In recent years, a growing number of scholars have embraced multispecies ethnography as they question the society-nature dichotomy that has long oriented the anthropological project (Kirksey and Helmreich 2010; Govindrajan 2018). The anthropologist Natasha Fijn (2011), for example, seeks to include both humans and animals as social actors who make up what she calls the "ecosocial sphere" or "co-domestic sphere" of the Mongolian herding encampment. For Fijn (2011, 58), the encampment is a bounded site of human-animal intimacy and "a world unto itself." In a sense, the village, that archetypal site of social intimacy (Herzfeld 2015), is here rescaled to the level of the encampment and repopulated with animals as well as humans. But herding households in Alasha are not worlds unto themselves. In the case of camels, these animals spend most of their time wandering far from the household; this implicates them in conflicts over pastureland access. Most of the time Batbagana and his wife, Sarna, engaged with their camels through binoculars. It was difficult to see how I could pursue multispecies ethnography, with its privileging of human-animal intimacies and its implicit emphasis on proximity, in the case of these animals. Instead of proceeding from an ontology of entanglement, then, I approach human-animal intimacy as itself the site of reflection and contestation.

Though ethnographic fieldwork in Alasha is at the heart of this book, my interest in how pastoralism is represented has necessitated a certain methodological eclecticism. Though the archives of Alasha were off-limits to foreign researchers, I have been able to consult a wide range of textual sources. Like other anthropologists working in China (e.g., Ptackova 2020), I have contextualized my ethnography with reference to official policy documents. However, my textual studies have revealed policy toward pastoralists in China to be a more negotiated field than is often thought. I have drawn, for example, on policy proposals advocating support for camel husbandry in Alasha posted on official national websites, including E-Polity Square (C. E-Zheng Guangchang), established in 2009. This website, which now appears to be defunct, allowed users to comment on existing policy proposals or submit new ones (Wei Zhang et al. 2016). Whatever the effectiveness of such proposals and suggestions, they illuminate how minority elites sought to defend pastoralism using official discourses. I also consulted Chinese academic journals, where policy suggestions in relation to pastoralism in Alasha have also been published.

While I was in the field, herders of all ages began to use the Chinese social media platform WeChat, thereby establishing a new digital space simultaneously occupied by both urban and rural Mongols (see also McDonald 2016). My analysis thus also draws on WeChat posts from people in Alasha, most of whom I was acquainted with offline. While Chinese was the dominant language here, people also posted images of Mongolian text. And though WeChat in the early 2010s could not be described as a space of free expression, it did enable certain forms of representational politics, as minorities called out offenses and discrimination (Grant 2017), as well as complaining about official corruption.

It was common for those in the penumbra of the state to have published at least one book, whether a memoir, a piece of local or family history, or an account of local cultural heritage. Some of the books I discuss are striking in their generic heterogeneity: one edited volume, *The Silk Road Camel Bell* (C. Silu tuoling; Batuchulu and Siqinbielige 2017), presented to me by a retired cadre, contains policy documents, speeches by officials, policy suggestions, ethnological descriptions of camel culture, poems in Mongolian, an account of Lenin's brief encounter with camel caravans from Alasha, and official livestock statistics. This heterogeneity, a blending of official materials and folklore, is characteristic of the penumbra of the state. That book, like some other material to which I refer, was published by the Alasha League branch of the Chinese People's Political Consultative Conference (CPPCC). While this organization, which exists across China from the national level to that of the county, is often dismissed as merely decorative, a means of co-opting possible opposition to the party, it is designed to play an intermediary role between state and society (Sagild and Ahlers 2019); like those retired cadres in the penumbra of the state, its existence muddles these binary categories. At the local level it also plays an important role in documenting local history and culture and publishes compendia of cultural and historical materials (C. *wenshi ziliao*), in the service of the party's nation-building efforts (Weiner 2020).

Most of the fieldwork on which this book is based took place in the first couple of years of the Xi era. A final piece of fieldwork was conducted in the summer of 2019. The following year, in the wake of the COVID-19 outbreak, China closed its borders to most foreigners. These did not open again until 2023, as this book was being finalized. In 2020 educational reforms were introduced in the Inner Mongolia Autonomous Region (IMAR) that reduced the teaching conducted in Mongolian (Atwood 2020). Protests and school boycotts followed, as well as several suicides (Bulag 2020), including a government official in Alasha. The recent ratcheting up of the nation-building processes described in this book, as well as heightened geopolitical tensions, have in turn limited the possibility of further sustained ethnographic engagement with this region.

1

Situating Pastoralist Heritage

ALTANUUL WAS ONE of the first people I met in Alasha. He lived in an apartment in a recently built complex in the center of Bayanhot, though he had been born in 1939 into a pastoralist family in Khöövör. He received a few years of schooling in the countryside, and following collectivization in 1958, when the state suddenly had a pressing need for administrators in rural areas, he began to work for one of the people's communes (C. *renmin gongshe*; M. *ardiin negdel*) in northern Alasha. After being violently persecuted during the Cultural Revolution, he was rehabilitated in 1974 and sent to work in the Alasha Left Banner CPPCC, where he remained until his retirement in 1999. Following a path typical of those in the penumbra of the state, he went on to become chairman of the Alasha Folk Song Society and published several books. As he guided me to his study on our first meeting, he pointed at the shelves lined with books in Mongolian and Chinese and told me with a wink that he couldn't read most of them, because his cultural level (C. *wenhua shuiping*) was not high. However, while he had not had much formal education, he had established a name for himself locally as an amateur scholar and had been formally declared a "transmitter of intangible cultural heritage" (C. *wenhua chuanchengren*) by the state. He was now planning, he told me, to write a book on Alasha camel culture.

Altanuul was not alone in his interest. While the term *camel culture* did not exist before the twenty-first century, in the last two decades the topic has been the subject of numerous works produced by retired officials, amateur scholars, and graduate students at universities across China, as well as documentary filmmakers. Pastoralism in Inner Mongolia has long been "formatted and reformatted as required by different ideological and cultural imperatives" (Bulag 2004a, 3). Once portrayed as an integral part of China's national economy that needed development, in the early twenty-first century pastoralism in Inner Mongolia, where it still existed, was increasingly reimagined as locally specific cultural heritage that required conservation.

Alasha camel culture has been understood in quite different ways by its various proponents. On the one hand, it referred to local intangible cultural heritage (C. *feiwuzhi yichan*), which could serve as a resource (C. *ziyuan*) for the development of tourism; at the same time, however, camel culture could be understood as a kind of traditional ecological knowledge, a form of positively valued cultural difference that stood in contrast to powerful representations of pastoralists as environmentally destructive. Discourses and practices of cultural heritage can be deployed as a form of politics by marginalized communities (Peutz 2018; Herzfeld 2021), and the framing of pastoralism as camel culture must be understood as a response to state environmentalism's stigmatization of pastoralists.

However, the making of pastoralist heritage in Alasha did not simply revalorize the stigmatized cultural practices of a minority nationality, thereby participating in a form of representational politics that anthropologists have documented across China in the reform era (Chao 1996; Litzinger 2000). At a time when the distinctiveness of minority nationalities is increasingly deemphasized in cultural production in China (Schein 2020), or even seen as an unnatural, undesirable product of earlier state policies (Bulag 2021), the representational politics of land use in Inner Mongolia, often understood to be synonymous with ethnic politics (Khan 1996; Baranovitch 2021), now also had to participate in the production of new local scales of culture and an emphasis on frontier interaction and exchange that transcended the bounds of nationality.

"A Remote, Purely Pastoralist Banner"

Alasha, Inner Mongolia, and the PRC

In 1947, two years before the establishment of the People's Republic of China (PRC), the Inner Mongolia Autonomous Region (IMAR) was founded in eastern Inner Mongolia. Mongol cadres in the Chinese Communist Party (CCP) succeeded in co-opting a Mongolian nationalist movement, which had leaned toward unification with the independent Mongolian People's Republic (MPR).[1] In 1956, Alasha was finally incorporated into the IMAR, having previously been part of Ningxia and then Gansu.[2]

Historically, Alasha Banner was administratively distinct from the rest of Inner Mongolia, answering directly to authorities in Beijing with a significant degree of autonomy. It had been ruled by a line of Mongol princes closely linked through marriage to the ruling Qing dynasty. During the second phase of the Chinese Civil War (1945–49), its remoteness led to it becoming the base of operations for the Inner Mongolian nationalist leader Prince Dem-chugdongrub (Prince De), who had been head of the Japanese-sponsored Mengjiang Autonomous Government in eastern Inner Mongolia prior to the defeat of Japan (Jagchid 1999). The prince of Alasha, Darijaya, initially welcomed him but was himself navigating the rapidly shifting political landscape and was also secretly in contact with the CCP. On October 1, 1949, when Mao announced the establishment of the PRC, the Alasha banner authorities declared the loyalty of what they described as their "remote frontier region" (C. *yaoyuan de bianjiang*) to the new regime in a congratulatory telegram sent to Chairman Mao (ALBG 2000, 35). Prince De fled through Alasha to the MPR, while Darijaya became the chairman of Alasha Khoshuud Banner Special Autonomous Region in Ningxia, later rising to become vice chairman of the IMAR (Bayar 2002).

The co-opting of Darijaya, whose wife was a cousin of the last Qing emperor, Puyi, was part of the CCP's United Front strategy. Emerging from the arduous conditions of the Long March through western China to escape the Nationalists during the Chinese Civil War, this involved downplaying class struggle and making strategic alliances with non-Han elites (Leibold 2007, 93–95). The fact that this aristocrat was able to enjoy such a career in the socialist state (until his death during the Cultural Revolution) is remarkable, but it also evidenced the regularization and administrative nesting of Alasha as merely one constituent—comparatively remote and unimportant—part of the IMAR, in contrast to its former status as a princely banner that enjoyed a special relationship, structured by kinship, with the imperial ruling house in Beijing.[3]

The accession of Alasha to the IMAR in 1956 appeared to fulfill a promise made by Mao in 1935 to abolish the Chinese provinces that had been established in Inner Mongolia and restore their territory to the Inner Mongols (Bulag 2002b, 110). With such assurances, the CCP sought to distinguish itself from the Nationalists and gain the support of what were termed "minority nationalities" (C. *shaoshu minzu*) in key border areas during the Civil War (Xiaoyuan Liu 2006, 264). The CCP's nationality policies were initially influenced by those of the Soviet Union, though they came to differ in important respects (Mullaney 2011). The 1924 constitution of the Soviet Union recognized the right of its constituent republics to secede, and as late as 1947, the CCP promised that autonomy for the Inner Mongols was a stepping stone to future self-determination (C. *zijue*; Xiaoyuan Liu 2006, 265). However, following the Chinese Civil War, and in the face of the perceived territorial threats from other countries, the CCP decided that a unitary state system, without the right of secession, would be adopted over a federal model (Xiaoyuan Liu 2006, 266–67). According to the 1982 PRC constitution, the head of government in minority regions must be a member of the titular minority. However, the party secretary of the region, in whom real power is vested, is almost always Han Chinese (Hoshino 2019).

The territorial expansion of the IMAR turned out to be a double-edged sword. Since the late Qing period, parts of Inner Mongolia had been settled by large numbers of Han Chinese farmers, who initially rented land from Mongol aristocrats.[4] Ethnic tensions over land resulted in sometimes violent conflict, including the massacre of thousands of Mongols in eastern Inner Mongolia by a Han Chinese secret society in the Jindandao Incident of 1891 (Borjigin 2004). With the expansion of the IMAR, its demographics were suddenly transformed and Han Chinese outnumbered the Mongols by four to one. The very desire on the part of Mongols to recover Inner Mongolian territory ironically resulted in closer integration (Bulag 2004b). It also involved the erosion of autonomy at the scale of the banner, which had characterized the Qing system of administration in Inner Mongolia, the defense of which had been a rallying point for Inner Mongolian nationalists in the first decades of the twentieth century (Bulag 2002a).[5] In the context of the PRC, however, Mongol leaders believed that autonomy at the scale of the region meant that local autonomy was no longer necessary (Bulag 2004b, 114).

After coming to power, the CCP had embarked on a program of nationality classification (C. *minzu shibie*), which eventually resulted in the formal classification of China's population into fifty-six nationalities. This classification project was informed by Stalin's four criteria for defining nationality: common territory, common economy, common language, and common psychological makeup (Bulag 2002b, 10), though these were not always strictly adhered to (Mullaney 2011). Scholars have emphasized that this process of *minzu* classification did not merely involve recognition of a preexisting reality. Inner Mongolian anthropologist Uradyn Bulag (2002b, 10) writes that the "minzu-building project is simultaneously a purifying process, designed to make ethnic traits congruent with the qualities said to define Mongolness." Pastoralism came to be seen as defining Mongolian identity, notwithstanding the fact that more than half of the Mongol population were agriculturalists who lived in the more densely populated eastern Inner Mongolia (Khan 1996; Borjigin 2017).[6]

According to the Marxist models of social evolutionism that guided CCP policy, pastoralism was deemed to be characteristic of a less advanced stage of social progress than agriculture. Since the Mongols were understood as pastoralists, they were also seen as more backward than the agrarian Han Chinese (Khan 1996). The role of the Han Chinese in Inner Mongolia was thus to help the Mongols advance (Bayar 2014a, 453). In the early 1950s, Mongol leaders in IMAR celebrated the fact that some Mongols had gone to work in factories and on the railways, representing an incipient Mongol proletariat (Wulanfu 1990, 115; Bulag 2010); in the face of land reclamation projects and increasing Han Chinese settlement, however, these leaders came to see pastoralism as a vital bulwark for the preservation of Mongol autonomy within the PRC.

In Alasha, the *minzu*-building project involved stretching a heterogeneous population on a Procrustean bed. This heterogeneity was a product of Alasha's status as a refuge zone (Humphrey 2015; Scott 2009), whose vast spaces absorbed those fleeing war, famine, and persecution elsewhere in the region. The banner was home not only to the descendants of the Khoshuud Mongols who had been settled in the area in the seventeenth century by the Qing, but also Khalkha Mongols who arrived in the 1920s fleeing religious persecution in the MPR (Bayar 2002). Han Chinese also came to prerevolutionary Alasha from neighboring impoverished agricultural areas to work as hired hands and were later adopted by Mongol families. They were then registered as commoners (M. *albat*) of the banner, liable for tax and military service, and were described in official documents as having "become Mongol" (C. *biancheng mengguren*; IMAR EG, 2009, 204). This model of ethnicity thus differed from the later *minzu* paradigm in that ethnic identity was linked to feudal duties.

In Khöövör in the northeast of Alasha, a community of Muslim Mongols was a classificatory anomaly, since they shared a religion with the Hui, who were Chinese-speaking Muslims.[7] They were the descendants of Turkic Muslims who had settled in the banner and intermarried with local Mongols while maintaining their religion, as well as more recent arrivals from Hui regions who were fleeing conscription by warlords.[8] Having registered as commoners of the banner, their use of the Mongolian language and their pastoral way of life were ultimately deemed to qualify them as members of the Mongol nationality (Ding Mingjun 2006, 39).

The *minzu*-building project also extended to the names of places and public events. In 1952 the Chinese name of the sole town in Alasha, Dingyu-anying (lit. Garrison for the Pacification of Remote Lands), was changed to the Mongolian Bayanhot (lit. Rich Town), since the former was believed to "offend public opinion" (C. *bu he minyi*; Li Wanlu 2007, 520).[9] In prerev-olutionary Alasha, the banner prince had hosted large games, including a variety of sporting contests, known locally as *üres*. In 1954, games were held to celebrate Alasha's incorporation into the IMAR. These were now referred to as *naadam*, a pan-Mongolian term that was preferred because it would be "accepted by all members of the Mongol nationality" (ALBG 2000, 923).

Under the gaze of state ethnographers, Alasha came to function as an archetype of traditional Mongol society. Unlike eastern Inner Mongolia, it had not been part of the Japanese Empire and thus was not subject to the kinds of modernizing projects implemented there, in terms of administra-tion, education, and animal husbandry, for example (Tighe 2005; Christmas 2019). The construction of railways in eastern Inner Mongolia in the early twentieth century had enabled rapid Han Chinese colonization of the region (Lattimore 1935); by contrast, the first railway in Alasha, a branch line used to transport salt, was not completed until 1965.[10] Its arid environmental conditions meant that most of the banner had still not been subject to the agricultural land reclamation and concomitant Han Chinese settlement that had transformed other parts of Inner Mongolia;[11] unlike eastern parts of Inner Mongolia (Borjigin 2017), pressures on land availability caused by Han Chinese settlement had not forced Mongols to become farmers, and Alasha appeared to preserve elements of the feudal social relations thought to be characteristic of prerevolutionary Mongol society.[12] After all, the region was represented by a former aristocrat in the person of Darijaya, in contrast to the Mongol revolutionaries from central (often referred to as "western") and eastern Inner Mongolia who vied for control of the IMAR (Sneath 2008).[13] Its apparent traditionalism meant that it was selected as the location of an extensive study of the society and history of the Mongol nationality in the 1950s (IMAR EG 2009). Along with the nationality classification project, such studies were conducted in minority areas across China as a central part of the CCP's nationality work (C. *minzu gongzuo*) in the years after it assumed power. Alasha's Mongols thereby became a synecdoche for the Mongol nationality. In 1963 the Inner Mongolian CCP designated Alasha Left Banner a "remote, purely pastoralist banner" (C. *bianyuan chun muye qi*), thus entitling it to subsidies (ALBG 2000, 48).

Ulanhu and the Defense of Pastoralism

Land reform was a central aspect of early CCP policy (DeMare 2019). By identifying classes and redistributing land from landlords to peasants, the CCP sought to gain the support of the masses and reorder Chinese society along socialist lines. In eastern Inner Mongolia they pursued violent land reform in the late 1940s, as they had in occupied agricultural areas of southern China. In Inner Mongolia, however, questions of land and class were crosscut by ethnic divisions, such that the peasants championed by the CCP were often Han Chinese settlers, while the landlords who were struggled against were frequently Mongols (Bulag 2000). In pastoral areas, land reform meant dividing large herds among many households, reducing the ability of herds to reproduce themselves. Richer herders often slaughtered their animals rather than have them confiscated (Sneath 2000, 64). The result was the rapid immiseration of many pastoral regions (Xiaoyuan Liu 2006, 278).

The Mongol chairman of the IMAR, Ulanhu, pushed back against this single-minded focus on class struggle in Inner Mongolia.[14] Rural areas were categorized as either agricultural, semipastoral, or pastoral zones—which, following its incorporation, included Alasha (Sneath 2000, 88)—and in 1948 Ulanhu announced the policy of Three Nos and Two Benefits (C. San Bu Liang Li), according to which there would be "no property distribution, no class labeling, and no class struggle" in pastoral regions, and "herd lords" (C. *muzhu*) and "herd workers" (C. *mugong*) were to be regarded as mutually beneficial (Bulag 2002b, 120). This form of Inner Mongolian exceptionalism was possible in the context of the CCP's emphasis on the importance of "implementing policy according to local conditions" (C. *yin di zhi yi*), a legacy of its successful revolutionary tactics (Heilmann 2008; Schmalzer 2019).

However, in the years that followed, Ulanhu frequently had to defend pastoral land use against those officials who wanted to expand agricultural production in the IMAR. He argued that they failed to understand "the political and economic significance of developing pastoralism in the IMAR," given its "*minzu* particularities" (C. *minzu tedian*; Wulanfu 1990, 198). Ulanhu declared that "the IMAR is a vital base of pastoralism [C. *xumuye jidi*] for the motherland. It is so now, and it always will be" (Wulanfu 1990, 198–99). His defense of pastoralism centered on its contribution to the national economy; in an earlier speech he claimed that "to develop pastoral production . . . is to assist China's socialist industrialization" (Wulanfu 1990, 121). This was in line with the overarching emphasis in Mao's thought on integration

(C. *zonghe*; Schmalzer 2022). When Mao thrust the agricultural commune of Dazhai into the limelight as a model to be emulated nationwide, Ulanhu faithfully echoed Maoist form but sought to ensure that the agricultural did not replace the pastoral by promoting the commune of Ushin as a "pastoral Dazhai" (Bulag 2002b; Hong Jiang 2006).

For Ulanhu, pastoralism was not culture to be preserved but a mode of production to be developed, which had to be understood as interdependent with agriculture and industry as part of an integrated national economy. His pronouncements on pastoralism also shifted according to changes in the political winds. While his speeches in the early 1950s suggested that no-madism would eventually give way to sedentarized herding, he also pointed out the benefits of nomadism in preventing the deterioration of the grass-lands (Wulanfu 1990, 57); as China embarked on collectivization in 1958, however, Ulanhu became more scathing about nomadism and stressed the importance of sedentarization as part of the process of collectivization, which would allow for "technological and cultural revolutions" among the herding population. "It is impossible to build socialism and communism on the basis of nomadism," he now insisted (Wulanfu 1990, 184). Stock improvement was also seen as key to the development of pastoralism, through importing improved breeds, such as the Soviet fine-haired sheep, but also by exploiting local improved breeds (C. *ben di gai xu*; Wulanfu 1990, 183).

Cultural Revolution and Settler Colonization

In 1958, Mao launched the Great Leap Forward, a program of rapid economic transformation that was supposed to allow China to surpass the United States in steel production in twenty years. These policies led to widespread famine, resulting in the deaths of millions across China and weakening Mao's posi-tion in the party. In an attempt to reassert his power, Mao claimed that the party had been infiltrated by Rightist elements and unleashed the Cultural Revolution in 1966. Young student Red Guards (C. Hong Weibing) traveled around China destroying the Four Olds (C. Si Jiu; old ideas, old culture, old habits, and old customs).

The effects of the Cultural Revolution were felt particularly severely In Inner Mongolia. Ulanhu's attempt to carve out spaces of Inner Mongolian exception from national policies was now attacked as local nationalism, and he was denounced publicly, accused of seeking to restore capitalism and split Inner Mongolia from China. He was detained in Beijing and then dismissed from his party posts. In 1968, a violent campaign against Mongols was launched in Inner Mongolia, under the guise of rooting out members of an alleged new Inner Mongolian People's Revolutionary Party (C. Nei Ren Dang), committed to splitting Inner Mongolia from China and merging with the MPR (Brown 2006).[15] Across Inner Mongolia, tens of thousands of people were killed and many more violently persecuted during the Cultural Revolution, most of them Mongols (Sneath 1994).[16] In 1969 the territory of the IMAR was reduced on grounds of national security, with certain areas given to neighboring Chinese provinces, including Alasha Left and Right Banners and Ejine Banner (Bulag 2017).

In Khöövör, local Mongols remember that much of the violence was perpetrated by recent Chinese migrants from Minqin County, in a part of Gansu bordering Alasha. As the famine that followed in the wake of the Great Leap Forward took hold in this arid region, thousands of starving peasants left Minqin and wandered through Alasha in search of food. Inner Mongolia's pastoral economy had been less severely affected than neighboring agricultural regions, and the recently established collectives took in these famine refugees. This fundamentally transformed the demographics of the banner. In 1949 there were 12,402 Mongols in the banner and 10,854 Han. By 1965 there were 14,372 Mongols and 36,934 Han (ALBG 2000, 206).[17]

According to local Mongols, once the Cultural Revolution started, their hospitality was quickly forgotten. Indeed, in the context of the renewed emphasis on class struggle brought about by the Cultural Revolution, their very ability to provide assistance was held against them, evidence of their class status as herd lords. Mongols were beaten and killed, with the Han Chinese attackers apparently claiming that this violence "served them right" (C. huogai) for their allegedly privileged position.

The 1960s also saw an aggressive emphasis on agriculture over pastoralism. Since the Han Chinese settlers were farmers, their arrival led to a huge increase in the amount of land under cultivation (ALBG 2000, 320). However, it was not only Chinese immigration that lay behind the expansion of agriculture in Alasha in the 1960s; following the Sino-Soviet split in 1960 and the withdrawal of Soviet aid to China, central state policies were increasingly driven by the notion of "taking grain as the key link" (C. yi liang wei gang; Shapiro 2001, 95). As self-reliance became a cardinal virtue, pastoralists were chastised for consuming grain they did not produce themselves, known as "grain of bad conscience" (C. kui xin liang; ALBG 2000, 320). Authorities in Alasha thus began to reclaim ever more pastureland for agricultural use, even though much of this new cropland failed, with disastrous ecological consequences, as members of the Alasha Camel Society would point out decades later in papers published with Han Chinese ecologists (Namuji-lecelin et al. 2012).

Localizing Pastoralism in the Reform Era

By the early 1970s, the Cultural Revolution was winding down in Inner Mongolia, signaled by the rehabilitation of Ulanhu in 1972. Mao's death in 1976 ushered in a new political climate, in which economic reforms were complemented by greater tolerance for certain forms of ethnic difference. Selected elements of Mongolian culture came to enjoy official support, and even Mongolian Buddhism was now tolerated (several of the larger monasteries in Alasha were rebuilt during the early 1980s). Following Mongol protests in 1981 against Han Chinese settlement in the IMAR, the 1980s also briefly saw the implementation of policies designed to limit agricultural expansion in the interests of preventing ecological degradation and the return of policies more favorable to pastoralism (Jankowiak 1988).[18]

In 1979 the two Alasha banners had been returned to the IMAR, in 1980 becoming part of the new Alasha League, along with Ejine Banner to the west.[19] In the context of economic reforms that emphasized comparative advantage and regional specialization (Hendrischke 1999; Liang and Xu 2004), the two most senior officials in Alasha League responded to pro-pastoralism shifts in IMAR policy with a paper titled *Exploiting the Strengths of Alasha League, Vigorously Promoting Camel Husbandry* (Liu Xiaowang and Wulunsai 2017 [1986]). They argued that development had to respect Alasha's unique environmental conditions, and thus could not be based on models from elsewhere in China, or even other parts of Inner Mongolia. In Alasha's arid environment, the authors claimed, only the camel thrived, this animal having a unique physiological adaptation to local conditions. These senior officials contrasted their sensitivity to local conditions to the Leftist (C. *zuo de sixiang*) policies of recent decades. In doing so, they could draw on a long-standing element of CCP strategy—eclipsed during the Cultural Revolution—that emphasized the importance of resisting uniform models and adapting to local conditions. Camel bodies thus materialized a particular post–Cultural Revolution politics that was critical of that period's fevered class reductionism.

However, pastoralism was not yet understood as a cultural tradition to be preserved but only as an economic form to be developed, as it had been for Ulanhu. The authors were on occasion explicitly critical of tradition, which they saw as an obstacle to the marketization of pastoralism: echoing negative stereotypes of irrational pastoralists found in other parts of the world, they lamented the influence of traditional pastoralism (C. *chuantong xumuye*) on herders, which apparently meant that in cases of severe drought, they preferred to hold on to their camels rather than selling them, with the result that the camels merely used up precious grassland resources before starving to death. The authors argued that when faced with a choice of getting rid of their camels or having them slowly perish in this way, herders had to be resolute and "sell, kill, or eat" (Liu Xiaowang and Wulunsai 2017 [1986], 108).

Neither cultural nor biological endangerment is evident in the document. There is no sense yet of the Alasha Bactrian camel as a genetic resource that needed to be conserved; indeed, the authors advocate developing new improved breeds by importing animals from Mongolia (Liu Xiaowang and Wulunsai 2017, 110). This desire for stock improvement also lay behind the local government's support for a sport—camel racing—that was later to be itemized as a central component of Alasha's camel culture. Large-scale camel-racing events were initially a way of encouraging herders and their camels from across Alasha to come together, affording the opportunity to exchange breeding stock. In the early 1980s, the Alasha League government had instituted a selective breeding program that sought to transform these former pack animals by selecting for quality hair, with meat a secondary consideration. In 1983 a small factory for processing camel hair was built in Alasha, and in 1984 sport and livestock improvement were combined when a large-scale camel-racing event was held alongside a stud camel evaluation and comparison event in the north of Alasha (ALBG 2000, 60).

The official promotion of camel racing was also influenced by broader shifts in policies toward minority cultures. As these began to thaw in the early reform era, China's Minzu Games (C. Minzu Yundong Hui), first held in 1952, were revived. In 1982 these were held in Hohhot, and in 1986 in Ürümqi in Xinjiang, an event at which the swift camels of Khöövör first gained their reputation. One anthropological observer noted that this event consisted of folkloric "exhibition displays of games or activities unique to particular groups," rather than competitive sports (Hann 1991, 228). Such competition as existed occurred between regions rather than nationalities. Camel racing had in fact only recently been codified by authorities in Alasha League, having previously been an informal activity that took place between households during New Year's celebrations, which had apparently been banned during the Cultural Revolution.[20] The state promotion of camel racing in Alasha in the 1980s must thus be understood in the context of developmentalist efforts at stock improvement but also of national policies that promoted spectacles of ethnic diversity but downplayed competition between nationalities in favor of national unity.

By 1994, however, the camel hair factory had gone bankrupt, and cryo-preservation and artificial insemination techniques, which had been developed as part of the 1980s breeding program, had been abandoned. Camel numbers plummeted as herders shifted to cashmere goats. Camel racing, however, outlasted its association with the selective breeding program, remaining popular in parts of Alasha, particularly Khöövör. As cashmere goats became the mainstay of the pastoral economy, camels were increasingly distinguished from the realm of the market, instead nostalgically associated with cultural vanishing.

Rescaling Culture in the Twenty-First Century

The Politics of Cultural Heritage

The first decade of the twenty-first century saw China gripped by "cultural heritage preservation fever" (Harrell 2013). Ideas of cultural heritage have quickly transformed how historical sites and cultural traditions are understood in China (Evans and Rowlands 2021). But they have also involved the extension of ideas of cultural tradition to practices that were not previously conceptualized in this way. In Alasha, camel husbandry, understood to be threatened by the forces of modernization, came to be regarded not simply as an economic matter but also as a valuable form of cultural heritage that needed to be preserved.

In 2006, the Mongolian-language *Alasha Camel Culture* (M. *Alasha temeen soyol*) was published as part of a series on the culture of the Oirad, or Western Mongols (Mönkhjargal 2006).[21] Its author was an Alasha herder who had initially made a name for himself locally as a poet. This was the first book-length treatment of camels in Alasha since *The Alasha Bactrian Camel*, published in the heady days of the late 1980s (Norbu and Jüngnei 1988), when local officials were enthusiastic about the development prospects of camel husbandry. The introduction to Mönkhjargal's book explicitly compares it with *The Alasha Bactrian Camel*, noting that this earlier work was written at a time when the population of camels was still over two hundred thousand and herders were contented (M. *setgel taivan*), whereas by the time *Alasha Camel Culture* was written there were fewer than fifty thousand camels left and herders were regretful and despondent (M. *kharamsan gashilj*). While the earlier book focused on research into the camel itself, the latter was concerned with customs and culture (M. *yos zangshil, soyol*) surrounding the camel. This cultural turn is evident in the language used to describe the practices involved in camel husbandry. Though the two works overlap in the practices they describe, such as shearing and milking, in the 1988 book these are merely skills (M. *mergejil*), while in Mönkhjargal's book they have become customs (M. *yos zanshil*).

In 2003, China became a signatory to the UNESCO convention on intangible cultural heritage (ICH). The years that followed saw the enthusiastic cataloging of practices and the compiling of provincial, as well as national, lists of ICH. Such listing has become an important part of nation-building in contemporary China (Oakes and Zuo 2022). In 2008, the camel husbandry customs of the Mongol nationality were officially included as part of Alasha's contribution to China's national ICH list. These customs were itemized as camel veneration (C. *jituo*), camel racing (C. *saituo*), and the craft of camel tack (C. *tuoju zhizuo gongyi*; Huqun 2010).

According to China's national ICH list, each item has a particular government department responsible for its conservation (C. *baohu danwei*). In the case of the camel husbandry customs of the Mongol nationality, responsibility lies with the Alasha League Mass Art Center (C. Qunzhong Yishu Guan), a repository of mass culture (C. *qunzhong wenhua*) that is a legacy of the Mao era. The CCP had early on looked to folk songs in particular as a form of mass culture that could be reworked to spread socialist ideas (Mackerras 1984). It is no coincidence that figures such as Altanuul who have helped to produce a discourse of camel culture have also been involved in preservation of local folk songs, which are one of Alasha's signature forms of ICH (D'Evelyn 2018). While the formation of camel culture was indebted to globally circulating ideas of heritage promulgated by UNESCO, it was also inflected by the Mao-era valorization of particular forms of cultural production on the part of the masses.

The concept of agricultural heritage systems, promoted by the Food and Agriculture Organization of the UN (FAO), has quickly gained traction in China, where the notion of agricultural heritage has a long history (Schmalzer 2019). This idea of agricultural heritage has recently been deployed to protect pastoralist land use, and in 2014 the Nomadic System of the Ar Khorchin Grasslands was recognized as Nationally Important Agricultural Heritage. Around this time, Baigal, a livestock technician and one of the founders of the Alasha Camel Society, had sought unsuccessfully to register Alasha's camel husbandry as part of China's agricultural heritage. He attributed his failure to the fact that senior officials from the local Bureau of Agriculture and Animal Husbandry, which is responsible for China's agricultural heritage listing, had not understood the initiative and so had not supported it.

Heritage-making is inevitably a selective process. As a result of the discursive localizing of pastoralism in the 1980s, the subsequent endangerment of the camel, and the association of cashmere goats with the ills of marketization, pastoralist heritage in Alasha came to focus on the camel. What is more, the institutional arrangements through which camel husbandry was conserved as culture objectified it as a limited set of aestheticized practices. Alasha League's listing of three practices—camel veneration rituals, camel racing, and the craft of camel tack—resulted from the administrative division of the league into three banners; one practice was assigned to each banner, and they were allotted funds to support that particular practice (Wu Ning 2018, 130).[22] The logic of comparative advantage and specialization was again at work, and cultural heritage was bent to the shape of the administrative structure of the post-1980 Alasha League.

In other contexts, pastoralist mobility has itself recently been listed as heritage. In 2019, UNESCO listed "transhumance, the seasonal droving of livestock along migratory routes in the Mediterranean and the Alps" on the representative list of the intangible cultural heritage of humanity (Bindi 2022). However, in Alasha the mobility that is an inherent part of camel husbandry in the region was not itself recognized as heritage. Instead, those who would defend this mobility and oppose enclosure of the grasslands were forced to adopt a different strategy, insisting on the modernity of mobility by articulating a vision of high-tech husbandry or *techno-pastoralism*, which I discuss in chapter 4.

The particular framing of pastoralist heritage that was possible in Alasha, as spectacles to be performed and objects to be displayed, was shaped by the local state's desire to foster tourism through cultural production. In 2003, for example, the IMAR government announced a plan for regional development that involved transforming Inner Mongolia into a Great Cultural Region (C. *wenhua daqu*; Liu Keyan 2003). In Alasha this was exemplified by the establishment of an annual Camel Naadam in 2012, the year the region was officially declared China's Camel Country. By 2013, when I first attended, the Camel Naadam was being billed as one of Alasha Left Banner's three unique cultural brands (C. *tese wenhua pinpai*), along with the Alasha Strange Stone Culture and Tourism Festival and the Alasha Heroes Meet (C. Yingxiong Hui), a huge off-road vehicle festival held in the Tengger Desert. A few years later, two of these cultural brands were combined for maximum tourist exposure, and a Camel Culture and Tourism Festival was held in tandem with the Heroes Meet.

For some, this exuberant heritage-making had gone too far. Jargal, a rather cynical local official in Khöövör, complained that "recently the state has been encouraging people to sing songs and worship *ovoo* (ritual cairns); some of these were never worshipped before! There are many fake things now." He also objected to the use of the term *naadam* in relation to camel racing, asserting that this word should be used only to refer to occasions when the traditional Mongolian three manly sports (M. *eriin gurvan naadam*) of horse racing, wrestling, and archery were performed (see Kabzińska-Stawartz 1991).

The Chinese state's policies toward minority regions shifted in the reform era from an earlier emphasis on coercive assimilation to an encouragement of circumscribed forms of commodified cultural difference that could be packaged for tourists. Some anthropologists have argued that in this context the preservation of cultural heritage should be seen as a political project on the part of the Chinese state to pacify minority regions (Shepherd 2006; Rippa 2020). Others, however, have argued that cultural heritage in minority regions of China is not simply imposed in a top-down manner but can be harnessed by minority actors seeking material improvements to their communities (in housing and infrastructure, for example). These actors can also use discourses of cultural heritage to frame particular issues, for example in contesting policies that ban hunting (Fraser 2020). Against the backdrop of state environmentalism that blames desertification on pastoralists, the discourse of cultural heritage has enabled Mongols in Alasha to assert the value of camel husbandry. This framing of pastoralism as heritage has helped justify local exemptions for the camel from the strict stocking limits that apply to sheep and goats. The local politics of cultural heritage can thus modulate the ways state environmental policies are implemented on the ground.

Ideas of camel husbandry as cultural heritage in Alasha have also created space for the selective valorization of pastoralists' traditional ecological knowledge. The 1980s saw the emergence of a global movement, with its roots in the struggles over land in the Brazilian Amazon, which advocated for the rights of indigenous peoples. This involved alliances between environmental NGOs in the Global North and certain indigenous groups (Conklin and Graham 1995). Such alliances were partly enabled by the development of concepts such as indigenous knowledge and traditional ecological knowledge, which cast indigenous peoples as stewards of nature rather than backward and inefficient resource users. These ideas entered China through the work of transnational conservation NGOs in the 1980s. Chinese intellectuals who worked with these NGOs began to apply ideas of indigenous knowledge to certain minority nationalities, defending practices such as swidden agriculture, which had been denigrated by the state as ecologically destructive and backward (C. *luohou*; Hathaway 2010).

In Alasha, where the presence of transnational NGOs has been much more limited, similar ideas have been transmitted through collaborations between the Alasha Camel Society and Han Chinese ecologists, as well as through the work of Inner Mongolian academics. Herders' knowledge is often justified with reference to Alasha's camel culture, demonstrating how heritage in this case is more than the aestheticized objects of tourist desire. Writing in a Chinese journal, one Inner Mongolian anthropologist, for example, writes that "camel husbandry and related traditional customs play a key role in maintaining the local ecosystem" (Wu Ning 2015, 70). This anthropologist criticizes the grazing ban policies and the state's tendency to regard nomadism as backward, which has led to the neglect of traditional knowledge (C. *chuantong zhishi*; Wu Ning 2015, 73). A better understanding of local ecological knowledge (C. *bentu shengtai zhishi*) would, the anthropologist asserts, make the state's environmental policies more scientific (C. *kexuexing*) and contribute to "the construction of ecological civilization." Here we can see how the discourse of ecological civilization is appropriated and routed away from coercive environmentalism (Yifei Li and Judith Shapiro 2020) toward a defense of nomadism as local knowledge.

In a short article in a compendium of camel-related material, *The Silk Road Camel Bell*, published by the Alasha League branch of the CPPCC, one young Mongol CPPCC official describes the ecological benefits of the semiwild herding style (C. *ban yesheng mutuo fangshi*) employed by camel herders, which involves allowing camels to browse freely on pastureland selected by herders according to the season. Camels are here described as an important part of the Gobi ecosystem. This official writes that "Gobi camel herding culture [C. *Gebi mutuo wenhua*] is the crystallization of herders' labor and wisdom" (Wuricaihu 2017, 174). And in a piece cowritten with a Han Chinese ecologist from the prestigious Tsinghua University in Beijing, three members of the Alasha Camel Society write that "Alasha people understand the region's harsh climate, the adaptation of breeds to this climate, and the characteristics of plants, and they themselves have adapted and developed a characteristic nomadic culture. They understand the laws of nature and have accumulated a rich store of knowledge" (Namujilecelin et al. 2012).

Scholars have identified the emergence of an ethno-environmental discourse in early twenty-first-century Inner Mongolia whereby Mongol intellectuals contested the stigmatization of pastoralism as backward and environmentally destructive and instead insisted that the traditional Mongolian lifestyle should be preserved because it is an important part of the grassland ecosystem (Baranovitch 2016b). While this ethno-environmental discourse has clearly informed discussions of Alasha camel culture, it is important to note that the officials above make reference not to Mongols but to Gobi herders (C. *Gebi mumin*) and Alasha people (C. *Alashan ren*). This indicates a shift in discourses of culture in Inner Mongolia in recent years, such that they foreground region and locality over ethnicity. Mongol intellectuals who seek to defend pastoralist land use increasingly have to adopt discourses of localization and cultural hybridity, weakening the connection between land use and nationality that was once at the heart of politics in Inner Mongolia.

Reimagining Alasha's Frontier Hybridity

The opening ceremony of the 2013 Camel Naadam included a speech by the Han Chinese party secretary of Alasha Left Banner, the most powerful local official. He referred to the *naadam* as a traditional festival of the people of the grasslands (C. *caoyuan de renmin*) but stated that the Camel Naadam was one of Alasha's unique cultural brands (C. *tese wenhua pinpai*). Absent from the speech was any reference to the Mongol nationality. This reflected an increasing tendency in Inner Mongolia, since the beginning of the twenty-first century, to scale culture in terms of grasslands, the biome that characterizes much of the region, while at the same time emphasizing the unique cultural brands of particular localities, such as Alasha (Ujeed n.d.). Following the 2003 announcement of a plan to turn the IMAR into a Great National Cultural Region, the first annual Grassland Culture Festival was held in 2004, and in subsequent years cultural festivals began to proliferate at subregional scales, including the Hongshan Culture Festival in eastern Chifeng Municipality, which began in 2006, and the Hetao Culture Festival in Bayannuur Municipality, starting in 2014.

Cultural branding at the provincial scale had been deployed in other parts of China since the 1990s, as economic reforms increased the powers and responsibilities of provinces, which now competed to attract foreign and domestic investment (Hendrischke 1999). In Inner Mongolia in the 1990s high-ranking officials, mainly Han Chinese, sought to develop a distinctive Inner Mongolian regional culture to attract domestic and foreign investment (Borchigud 1996). The promotion of tourism has been an important aspect of cultural branding in China, especially in certain poorer provinces, such as Guizhou, which lacked other avenues for development (Oakes 1999), but fostering distinctive provincial cultural identities is also about attracting economic investment more broadly. This is also evident at other administrative scales. According to one of the founders of the Alasha Camel Society, camel culture and the Camel Country brand would help distinguish Alasha League and thus encourage investment.

However, the example of Inner Mongolia shows how cultural branding has political as well as economic significance and is bound up with the Chinese state's nation-building project at its ethnic frontiers. Mongol intellectuals formulated the concept of grassland culture (C. *caoyuan wenhua*) in the early twenty-first century, in response to ideas of nomadic civilization that were being promoted across the border in Mongolia (Bayar 2014a). In one respect, the idea of grassland culture works to counter long-standing stereotypes of nomadic peoples on China's periphery as barbarians in need of civilizing (Harrell 1995). Indeed, grassland culture is said to be one of the three core components of Chinese civilization, along with Yellow River culture and Yangtze River culture (Bayar 2014a, 450). It is thus part of broader intellectual currents in reform-era China that have sought to emphasize the role of frontiers, both steppe and maritime, in the construction of China, rather than thinking solely in terms of a Chinese civilization which emanates out from center to periphery (Dirlik 2006).

However, grassland culture is also a scaling device that works to circumscribe the Mongols within the bounds of Chinese civilization and the contemporary Chinese state, as links with other Eurasian nomadic peoples are deemphasized. Furthermore, grassland culture is explicitly multiethnic, encompassing all nationalities who live in this geographical region, and is said to include hunting, farming, and even industry (Bayar 2014a, 450). Rather than belonging to a particular nationality, proponents of the term argue that grassland culture is defined by a geographical area. In the words of one member of the Inner Mongolia Academy of Social Sciences, "Grassland culture is a regional culture [C. *quyu wenhua*] formed in the particular natural environment of the grasslands" (Shi Shuangzhu 2011).

While grassland culture reworks long-standing hierarchies and narratives of Chinese civilization and Inner Asian barbarism, it also has the effect of obscuring the Han Chinese settler colonization of Inner Mongolia. This is evident in the case of some of the regional cultures (or cultural brands) that are conceptualized as nested within grassland culture or formed by its intersection with the other great cultures of Chinese civilization. To the east of Alasha, Bayannuur Municipality, for example, now styles itself as the home of Yellow River Bend culture (C. *Hetao wenhua*), in reference to this river's detour into Inner Mongolia, which enables irrigated agriculture in this arid region. This culture is said to be a product of the "blending [C. *jiaorong*] of grassland culture and agrarian culture" (Ba 2005). Obscured here are the contested processes through which Chinese counties were formed out of Mongolian banners (Bulag 2017) and agriculture came to replace pastoralism across much of this region. Indeed, some formulations of Yellow River Bend culture in fact regurgitate the denigration of nomadism that grassland culture was supposed to counter. One article, for example, celebrates the contribution made by the formation of Yellow River Bend culture to the "sedentarization of nomads [C. *youmu dingju*] and the development of wasteland reclamation [C. *kenzhi fazhan*]" (Ba 2005).

Of the various regional elements of grassland culture proposed in recent years, one of the few that correspond to a preexisting Mongolian politicocultural unit is Alasha culture (C. *Alashan wenhua*). This builds on the long-standing sense of Alasha as distinct from the rest of the IMAR because of its historical ties to the western Mongols (Oirad), its historically distinctive administrative status, and its relatively late incorporation into the region. However, that Alasha culture is a recent invention is evident in the way it is mapped onto contemporary Alasha League, itself only established in 1980. It thus amalgamates the Torghud Mongols of Ejine and the Khoshuud Mongols of the two Alasha banners, as well as the more recent Khalkha arrivals.[23]

One local intellectual who played a key role in elaborating Alasha culture was Nasun, a Mongol who hailed from eastern Inner Mongolia. In 1985 he had been sent to work in the Alasha League Party School, which trained cadres. Lamenting the fact that Alasha did not have much of a "cultural atmosphere" (C. *wenhua qifen*) and that many cultural and historical resources (C. *lishi wenhua ziyuan*) had not been excavated (C. *wajue*), in 2001 he resolved to set up a website, which went on to publish numerous articles on Alasha's history and culture.[24]

According to Nasun, Alasha's cultural distinctiveness was partly a product of its administrative status under the Qing, separate from the rest of Inner Mongolia. He also argued that culture is shaped by both humans and their natural surroundings. He stressed the importance of a particular geographical environment (C. *teding dili huanjing*) in creating distinctive cultures. He was critical of those who speak of "Alasha religious culture" or "Alasha oboo culture," since they described things that are not unique to Alasha. By contrast, it was correct to speak of "Alasha camel culture," since the Alasha Bactrian camel was a "breed with unique biological characteristics" (C.

shengwu tezheng dute de pinzhong) created by this environment, and Alasha camel culture had been formed by a long process of interaction between Alasha people and these animals. Environmental specificity is seen to produce both biological and cultural specificity.

Some members of the Alasha Camel Society echoed these ideas. Baigal explained to me that Alasha Culture had been strongly influenced by the region's arid grasslands. He told me that culture consisted of the survival skills (C. *shengcun de jishu*) required in a particular environment and was not the marker (C. *fuhao*) of any particular nationality. According to Baigal, Alasha camel culture was not merely the preserve of Mongols; he pointed out that the winner of the camel milking competition at the Camel *Naadam* had been Han. "Culture is a product of the natural environment [C. *ziran huanjing*] and does not belong to a single nationality," he insisted.

Alasha culture, then, was not treated as the exclusive property of the region's Mongols. Instead, its elaborators referred to the history of the region before the arrival of the Oirad Mongols, arguing that when it was part of the Tangut Empire (1038–1227), it was inhabited by Tanguts and Han Chinese. During the Yuan dynasty (1271–1368), Muslims moved into the area, with the result that Alasha "gradually became a place where Mongolian culture, and the Han and Hui cultures of China's northwest, came together and blended with one another" (Pan Zhaodong and Liu Junbao 2005).

This emphasis on hybridity was central to many articulations of Alasha culture. It was also nested underneath a superordinate Chinese culture (C. *Zhonghua wenhua*), with *Chinese* here referring to the Chinese nation (C. *Zhonghua minzu*) rather than the Han Chinese nationality. In an interview with the *Alasha Daily News* (Tang Jinwang 2013), Nasun argued that "Alasha culture is a branch of Chinese culture and of grassland culture, with its own unique [C. *dute*] charm. This culture has evolved over a great swathe of time, beginning with the rich culture of [Mongol] migration [C. *qianxi wenhua*] later merging [C. *ronghe*] with Han culture and Hui culture, which eventually created this unique local [C. *bendi de*] culture."

Other discussions of Alasha culture single out the Muslim Mongols of Khöövör as an example of the inclusiveness (C. *baorongxing*) of Alasha, since they have the same language and way of life as the Mongols but share their religion with the Hui (Xinhua 2012). Where the nationality classification project of the 1950s had no place for the Muslim Mongols as a distinct group, today they are celebrated as a microcosm of the blending of multiple nationalities (C. *duo minzu ronghe*) that is said to be characteristic of Alasha. On the occasion of a *naadam* held in 2013 to celebrate the reconstruction of one of the mosques of the Muslim Mongols, the opening speech explained that Khöövör was characterized by "the blending [C. *jiaorong*] of nomadic culture and the agrarian civilization of the Yellow River Bend."

In the context of this celebration of frontier hybridity, the association of camels and culture has also been expanded. Rather than merely giving rise to certain forms of local intangible cultural heritage, they are celebrated for their role as a kind of cultural infrastructure, enabling cultural exchange between nationalities. The camel caravan is central to this imaginary of exchange and interaction. One local historian, for example, writes that "not only did camel caravans play an important role in trade; what is even more significant is the way that they strengthened and deepened connections [C. *lianxi*] and friendship [C. *youyi*] between nationalities" (Shi Youtian 2007, 419).[25]

Since the start of the twenty-first century, intellectuals and cultural producers in China have increasingly represented China's frontiers as spaces characterized by cultural contact and exchange (Oakes 2012; Yu Luo et al. 2019). Others argue that such processes need to be intensified through policy reform. In the early 2010s, prominent Han Chinese intellectuals began to discuss proposals for a "second generation" of *minzu* policies (Hu Angang and Hu Lianhe 2011; Ma Rong 2014). The American melting pot model has proved influential among these scholars, and they call for increased contact (C. *jiaowang*), exchange (C. *jiaoliu*), and mingling (C. *jiaorong*) among China's ethnic groups (C. *zuqun*) in order to bring about the integration (C. *yitihua*) of the Chinese nation (C. *Zhonghua minzu*). These ideas were soon echoed in official pronouncements and in policies toward minority nationalities, including the promotion of Mandarin in education at the expense of minority languages (Roche and Leibold 2020) and cash incentives for interethnic marriages (Kaiman 2014). On a visit to Inner Mongolia in 2014, Xi Jinping spoke of the need to "bind the people of each ethnic group into a single strand of rope" (Leibold 2014).

Ideas of cultural exchange and hybridity have been promoted as part of China's Belt and Road Initiative (BRI), launched by Xi Jinping in 2013. This is a grand vision of infrastructural investment and "people-to-people exchange" across Eurasia and beyond, which draws on the imagery of the Silk Road to suggest the return of an era of peaceful exchange between China and the rest of the world. Since its launch, the BRI has generated a vast amount of commentary from scholars, journalists, and politicians (e.g., Phillips 2017; Jones and Zeng 2019; Rogelja and Tsimonis 2022). While much of this focuses on its economic and political implications, some have looked more closely at how the BRI is suffused with ideas of a historical Silk Road (Winter 2019;

Qian 2022). Silk Road imagery is more than just window dressing, a way of casting the boring stuff of logistics and infrastructure in a romantic light. In fact, international cultural heritage cooperation is an important part of the BRI, and ideas of cultural exchange (C. *wenhua jiaoliu*) feature prominently in Chinese BRI discourse. Moreover, the revival of the notion of the Silk Road is fundamentally related to conceptions of China as a civilization-state characterized by historical continuity and enduring values and by routes and networks that emanate from Beijing rather than by Westphalian borders (Grant 2018).

Such civilizational visions coexist with a nation-building project that continues to grapple with the ethnic diversity of China's borderlands. Indeed, China's recent "going out" (C. *zou chuqu*) into the world has occurred in conjunction with an intensification of nation-building in the country's western regions (Nyiri 2006). "Mobility narratives" (Sigley 2020) such as the Silk Road are thus not only of geopolitical significance but also shape understandings of frontier regions and the minority nationalities who inhabit them. In recent years, for example, minority scholars in southwest China have promoted the idea of a Tea Horse Road that historically connected communities in this region to each other and to other parts of China. The connectivity afforded by this route is seen to have enabled among disparate minority groups the development of a consciousness of their membership of the Chinese nation (C. *Zhonghua minzu*; Sigley 2020).

In 2015 the China Camel Culture Museum opened in a large new building on the outskirts of Bayanhot.[26] Having walked past a life-size cross-section of a camel, which provides information about the distinctive biological features of the camel, visitors enter an exhibition room where they are confronted with a large image of President Xi Jinping superimposed on a string of camels. This exhibition, titled *The Silk Road*, features a huge map of Eurasia across which red lines show the route of two historical Silk Roads. At the bottom of the map, a Chinese high-speed train the size of half of Eurasia speeds toward Europe.

The emphasis on the Silk Road accompanying the BRI has stimulated narratives and practices of place-making in Alasha that work to transform its long-standing characterization as a remote periphery and, in turn, the association of camel husbandry with remoteness. This can involve banal acts of touristic rebranding, such as the construction of new rest stops alongside highways that go under the name of caravanserais (C. *yi zhan*). But it has also given rise, for example, to archaeological expeditions. In 2014, the chairman of the Alasha League CPPCC began an investigation into Alasha's caravan routes and the Silk Road (Wang Qiucai 2016).[27] This official was eager to connect the history of this route to the Silk Road, claiming that the caravan routes across Alasha were originally "the northern route of the Grassland Silk Road." He writes that "Silk Road culture, which depended on the caravans, is intimately linked to Alasha."

As in other Chinese border regions (Yongming Zhou 2013), this reinterpretation of local history in order to align it with policy initiatives has the effect of repositioning Alasha: it is no longer on the margins of the nation-state but instead plays an important role in an expansive civilization-state. Camel culture is now scaled up, no longer merely a local phenomenon but rather bound up with the interaction and exchange between civilizations. Writes one Alasha scholar, "It was camels that traveled the Silk Road, the Porcelain Road, the Tea Road, bringing agrarian and nomadic civilizations together and helping them to blend, causing Eastern civilization and Western civilization to influence one another" (Liu Yuelian 2017). It is notable in this respect that the camel culture museum in Bayanhot is not the *Alasha* but the *China* Camel Culture Museum.

The new camel culture exhibition hall in the Alasha Right Banner Museum features an introductory panel that reads, "Camel husbandry has an ancient pedigree. It not only supported the ceaseless development of the local economy but also nourished a camel culture with distinctive regional and ethnic characteristics, and a historical and contemporary Silk Road culture, manifesting the traditional charm and contemporary value of grassland civilization." Where once it had been counterposed to modern civilization, the camel in Alasha now becomes a bridge between Silk Roads old and new. One retired official, for example, argues that the local government should seize the historic opportunity offered by the BRI and exploit Alasha's status as a "vital node on the Silk Road" to establish Silk Road–themed tourism, with tourists following an old caravan route across Alasha (Batuchulu 2017). This is imagined as an aspect of Alasha's "opening up to the north," situating itself on the China-Mongolia-Russia Economic Corridor, which is a key element of the BRI. Ancient and contemporary connectivity are thus sutured together, as tourists instantiate a new economic corridor by following the alleged route of the ancient Silk Road.

THE REMAKING OF PASTORALISM as heritage in Inner Mongolia is an ongoing process. In 2015, Sunit Banner in Shilingol League was declared China's Camel Culture Country (C. *Zhongguo Luotuo Wenhua Zhi Xiang*) by the China Folk Artists Association (C. *Minjian Yishujia Xiehui*), and in 2020 the Gobi Red Camel Herding System in Urad Rear Banner, Bayannuur Municipality, was listed as part of China's national agricultural heritage.[28] Thus local governments in the IMAR jostle for the attention of tourists and investors through the creation of locally specific cultural heritage brands, even when these appear to step on the toes of other localities.

While this exemplifies the broader commodification of culture in China that has been underway since the 1980s, pastoralist heritage must also be understood in the context of Inner Mongolia's political ecology. In Inner Mongolia, the Chinese state's embrace of globally circulating ideas of cultural heritage has provided local minority elites with a way of reframing the issue of pastoralist land use and countering the stigmatization characteristic of recent policies such as ecological migration and grazing bans. Questions of heritage and political ecology have only rarely been considered alongside each other (e.g., Heatherington 2010; Peutz 2018), but attending to their interrelation is vital for an understanding of the politics of state environmentalism in contemporary China.

Even as they revalorize pastoralism, however, these processes of heritage-making also represent a novel rescaling of culture. The twentieth century saw pastoralism become firmly established as the central marker of Mongol identity. Urban Mongol intellectuals played an important role in essentializing Mongols as pastoralists as they sought to resist assimilation into the Han Chinese majority (Khan 1996). However, novel representations of pastoralism in Inner Mongolia have emerged in the early twenty-first century, whereby pastoralist heritage assumes distinctive *local* forms. In these representations, pastoralism no longer marks a straightforward binary opposition between Mongol pastoralists and Han Chinese agriculturalists. In their defense of pastoralism, Mongol elites have adopted this localizing discourse.

However, transcending this binary through localization glosses over the demographic and ecological transformation that accompanied post-1949 Han Chinese settlement by treating it as part of a long history of migration and benign cultural exchange said to characterize this frontier region. In recent years, Alasha's camel culture has also been scaled up to become both local and continental, part of the Silk Road narratives that have accompanied the Belt and Road Initiative. In the context of China's increasingly assimilationist policies toward minorities, the defense of pastoralism as heritage has thus been strategically decoupled from questions of nationality autonomy and exception and must make use of powerful new scales of culture.

Despite these discourses of hybridity and cultural rescaling, however, the *minzu* paradigm remained important in shaping how culture was understood and performed on the ground in the early 2010s. At the *naadam* to celebrate the renovation of a mosque in Khöövör in 2013, a parade followed the opening speech, which had praised the Muslim Mongols as exemplars of hybridity. This parade saw Muslim Mongols dressed in Mongolian robes carrying various items of camel tack, while local Hui, many of them in fact from local camel-herding households, were dressed in waistcoats and white hats and merely given small flags to wave. When I asked a local Muslim Mongol herder about this, he told me that the Hui, unlike the Mongols, had "no culture of their own" (M. *ööriin soyol baikhgüi*). When he later complemented the skills in camel husbandry of a local Hui, he said that this man was "a true Mongol herder" (M. *jinkhene Mongol malchin*). Whatever the post-ethnic formulations of intellectuals in Bayanhot, on the grasslands of Alasha pastoralism remained strongly associated with the Mongols, and culture was commonly scaled to nationality. As people like Altanuul and his herder relatives were encouraged by local heritage policies to organize camel culture events in rural Alasha, they thus had to navigate tensions between locality, religion, and nationality.

2

The Politics
of Livestock
Rituals

THE MONASTERY at Bull Camel Mountain, straddling the contemporary border between Alasha League and Bayannuur Municipality, was destroyed during the Cultural Revolution. Today locals can still point to bullet holes on the cliff face, where Red Guards took potshots at the magical image of a bull camel, which gives the mountain its name, as they sought to expunge any vestiges of the Four Olds. The ruins of the former monastery are still clearly visible, but there has been no attempt to protect or restore the buildings. In 1986 herders from neighboring Dengkou County began to organize the annual veneration ritual at the mountain, but it was not until 2004 that a small one-room temple was built, thanks to the efforts of several Mongol elites based in Bayanhot, including Altanuul. They were members of the local branch of the China Federation of Literary and Art Circles (C. Zhongguo Wenxue Yishu Jie Lianhe Hui), a part of the CPPCC that represents cultural elites.

While the material heritage of the ruined Buddhist monastery has been neglected, the rituals conducted here, by contrast, now enjoy official protection. Classified as "camel veneration rituals," they represent perhaps the most surprising element of the camel husbandry customs registered as part of China's national intangible cultural heritage in 2008. Practices that had been denounced only a few decades earlier as superstition (C. *mixin*) were now officially celebrated as local culture. This was all the more striking in the context of the state's destocking policies, which addressed herders as irresponsible resource users and understood livestock in relation to the carrying capacity of the grasslands. Scholars of pastoralism in China have often contrasted the state's ecological and economic understandings of livestock with those of minority herders, which the state deems irrational (Levine 1999; Kabzung and Yeh 2016). Listing camel veneration rituals as intangible cultural heritage, by contrast, appeared to valorize local understandings of livestock and recognize the importance of ritual to Mongolian pastoralism (Wallace 2012).

Across the world, many environmental organizations now proclaim their respect for the beliefs and rituals of indigenous peoples and highlight their compatibility with the goals of conservation (Brosius 1997; Delcore 2004). In China, positive understandings of beliefs in sacred forests, for instance, were promulgated by Chinese intellectuals who worked with transnational NGOs in the biodiversity hot spot of Yunnan (Hathaway 2010). This represented a significant shift from the Cultural Revolution era, when such beliefs had been attacked as superstition, and was in line with a broader relaxation of policies that marked the first decades of the reform era (Chau 2011). In some parts of China, officials have begun to regard animism or "nature worship" (C. *ziran chongbai*) positively, as a means of galvanizing environmentalist sensibilities toward state-approved ends (Swancutt 2016). Analyses of state environmentalism in China, then, must not merely account for restrictions on the land use practices of ethnic minorities but also address the apparent rehabilitation, and official approval, of certain beliefs and ritual practices related to the natural world.

However, rather than representing simply a revival and revalorization of folk traditions briefly interrupted by the Cultural Revolution, these rituals have in fact been transformed through their categorization as local intangible cultural heritage. In this respect, two overlapping aspects of the rituals were particularly important: their *ontology* and their *organization*. In becoming heritage, the relationship of these rituals to Buddhist lamas and landscapes was obscured, as they were ontologically reformatted by intellectuals and officials as a distinctive local folk culture directed at the veneration of the natural world in the form of camels. The creation of a category of camel veneration rituals in Alasha thus reveals how conceptions of the "ecologically noble savage" (Redford 1991) have circulated throughout China (Yeh 2014b). However, its local manifestation—the ecologically noble herder—must also be understood in the context of attempts to distinguish Mongolian culture from Tibeto-Mongolian Buddhism, a legacy of early twentieth-century Mongolian nationalism.

In terms of organization, remaking these rituals as heritage involved the discursive construction and performance of a local society, represented by certain "transmitters" (C. *chuanchengren*) of cultural heritage, which could be clearly demarcated from the state. Some scholars have argued that the revival of rituals in reform-era China involves carving out a space of community autonomy apart from the structures of the state (Dean 2003; Maags 2018). However, in Alasha, the nonstate realm was the site of multiple, at times contested, sources of authority: that of the lay transmitters of cultural heritage and that of Buddhist lamas. Furthermore, the organization of the rituals showed that the boundary between state and society, like that between culture and religion, was contested and contingent: rituals organized by those in the penumbra of the state eventually became embroiled in Xi Jinping's anticorruption politics, and pastoral heritage was commodified as a spectacle for tourists through the conjuncture of local state and mining capital, in line with processes documented elsewhere in China (Chio 2014). The Chinese state's relationship to pastoralism was not simply characterized by an aggressive modernizing agenda, according to which livestock rituals would be exemplary of "irrational" and "backward" pastoralism and either repressed or ignored by the state; instead, these rituals were a key site at which the relationship between state and society in rural Alasha was imagined, performed, and remade.

Ritual at Bull Camel Mountain

On a cold dawn in early spring 2013, in a large yurt (M. *ger*) at the foot of a cliff, Batbagana was preparing a ritual offering. With a pocket knife he cut out the breastbone (M. *övchüü*) from a slab of boiled mutton and placed it on a metal tray before making a kind of cradle on top out of lengths of string. His preparation was interrupted by an elderly lama, Tsetsen, who wandered over to the table and began to advise Batbagana. A blue silk scarf (M. *khadag*) was then placed on top of the cradle, followed by strips of red, yellow, and green cloth, a sweet pancake, and some jujubes. An hour later, this breastbone was placed in a large bonfire outside as part of the fire veneration ritual (M. *galiin takhilga*) that marked the start of this annual ceremony to venerate Bull Camel Mountain. Batbagana and several others circumambulated the fire, tossing yogurt and alcohol into the flames. They were dressed in traditional Mongolian robes (M. *deel*) but were soon joined by several Han and Mongol officials from Khöövör Town, including the local (Mongol) party secretary, all dressed in crisp white shirts and zippered windbreakers.[1]

They then returned to the yurt. Flanked by two other lamas, Tsetsen occupied the seat of honor in the middle of the table, with Altanuul, the officials, and me at one end. Set out in front of the lamas was the boiled sheep's back and fatty tail (M. *uuts*), which is customarily served on ceremonial occasions in Alasha. As the organizer of this revived ritual, Altanuul assumed the role of host and began to make a speech in halting Chinese explaining the history of the temple and the revival of the veneration ritual, which he claimed was "spontaneously" (C. *zifa*) organized by local farmers and herders (C. *nong-mumin*). He boasted that the revived ceremonies, which included "cultural activities" (C. *wenhua huodong*), like camel racing and wrestling, had been covered by media organizations from across Inner Mongolia.

The metal door of the yurt then creaked open, and an official in an elegant trenchcoat entered, carrying the traditional Mongolian gifts of brick tea and bottles of alcohol with a blue silk scarf draped over them. A thick wad of red hundred-yuan notes was placed on top of the *khadag*. "It's the head of the Banner!" (C. *qizhang*)—the excitement was evident in Altanuul's voice as he stood up to receive the important new guest and his gifts. He told the Han Chinese head of the Banner, "I will be sure to pass this on to the ordinary people" (C. *laobaixing*), adding, "On behalf of the masses [C. *renmin qunzhong*] of Khöövör, I thank you."

Tsetsen then stood up, announcing in Mongolian that he wanted to say something about how "our homeland has been destroyed" (M. *gazar nutagaa evdesen*). An awkward silence fell on the assembled Mongols. Referring to the numerous mines in the Kharuuna Mountains behind us, he complained that the mountains had been continuously "developed" (C. *kaifa*). "Digging up the mountains is wrong" (M. *uul maltaj bolokhgüi*), he insisted. Altanuul tried to interject to restore the genial atmosphere of hospitality, but Tsetsen continued. He told them it was important to "venerate the Bull Camel [mountain] properly" (M. *Buuraa sain takhih yostoi*). He had not finished with his criticism, and he now moved on to the lay organizers of the event, Altanuul and Batbagana. They needed to prepare the sheep's breastbone properly, he said, to bring about the flourishing of the five kinds of domestic animal (M. *tavan khoshuu mal*): horses, camels, cattle, sheep, and goats. Altanuul whispered to the Han Chinese official sitting between us that Tsetsen was "criticizing our mistakes" (C. *piping women de cuowu*).

Buddhist Geographies

The previous evening, when we met in his hotel room in Khöövör Town, Altanuul had handed me a small laminated card. This contained a photo of Bull Camel Mountain and retold the legend associated with it in both Mongolian and Chinese. According to this legend, the Indian Buddhist sage Padmasambhava, having suppressed local demons in various parts of Tibet, traveled to this northeastern corner of Alasha, where he fought and defeated a demon in a cave in the Kharuuna Mountains, which mark the northern boundary of Khöövör. The famous Monastery of the Caves (M. Aguin Süm) was later constructed around a complex of caves here, the central one of which contains a huge stone said to have been used by Padmasambhava to pin the demon in place. Another cave is reputed to lead to a tunnel that allows one to reach central Tibet in only a day's walk (Charleux 2002). Annual ceremonies at the monastery attract people from across the region, and many of the herders in Khöövör, including Muslim Mongols, attend.

Padmasambhava is said to have ridden a bull camel on his way to destroy the demon in the cave. The hoofprints of this animal are still visible at the Monastery of the Caves, etched into a large rock in front of the main cave. After Padmasambhava destroyed the demon, the bull camel was transformed into a dark imprint on the cliff face at nearby Bull Camel Mountain. This image of a camel is said to change according to the season: in the winter, for example, a covering of rime makes it appear as if the camel is frothing at the mouth, as bull camels do when they are in rut at this time of year. A monastery built later at the foot of Bull Camel Mountain was historically a subsidiary of the Monastery of the Caves. The mountain is regarded as a particularly potent place, and many in Alasha credit it for the flourishing of camels in Alasha and, in particular, the speed of Khöövör's camels, which are said to resemble the image of the camel on the cliff face. It is said that if a cow camel (M. *inge*) that has repeatedly miscarried is brought in front of Bull Camel Mountain when the camel on the cliff is "in rut" in the winter, it will conceive successfully.[2]

The recent prominence of the Silk Road in Chinese public culture, following the launch of the Belt and Road Initiative (BRI) in 2013, has led to much discussion in Alasha of the various historical routes that passed through the region. While these are often talked about in nebulous Silk Road terms, local Mongols also refer to these routes as "yellow roads" (M. *shar zam*). Bull Camel Mountain lies on one of these historical east-west routes. The yellow roads also included important connections between Mongolian regions (including Ikh Khüree, today's Ulaanbaatar) and Lhasa in Tibet, along which lamas and pilgrims traveled. Indeed, some suggested that the yellowness of these roads was related to the Yellow Religion (M. *shariin shashin*), as the reformed Gelugpa sect, and Tibetan Buddhism more broadly, are known locally.[3] One unexpected effect of BRI discourse, then, has been to stimulate memories of historical Buddhist geographies among Mongols in Alasha, situating the region as part of a larger Buddhist ecumene (Sneath 2014) that transcended the bounds of contemporary states and of the modern Mongol *minzu* (Bulag and Diemberger 2007).

Navigating Culture and Religion

However, the creation of the category of camel veneration rituals as part of Alasha's intangible cultural heritage has involved discursive erasure of their Buddhist elements. Unlike the card produced by Altanuul, official publications on Alasha's cultural heritage make little, if any, mention of the legend of Padmasambhava and the Buddhist geographies it manifests, or the connection between Bull Camel Mountain and the Monastery of the Caves; instead the rituals are described as part of the camel husbandry customs of the Mongol nationality or as an example of the folk culture (C. *minjian wenhua*) of the Alasha Mongols.

Across China, numerous practices once denounced as superstition are now celebrated as cultural heritage. Actors involved in the revival of rituals often seek to downplay their religious aspects, emphasizing instead their status as culture, since the Chinese state remains suspicious of religion, especially noninstitutionalized folk religions, which are not legally recognized. For example, rebuilding a temple in Hebei dedicated to the worship of the Dragon Tablet, part of Chinese folk religion, was enabled through its official classification as a cultural museum (Gao 2014).

In Alasha, the cultural status of rituals is additionally inflected by the fraught question of the relationship of the Mongols to Buddhism, which goes to the heart of Mongol national consciousness in Inner Mongolia. During the Qing period, Mongol identification with Buddhist communities and geographies at the scales of both the multiethnic Qing empire and the local banner came to predominate over identification with a distinct Mongol political community (M. *ulus*; Elverskog 2006). In the early twentieth century, however, a mood of intense anticlericalism prevailed among many Mongol intellectuals, who blamed Buddhism for the comparative weakness of the Mongols since the Qing period, as the monasteries limited their reproduction and curbed their military prowess (Bulag 2004b). At the same time, they resented the prominence of the Tibetan language in Buddhism, which they saw as an impediment to the development of a modern national culture (Bulag 2007). As a result, Mongol scholars, in the words of the historian Christopher Atwood (1996, 116), "sought in the unsullied spirit of the folk a tradition antipathetic to the feudal Buddhist church." In their interpretations, Buddhism was seen as exploitative, and practices such as *ovoo* (ritual cairn) veneration were recast as lay, folk rites, emblematic of an unchanging nomadic way of life.[4] Fire rituals were also seen to be originally shamanic and only later subject to Buddhicization, when the lamas sought to assert their authority over the laity and their rituals (Atwood 1996).

The Chinese state has sought to curb the influence of Buddhism among the Mongols. While it has allowed the reconstruction of temples destroyed during the Cultural Revolution, in practice it has granted permission only for larger temples capable of being turned into tourist attractions (Mair 2013). Such permission had not been granted in the case of Bull Camel Monastery, and the small temple, whose restoration was coordinated by Altanuul, was not officially recognized as a religious site. Since 1958, the state has also forbidden the reincarnation of lamas in Inner Mongolia and remains wary of the religious connections between Mongols and Tibetans (Bulag and Diemberger 2007; Humphrey and Hürelbaatar 2013).

Given the region's distinctive history and geography, Mongols in Alasha tend to be particularly preoccupied with the relationship of Buddhism, Islam, and a Mongolian "folk tradition." Mönkh, a retired Muslim Mongol official who published a history of Alasha's Muslim Mongols (An 2005), told me that "venerating *ovoo* and fire is not Buddhism." Instead, he explained, these practices had been "exploited" (C. *liyong*) by lamas to convert the Mongols to Buddhism. He stressed that it was important to distinguish between religion and "the customs of a nationality" (C. *minzu xiguan*). From this perspective, Muslim Mongols took part in *ovoo* and fire veneration rituals not because they had adopted Buddhism but because they were Mongols.

Mönkh acknowledged that Muslim Mongols had historically attended ceremonies at Bull Camel Mountain and the Monastery of the Caves but explained that they had only gone there to "enjoy the hustle and bustle" (C. *cou renao*) and the entertainment in the form of masked *tsam* dances.[5] They had little option, suggested Mönkh, because "cultural life" (C. *wenhua shenghuo*) in remote rural areas like Khöövör had been "very backward" (C. *hen luohou*). Their participation was thus a matter of culture rather than religion.[6]

Other Muslim Mongols, however, did not feel the need to disassociate themselves from Buddhism; in fact, rather than looking to a pre-Buddhist Mongolian essence, these people regarded Mongol identity as inextricably linked to Buddhism.[7] "Of course we worship [M. *shütekh*] the Buddha," one Muslim Mongol herder told me. "Otherwise we wouldn't be Mongols!" Still others claimed that while they did go to Buddhist temples to "make merit" (M. *nom buyan khiikh*), they differed from other Mongols in that they did not bow or prostrate themselves (M. *mörgökh*) before statues of deities; this bodily practice was reserved for the mosque.

The Veneration of the Cow Camel's Fire

A few weeks after the event at Bull Camel Mountain, Ma Jun, the Hui head of the local culture station (C. *wenhua zhan*), invited me to what he described as a "camel culture event" (C. *luotuo wenhua huodong*) being organized by Batbagana at his home on the grasslands of Bayantal.[8] Upon arrival, we greeted Batbagana's middle-aged nephew, an officially recognized transmitter of the craft of camel tack, who was dressed in Mongolian robes and surrounded by journalists from Bayanhot asking him to explain the technical terms for the various items displayed on a table. With the help of several other Bayantal locals, he began to use spools of camel hair to braid a long rope, to the excitement of several photographers and a cameraman. There followed a short camel race on the level ground behind Batbagana's house. Two of the three elements of Alasha's camel husbandry customs were thus already accounted for.

The centerpiece of the day's events, however, was the cow camel's fire veneration (M. *ingenii galiin takhilga*). A cow camel was first blessed (M. *myalaakh*) by dabbing her muzzle with yogurt, and a colorful bridle was placed on her calf (M. *botog*). They were then led between the fire and a makeshift rostrum, where various local officials, including the party secretary from the local township, as well as Altanuul, surveyed the proceedings. Batbagana brought over a sheep's breastbone wrapped in a *khadag* and placed it on a low table in front of the fire. He and the members of his household, eventually accompanied by the other guests, then began to circumambulate the fire, sprinkling it with offerings of yogurt and alcohol. One senior relative, a retired official, led the cow camel around the fire, as the skittish calf attempted to seek refuge underneath its mother. This time there was no lama in attendance to advise on proceedings or chant scriptures.

After the ritual, we retired to the large main room of Batbagana's house, where the officials were seated at the table of honor, farthest from the door. As we began to enjoy the numerous dishes spread in front of us, Batbagana essayed a speech through the echoing speakers. He explained that his aim in holding this event was to "protect and develop" (M. *khamgaalakh khögjüülekh*) Mongolian culture and camel culture. The climax of the meal came when a steaming plate of boiled sheep's back was carried in, and the assembled guests broke into song. Slabs of fatty meat were then cut off and thrust into the hands of the guests before rounds of toasting began, beginning with the officials at the far end of the room.

Not long after this 2013 event, I came to live with Batbagana. One evening, after his son Mönkhbayar had returned from a trip to Bayanhot, talk turned to the event that had taken place a few weeks previously. Mönkhbayar, it emerged, was concerned that the ritual had not been carried out properly. He had been speaking to his friend, an important monk at the monastery of Baruun Khiid near Bayanhot, who told him that a lama should have been present to chant scripture, and in not having one they risked offending the local tutelary spirits (M. *sabdag*). Batbagana thought about this and then said that they did not need to worry since "we Muslim Mongols don't worship [such spirits]" (M. *manai Mongol Khoton shütekhgüi*) and thus would not be affected.

And yet it seemed Batbagana was somewhat perturbed by the lama's words, and he eventually decided that when the event was held the following year, he would invite a lama. Clearly he was not as comfortable as the scholar Mönkh in drawing a neat line between Mongolian folk culture and Buddhism. Some scholars of Mongolian religion have suggested that rural Mongols are unconcerned with the question of whether certain rituals are Buddhist or folk practices and are instead merely interested in the practical effects of ritual (Wallace 2012, 172). In Alasha, however, remaking these rituals as pastoral heritage has forced local Muslim Mongols to reflect explicitly on precisely such questions, as they grapple with the unstable delineation of culture and religion that has characterized Mongol identity in Inner Mongolia.

Making Nature Worshippers

On the day of the cow camel fire veneration, I had tried to ask several of those present about the ritual but was met by professions of ignorance. When I put my questions to Batbagana, he told me that the cow camel fire veneration was supposed to "revive the vitality" (M. *khii-mori sergeekh*) of the livestock and humans in one's household. The object of the veneration, he said, was the hearth deity (M. *galiin burkhan*). He compared it to the domestic fire veneration ritual (M. *galiin takhilga*) held just before Mongolian New Year.

This was the first time in many years that the ritual had been held in this part of Alasha, and many had not heard of it or had never seen it performed. Searching for more information, I came across a brief passage in the book *Alasha Camel Culture* by the local poet and herder Mönkhjargal. He writes that traditionally the cow camel fire veneration was held in the spring before the cow camels gave birth to ensure that their young were not killed by wolves.[9] The ritual was also held to increase the fortune (M. *buyan-khishig*) of the household as manifested in its camel herd (Mönkhjargal 2006, 12). According to Danzan of the Alasha Camel Society, Mongols venerated the "fire of the cow camel" (M. *ingenii gal*) to increase their camel herds. "Mongols have always greatly respected fire," he explained.

Antoine Mostaert, a Belgian Catholic missionary stationed from 1906 to 1925 in Ordos, to the east of Alasha, described a ritual he referred to as "worshipping the fire for the prosperity of the camels" (cited in Chabros 1992, 36). The Mongolist scholar Krystyna Chabros argues that the object of this ritual is to obtain the "benefit" of the camels, and classifies it as a "fortune beckoning" ritual. Fortune, in this sense, is understood as a fleeting quality that must be caught and stored in order for herds and the households that rely on them to prosper. In Mongolian pastoral regions, this catching and storing is achieved through a variety of everyday practices, including keeping behind a piece of the tail hair of a bull that is being sold (Empson 2012). But it is also central to more elaborate rituals, which often involve inviting a Buddhist lama to chant prayers. These include the practice of consecrating (M. *seterlekh*) an animal in the herd, which is then not ridden, milked, or slaughtered but instead becomes a vessel for the accumulation of fortune (Empson 2012, 122).[10]

These various rituals can be understood as expressions of the "ideology of pastoral plenty" that is characteristic of rural Mongols (Bristley 2020). This celebrates the expansion of livestock herds, often through invocation of the number 10,000 (M. *tüm*), which suggests a "qualitative sense of expansiveness" (Bristley 2020, 64), a stark contrast to the enumerative, delimiting logic of the stocking limits that characterize state environmentalism in Inner Mongolia. This ideology valorizes the five kinds of domestic animal (the "five muzzles"; M. *tavan khoshuu mal*), the possession of which typifies the ideal Mongol household. On the walls of homes in rural Alasha, it is common to find posters featuring the five kinds crudely photoshopped onto an idyllic grassland scene, and the presence of all five is considered to signify a household's fortune (fig. 2). Shortly after I came to live with Batbagana, Mönkhbayar had arranged for his friend, the lama from Baruun Khiid, to conduct a fortune-beckoning ritual for his sheep and goats. He also pinned a wind horse flag (M. *khii-moriin dartsag*) given to him by this lama to the inner wall of the sheepfold. These rituals, however, were conducted privately and not performed as heritage.

Creation of the category of camel veneration rituals as part of Alasha's

FIG. 2. A poster showing an idealized image of the five kinds of domestic animal on the wall of a herder's home, beckoning fortune. This herder possessed only goats, sheep, and a few camels.

intangible cultural heritage has detached the cow camel fire veneration from these other fortune-beckoning rituals, which involve other kinds of livestock, and assimilated it to the veneration of Bull Camel Mountain. Reframing pastoralism as heritage in Alasha thus privileged camel husbandry as distinctive local culture, while obscuring the continued herding of sheep and goats, animals that were increasingly subject to the economic and ecological rationales of state environmentalism (fig. 3).

Such compartmentalizing has been accompanied by interpretations on the part of some intellectuals in Alasha, at odds with those of herders, that suggest these rituals should be understood as a form of proto-conservationist nature worship, in which the camel itself is venerated. This is exemplified in an article published in the three-volume *History of Alasha* (C. Alashan wangshi), by Li Wanyu, a local Han Chinese cadre, on the camel veneration customs (C. *ji luotuo xisu*) of the Mongols of Alasha (Li Wanyu 2007), parts of which are reproduced in the official catalog of Alasha's intangible cultural heritage (Huqun 2010). These customs include the cow camel fire veneration and the ritual at the Bull Camel Mountain, thereby yoking together a domestic ritual and one that takes place at a Buddhist religious site. Li's article

FIG. 3. Multispecies pastoralism characteristic of Bayantal in the early 2010s, before small ruminant destocking policies had been strictly applied

begins by contrasting these customs to the worship of the stove god and the dragon king (C. *longwang*) among the Han. Unlike those forms of ritual, Li claims, camel veneration is directed not at a deity (C. *shenling*) but at one's own camels (C. *ziji siyang de luotuo*), such that the very substance (C. *shiti*) of the camel is regarded as sacred (C. *shen*; Li Wanyu 2007, 369). Whereas most of my Mongol informants reserved the term *sacred* (M. *onggon*) for Bull Camel Mountain, Li applies the term to herders' own livestock. The camels themselves, rather than the fire, have become the object of veneration. The rituals are thus said to be an expression of "harmony between humans and Nature, and between humans and livestock."

Further elaboration of this idea can be seen in an article by two Han Chinese anthropologists from nearby Ningxia University (Wu Yihang and Sheng Lianxiang 2016). They claim that these rituals are distinctive in that they are directed at camels raised by herders themselves rather than a symbol (C. *fuhao*) or deity (C. *shenling*). In this respect the rituals are said to differ from Mongolian totem worship (C. *tuteng chongbai*) and *ovoo* worship (C. *aobao chongbai*). These anthropologists claim that the camels are worshipped (C. *chongbai*) as an incarnation (C. *huashen*) of a spirit (C. *shen*) and argue that these rituals are an "important component of Alasha folk culture" that manifest local people's "simple philosophy of respect for nature" (C. *chong-shang ziran de pusu zheli*).

This emphasis on the sanctity of the camel, I suggest, was influenced by the protected status of the Alasha Bactrian camel and the discourse of conservation that came to surround it in the early twenty-first century. It was also enabled by the ideas of the "ecologically noble savage" that began to circulate in China in the 1990s in the context of interactions between Chinese scientists and transnational environmental NGOs in the 1980s and 1990s (Hathaway 2010). These ideas revalorized once-stigmatized beliefs and practices. During this period, the global environmental movement often framed indigenous environmental knowledge in terms of the sacred (Brosius 1997), and the reverberations of this are evident in Alasha in the interpretations of camel veneration rituals that have accompanied their remaking as heritage.

However, in the Chinese context the celebration of the ecologically noble savage must negotiate the legacy of twentieth-century attacks on superstition central to the Chinese state's quest for modernization (Goossaert and Palmer 2010). Whereas the Mongols' reverence for camels was regarded as superstition during the Cultural Revolution, camel veneration has come to be distinguished from other "religious veneration activities" (C. *zongjiao jisi huodong*) and seen not as a "purely superstitious activity" but instead as "a mixture of faith [C. *xinyang*] and pragmatism [C. *wushi*]" (Li Wanyu 2007, 370).

Interpretations of this ritual are also shaped by strong Marxian strains in Chinese anthropology. The anthropologists from Ningxia University offer a materialist explanation for what they call "camel worship" (C. *luotuo chongbai*), pointing to the historical centrality of camels to the livelihoods of Mongols in Alasha and citing a letter from Engels to Marx where he glosses Feuerbach's *The Essence of Religion*: "In his development man was assisted by other beings which, however, were not beings of a *higher* order, angels, but beings of a lower order, *animals*. Hence animal worship" (Marx and Engels 1982, 76). Their analysis is thus rooted in nineteenth-century evolutionist approaches to religion, even if locals' "simple philosophy of respect for nature" is now celebrated for its alleged congruence with state environmentalism.

The reference to Mongolian totem worship suggests that these anthropologists have been influenced as much by recent artistic representations of Mongols in China that extol the close relationship between Mongols and the natural world, such as the 2004 novel *Wolf Totem*, as by ethnographic observation. However, it would be wrong to dismiss their interpretation as merely a manifestation of the distanced, primitivizing gaze of Han Chinese intellectuals toward the minorities of the country's borderlands. Celebrations of Mongolian ecological wisdom also come from Mongol academics. Indeed, these scholars from Ningxia draw heavily on accounts of the ritual produced by Alasha intellectuals, many of whom are Mongols. A similar interpretation of these rituals as a form of nature worship was in fact offered by Baigal, of the Alasha Camel Society, who told me that the camel was indeed venerated in these rituals, and this showed how Mongols "respected Nature" (M. *baigalig khündetgekh*).[11] Switching to Chinese, he said, "It's about cherishing nature [C. *da ziran*], protecting the environment, protecting nature."

Through the production and circulation, by intellectuals in Alasha and beyond, of interpretations that are part of the process of heritage-making, these rituals have been reframed as a form of benign animism rather than superstition. They are glossed as an expression of the harmonious relations between local Mongols and nature, interpretations that participate in broader trends in the representation of Mongols in Inner Mongolia (Baranovitch 2016b), countering the logic of grassland conservation policies. For example, official interpretations of *ovoo* worship that have accompanied its rendering as heritage at the IMAR level portray it as an important example of how "people of the grasslands venerate nature" (Dumont 2021, 22).

However, in Alasha, these interpretations of the ontology of ritual are also part of the production of a distinctive *local* camel culture, and they obscure the connections between these rituals and those involving other livestock, while also downplaying Buddhist elements. The Alasha Bactrian camel and camel veneration rituals become local forms of nature and culture, both seen as endangered. At the 2013 event, however, the lama Tsetsen provided an alternative interpretation that emphasized the importance of venerating the sacred mountain; he used this to criticize local officials for allowing mining in the Kharuuna Mountains behind Bull Camel Mountain. Ritual performance thus provided space for alternative interpretations and enabled the expression of a kind of Buddhist environmentalism that, while common in Tibetan regions (Yeh 2014a), is less prominent in Inner Mongolia.

Imagining *Minjian* Society

For intellectuals and officials, these rituals also had an important "social value" (C. *shehui jiazhi*), because they manifested "the masses' capacity for organization and coordination," representing the "spontaneous and sincere" (C. *zifa er youzhong*) emergence of "folk society" or "civil society" (C. *minjian shehui*; Li

Wanyu 2007). The Chinese term *minjian* here refers very broadly to nonstate actors, and the same word is also used to refer to folk culture (C. *minjian wenhua*).[12] From the mid-1990s in China, public discourse increasingly featured positive assessments of the idea of a public sphere where citizens pursued their own initiatives, in contrast to earlier conceptions of the masses mobilized by the state. As the reform-era state retreated from direct management of everyday life, discussions proliferated over what kinds of institutions and forms of organization could take its place and help achieve its goals, for example in social service provision, while also combatting the erosion of social cohesion that had come about as a result of economic liberalization (Salmenkari 2011). With the taint of superstition now diminished, revived popular ritual was one site where the self-organizational capacities of ordinary people could be manifested and honed (Litzinger 2000; Chau 2006).

During the event at Bull Camel Mountain in 2013, Altanuul drew on this discourse when he claimed in his speech that the rituals had been spontaneously revived by local farmers and herders. The ritual allowed him to present himself as the representative (C. *daibiao*) of the local community in its interactions with the state. In performing this role he drew on his status as a retired cadre and cultural expert in the penumbra of the state. However, the events of that day showed how this conception of a self-organizing local society was crosscut by an alternative, older social schema, characterized by the relationship between laity and lamas. In Alasha during the early socialist period, as in other parts of the IMAR (Humphrey and Hürelbaatar 2013), lamas were expelled from the monasteries and ordered to engage in productive work and to abandon their vows of celibacy and take wives. But despite such attempts to collapse the distinction between lamas and laity, the authority of the former in Alasha, as in many other Mongolian regions, while certainly diminished, has not disappeared.

In his short speech, Tsetsen criticized both the assembled officials, for allowing mining in nearby mountains, and the laity, for their conduct of certain aspects of the ritual, insisting that they had to "properly venerate Bull Camel Mountain." He thereby sought to position the ritual not as a manifestation of Alasha camel culture but instead as an instance of mountain worship that should have been under the direction of Buddhist lamas from the Monastery of the Caves, of which Bull Camel Monastery was historically a subsidiary and to which it was connected through the legend of Padmasambhava. He also foregrounded a sacred landscape that transcended the borders of contemporary Alasha and was part of a broader Tibeto-Mongolian Buddhist ecumene (Bulag and Diemberger 2007).

While official interpretations downplayed the authority of the lamas in favor of the self-organization of ordinary people, the actual practice of the ritual revealed the awkward prominence religious experts could still assume. This brief moment of ritual politics unsettled classification of the ritual as a kind of local Alasha folk culture but also implicitly called into question the authority of Altanuul, who was positioned by Tsetsen's speech as a member of the laity with insufficient ritual expertise. Indeed, his role in organizing these rituals was regarded unfavorably by some. Mönkh, the retired Muslim Mongol cadre and amateur scholar, argued that this organization should be the business of the monastery (C. *miao shang de shi*); in the past, he said, it was lamas who took charge, not ordinary people (C. *laobaixing*).

Processes of heritage-making involve bestowing authority on certain cultural transmitters, such as Altanuul. As other scholars have noted, this can create hierarchies and conflict in communities as competition for transmitter status ensues (Maags 2018). However, in the case of the camel veneration rituals, conflicts of authority occurred not so much over competing claims to this status; instead the role of cultural transmitter confronted that of religious authority figure, in the form of the Buddhist lama Tsetsen. These tussles over authority, which are part and parcel of the process of making heritage, thus reveal the continued influence of past social orders. They show how religious practitioners with exclusive access to sacred knowledge, who position themselves as representatives of broader communities of humans and nonhumans, can contest the construction of local cultural heritage.

As commentary on the social value of camel veneration rituals suggests, cultural heritage is a key site where conceptions of state and society are produced and negotiated in contemporary China. This is evident in the changing role of the local culture station (C. *wenhua zhan*). In the 1990s, the station had undertaken activities such as the production and distribution among herders of the *Culture, Science and Technology Bulletin* (Alasha Right Banner Media Center 2000, 863). Culture, then, was to be bestowed on the masses from above. By the time I began fieldwork, however, something had clearly changed. The head of this culture station, Ma Jun, enjoyed a friendly, collaborative relationship with Batbagana. His role appeared to be that of a facilitator helping Batbagana organize events such as the cow camel fire veneration, rather than a state expert pursuing a project of top-down improvement. He even engaged in physical labor, helping assemble the stage next to Batbagana's house on the day before an event.

Batbagana took pride in the fact that not only local officials but also journalists from all over China had visited his house to consult with him as an expert on camel culture. On the bookcase in the main room of his house he had attached a laminated copy of an article from the local Mongolian-language newspaper that reported on the cow camel fire veneration he had hosted and featured a photo of him in Mongolian dress holding up a raw sheep's back. While acknowledging that cultural heritage in China often involves top-down processes whereby state officials are responsible for selecting cultural heritage items, scholars have also argued that it can provide spaces in which "local communities demonstrate agency and autonomy" (Maags 2018, 125).

The making of Alasha camel culture has certainly involved a recalibration of relations between state and society, as some herders in Khöövör assumed prominent roles in organizing cultural events. Indeed, Mongols in Bayanhot occasionally muttered at the swagger (C./M. *jiazitai*) some Khöövör herders had begun to assume as a result of their cultural prominence. However, rather than representing a desire for autonomy from the state, these rituals provided a means by which certain people in Khöövör could cultivate relations with state officials, thereby bringing prestige and, potentially, resources to the household. The attendance of state officials was thus desired by organizers such as Batbagana, himself of course a former local party secretary. Ma Jun explained to me that when officials attended such events, they gave the organizers face (C. *mianzi*), increasing their standing in the eyes of their neighbors. If officials failed to show up, people felt they had lost face. However, toward the end of 2012, shifts in national politics began to close off this avenue for engaging with the state in rural Alasha, and heritage rituals became a site at which herders experienced the political changes ushered in by Xi Jinping.

Culture as Corruption

In November 2012 Xi became general secretary of the Chinese Communist Party. He immediately made his mark by launching a wide-ranging anticorruption campaign, seeking to root out "tigers and flies": corrupt officials at both the central and local levels of government. Xi realized that the numerous corruption scandals involving the lavish spending habits of officials during the previous Hu Jintao era had seriously undermined public confidence in the CCP, threatening its rule (Brown 2018). The anticorruption campaign was combined with Xi's careful cultivation of his image as a humble man of the people by standing in line to order steamed buns at a cheap Beijing restaurant, for example. His frugal habits were the subject of much approving talk in Alasha. During one dinner together, Altanuul claimed that Xi traveled around Beijing in ordinary taxis and that he had announced there should only be one dish served per person at banquets. Such meals are where much of the business of officials is conducted, and they had become synonymous with waste and extravagance.

In China, corruption is closely related to food, not only because currying favor with officials commonly happens via the medium of banquets but also because eating is used as a metaphor for corruption in both Chinese and Mongolian, such that it was common to hear people mutter about local officials who were said to have "eaten" (C. *chi le*; M. *idsen*) public funds. In rural Alasha, particular delicacies, such as sheep's intestine (M. *gurguldee*), had also become associated with officials, to whom they would be served when they visited a household. It was not surprising, then, that it was through the medium of food that the anticorruption campaign was initially experienced and understood by herders in Khöövör. As the year wore on, talk at Batbagana's increasingly touched on the strictures the campaign had imposed on local officials, including, apparently, a ban on the consumption of sheep's back, due to its ostentation. This news was initially positively received, and Xi was praised for cracking down on the corruption of the "lords" (M. *darga noyan*), as senior officials are referred to in Inner Mongolia.

However, it gradually became clear that the effects of this new frugality and abstemiousness demanded of officials in the Xi era would be felt even in those rituals whose organization was supposed to be a purely nonstate (C. *minjian*) affair. Official rhetoric was becoming increasingly hostile to the idea of civil society (Pils 2012).[13] Instead, references to the masses now proliferated, particularly in the form of the "mass line" (C. *qunzhong luxian*), a Maoist concept that referred to the practice of cadres "consulting the masses, interpreting their will, and implementing policies in their interests" (Chun 2019). However, under Xi their earlier revolutionary thrust had been tempered and focused on self-criticism on the part of officials rather than the agency of the masses (Tiezzi 2013).

Batbagana was now concerned that cold water was being poured on his plans to host another cow camel fire veneration in the spring of 2014. The scenes I had witnessed at the previous year's event, which involved such overconsumption on the part of several officials that cars ferrying them back to their hotels had to stop by the side of the road so they could vomit, were very much not in keeping with the new spirit of the age. The list of items forbidden to officials was growing: they were no longer allowed to consume alcohol or smoke cigarettes at such events. In fact, Batbagana inferred that officials were now "scared" (M. *aij baina*) of any kind of festive occasion (M. *nair naadam*).

The new political winds prompted others to reassess the relations between state and society as manifested through cultural heritage. Ma Jun, despite his friendship with Batbagana, criticized the habit of inviting officials to these events. As soon as the officials arrived, he said, the atmosphere of the event changed, and what had been very "natural" (C. *zirande*) became "fake" (C. *xuwei*). You had to provide more elaborate food and drink, and the event had to go on for much longer.

Jargal, the official from Khöövör Town, muttered about a "gang" (M. *büleg*) of retired officials, including Altanuul, who used their connections to tap into state funds for cultural heritage that then also found their way into select rural households, including Batbagana's. The circulation of such funds, or rather the perception of the circulation of such funds, again cast doubt on official understandings of cultural events, such as the camel veneration rituals, as emerging from the spontaneous initiative of local people. For cynics like Jargal, then, these rituals were a means by which well-connected people got their hands on public funds under the guise of cultural heritage.

While he approved of Altanuul's organizational abilities, Ma Jun also questioned whether the rituals represented the authentic revival of a folk tradition. He suggested that Altanuul had "got hold of some documents" while working for the state and had tried to reconstruct the rituals from the information they contained. With this claim, Ma Jun implied that the revived rituals might in fact have their immediate origin in state archives accessed by a state employee rather than in some timeless collective folk wisdom.

Expropriating and Commodifying Heritage

In the winter of 2013, it emerged that local officials were planning to hold a large camel culture festival (C. *luotuo wenhua jie*) at Bull Camel Mountain the following spring to attract tourists and promote the area's economic development. The temple was apparently going to be purchased by a businessman from the nearby city of Wuhai who had mining interests in the Kharuuna Mountains but was now expanding into tourism. Jargal told me that this businessman was funding the event to publicize his other tourist ventures, including a hotel and scenic lake nearby.

Altanuul was angered by these new plans. When I asked him about organizing the rituals the following year, he told me, "It's got nothing to do with me anymore. . . . I'm no longer in charge. It's been stolen" (C. *qiang zou le*).

He went on to complain that the government had also decided to "get rid of Batbagana's event," meaning the cow camel fire veneration, or rather to combine it with the event at Bull Camel Mountain, saying that the local party secretary was now in charge. According to Altanuul, since the state had taken over what was originally a *minjian* event, it was "no longer worthwhile" (C. *mei you yisi*). He also protested the ontological elision at work, claiming that the combination of rituals was not correct.

Batbagana also disagreed with the plan to combine these events. He had learned that local officials now wanted to postpone the ritual at Bull Camel Mountain because it coincided with a large meeting of officials in Bayanhot. Bureaucratic time would thus take precedence over ritual time. Batbagana was scathing about these suggestions that the event should be postponed; for him it indicated that the officials were not up to the job of organizing it. "You need people who understand custom [M. *yos medekh khün*], people who have the ability to organize it [M. *khiij chadakh khün*]." He had told local officials that the mountain was "a place that had had a monastery, lamas, deities, and which had been venerated for hundreds of years."

This insistence on the sanctity of Bull Camel Mountain came at a time when many Mongols in Alasha were unhappy with the government's sale of the most prominent monastery in Alasha, Baruun Khiid, to a large coal-processing company, which would run it as a tourist site. Mongols feared that high ticket prices would be charged, even to local worshippers. Batbagana had criticized this, saying that "on the one hand you have making money [M. *zoos olokh*], while on the other you have making merit [M. *buyan khiih*]—the two things are completely different."

The local officials who were now in charge of the event eventually decided to hold it on the fifteenth of the second month of the lunar calendar, as dictated by custom. When the day arrived, we made our way to Bull Camel Mountain to find that a large stage had been erected on the plain in front of the mountain (fig. 4). A banner announced the event as the Inner Mongolia Alasha Sacred Camel Veneration Folk Culture Festival, in Chinese and Mongolian. Whereas Altanuul and Batbagana had always talked of the "sacred bull camel" (M. *onggon buur*), the Mongolian version of the event's name now referred in broader terms to the "sacred camel" (M. *onggon temee*), perhaps to encompass the cow camels that now had pride of place, but also in keeping with interpretations of the ritual as nature worship. To one side of the stage was an exhibition of items of camel tack, with text explaining them, as in a museum. Next to this was a prominent advertisement for a hotel owned by the Wuhai businessman. On the other side of the stage was a red

FIG. 4. A herder leads his camel and calf at the 2014 Inner Mongolia Alasha Sacred Camel Veneration Folk Culture Festival held at Bull Camel Mountain.

banner with white Chinese and Mongolian script, of the kind used to convey official messages across China, which read, "Develop the tourism industry!" (C. *fazhan lüyou chanye*).

Following the cow camel fire veneration ritual, lunch was served in a large tent. It consisted of bowls of mutton stew (C. *dun rou*) with steamed buns. There was no sign of sheep's back. As I wandered around the site, I noticed that monks from the Monastery of the Caves were present, chanting inside the small temple, but their role was far less prominent than the year before. During the cow camel fire veneration ritual on the plain below, which was the centerpiece of the event this year, scriptures were chanted instead by two lamas from the monastery of Baruun Khiid, one of the two largest Buddhist institutions in Alasha. One of these was Dorji, the lama who told Mönkhbayar that Batbagana had erred in failing to have a lama chant at his cow camel's fire veneration ritual the year before. In addition to being a high-ranking figure at Baruun Khiid, Dorji was a member of the Alasha Left Banner Buddhist Association (C. Fojiao Xiehui), the official institution representing worshippers to the state. Whereas the previous year the most prominent lama had come from the Monastery of the Caves across the border in Bayannuur Municipality, now religious and state territories were brought into alignment.

Unlike the previous year, the lamas were afforded no opportunity to speak publicly. Indeed, while many of the local herders who attended made their way into the tent where a senior lama was bestowing blessings, this was not part of the official script of proceedings. Instead, the cow camel's fire veneration ritual was followed by camel races and a wrestling match, before the event was brought to a close in late afternoon with an awards ceremony. The winner of the camel race was presented with a sheep before the adjudication of another competition began. Officials had instructed each local household to bring a decorated sheep's breastbone, of the kind that usually constituted the offering to the fire. These were then set out on tables in front of the stage and judged by none other than Altanuul. He was also interviewed by a television crew, where he explained the significance of the breastbone. Indeed, the whole event appeared to be an anticipatory performance of local culture for the tourists who would eventually visit.

At the event at Bull Camel Mountain a year previously, the lama Tsetsen had criticized the single breastbone prepared by Batbagana, who linked its correct preparation to the need to "properly venerate" the mountain. This year, however, assessment of the breastbones was no longer the domain of the lamas but rather of the lay cultural expert Altanuul. And rather than being offered to the fire as part of the ritual, they were displayed as part of a competition, a form often taken by peformances of minority culture in China. One of the winners of the competition was Batbagana's household; they were presented with their winnings of tea, a silk scarf, and a red envelope of cash by a local official. By the time of the awards ceremony, the lamas had long since left.

Despite his appearance on television, Altanuul grumbled that the event had not been done well. "It was chaotic" (C. *luan*), he told me a week later, adding, "This ritual used to be held at home but now it's been *developed*" (C. *bei fazhan le*). With his use of this term, fundamental to reform-era China, Altanuul criticized scaling up the cow camel fire veneration from a domestic ceremony as well as its incorporation into the local state's model of development based on tourism, now that Camel Country had become a refuge for mining capital seeking profit from tourist sites.

Through spectacles of ritual, competition, and material culture, the event sought to attract tourists by commodifying a regionally distinctive Alasha camel culture. This rescaling of culture obscured the historical and legendary connections between Bull Camel Mountain and the Monastery of the Caves, with the latter now lying beyond the borders of contemporary Alasha. Despite taking place at a historically Buddhist site with a small revived temple, the state-sponsored event was officially framed not as religious activity (C. *zongjiao huodong*) but as folk culture (C. *minjian wenhua*), and the lamas were reduced to a peripheral role.

The combination of two previously distinct rituals was discursively enabled by their common classification as camel veneration rituals, part of the reframing of pastoralism as positively valued local heritage in Alasha. This ritual elision foregrounded a distinctive local Alasha camel culture at the expense of Buddhist landscape and authority. And while the event reaffirmed the camel's exceptional status in the context of state environmentalism and celebrated livestock abundance in stark contrast to the prevailing destocking policies, for those Mongol folk who had organized the rituals in previous years it was also an unhappy example of cultural expropriation.

STATE ENVIRONMENTALISM in contemporary China has seen ethnic minorities subjected to ecological migration or strict controls on land use in the interests of environmental protection. At the same time, however, globally circulating ideas of indigenous peoples' reverence for nature have also created an "indigenous space" (Hathaway 2010) in parts of China and led to the revalorization of certain folk beliefs and practices once denounced as superstition, now understood as aligned with the state's environmental goals.

In Alasha, camel veneration rituals were a site at which the local instantiation of the ecologically noble herder was produced. But rather than merely revalorizing existing practices, the making of heritage produced new discursive objects through classification and objectification. The listing of camel veneration rituals amalgamated a variety of ritual practices related to camels, while disconnecting them from other livestock rituals and from Buddhism. The creation of this category had ontological implications, as commentators described the camel, and metonymically nature, as the object of veneration. Rather than reflecting a Mongolian animism (Fijn 2011), however, this ontology was shaped by the recent transformation of the Alasha Bactrian camel into an object of conservation—and thus distinct from other livestock subject to strict stocking limits—and by the global circulation of ideas of the "ecologically noble savage."

As geographer Tim Oakes (2005, 33) has argued, "Local scale expressions of popular culture should be seen not as confined by scale but rather as components in the on-going production of scale." Camel veneration rituals were instrumental in the production of the local, part of the broader rescaling of culture that Alasha camel culture represented. However, the figure of the ecologically noble herder and the local scale at which it manifested were haunted by the enduring power of Buddhism in Alasha and its contested relationship to the Mongol nationality. Late twentieth-century ideas of indigeneity and environmentalism thus do not straightforwardly map onto existing ideas of cultural difference, simply producing an ethnic environmentalism (Baranovitch 2021). Instead, they confront an earlier, unfinished scaling project that sought to separate national culture from Tibetan Buddhism.

The creation of the category of camel veneration rituals in the early 2000s was accompanied by imaginings on the part of local intellectuals of self-organizing rural communities, part of broader currents of thought in China during the Hu Jintao era, when notions of civil society were widely discussed (Froissart 2017). But while these rituals bestowed on some herders the status of cultural experts, this cannot be understood simply in terms of the opportunities for grassroots agency and autonomy that heritage can provide. For the Muslim Mongol lay organizers, the role of cultural expert could at times prove an awkward one, characterized as much by uncertainty as by agency, as they confronted the expertise of Buddhist lamas and grappled with their own relationship, as members of the Mongol nationality, to Buddhism. This role was unstable, as lay organizers were forced to cede rituals to the state as it collaborated with mining capital to commodify ritual landscapes as tourist sites.

The role of the state was thus contested and shifting. Although revived ritual in China may appear to be a space of community autonomy, these rituals did not constitute a space neatly set apart from the state. Instead, they were a site at which different visions of state-society relations were performed, at a time when such relations were under particular scrutiny in light of Xi Jinping's politics of anticorruption.

3

The Rural Sociality
of Camel Husbandry
in Urbanizing Alasha

IN THE NORTH of the Khöövör region lies Bayantal, today officially an administrative village (*gatsaa* in Mongolian). Locals, however, still refer to it as "Ba[yantal] Brigade" (C. Ba Dui), a legacy of its status during the collective period (1953–84) as one of several production brigades (C. *dadui*; M. *brigad*) that made up the local people's commune.[1] Bayantal covers 780 square kilometers of desert grassland between the Kharuuna Mountains to the north and the Ulaan Bukh desert in the south. In 2013, 109 households were registered to Bayantal, though of these only seventy were actually resident in the *gatsaa*, according to local officials. Almost all of the households that remained herded sheep and goats; around twenty of them also kept small herds of camels.[2] Horses and cattle had once been herded, but there were now very few of these animals, due to the ongoing drought. Several households also kept small herds of donkeys.[3]

Pastureland had been allocated to individual households in 1997, but in 2013 much of the *gatsaa* was still unfenced. Herders lived in permanent brick homes of varying size, often separated by several kilometers, and no longer moved seasonally with their livestock. They had not, however, been subject to the ecological migration policies that, in parts of China deemed to be ecologically fragile, have seen herders moved to expressly constructed concentrated settlements, where they are expected to engage in new economic activities (Ptackova 2020). Nevertheless, several abandoned houses in various states of disrepair bore witness to rural depopulation. While in agricultural areas of China out-migration tends to be driven by a search for economic opportunities, in pastoral regions it is more a product of environmental and educational policies (Gongbuzeren, Li, and Lai 2021). The local township had provided subsidies to purchase apartments in Bayanhot, and Payments for Ecosystem Services (PES) policies, which provided compensation for destocking, had encouraged some households to sell their entire herds and seek employment in the city.

Even in the case of resident households, several members were rarely present in the *gatsaa*: women often lived with their children in the city while the latter attended school. During the collective era, and for some years afterward, herders had attended school in the center of the local people's commune, but in recent decades a policy of school consolidation across rural regions of China (Gyal 2019) meant that Mongol children had to attend school in Bayanhot if they wanted to be educated in Mongolian.[4] This policy has contributed to a feeling across Inner Mongolia that *gatsaa* are disintegrating socially; in central Shilingol, for example, one herder lamented that "children in the *gatsaa* no longer recognize each other" (Han Niantong 2011a, 18).

The sense that rural life was being rendered increasingly unviable found material form in the crumbling buildings of the people's commune of Tsengel, which borders Bayantal to the west. In 2002 Tsengel was administratively subsumed into the small industrial town of Jirtei, some hundred kilometers to the south. This was done in accordance with a national policy of abolishing townships and amalgamating them into towns (C. *che xiang bing zhen*; Yeh and Henderson 2008), part of China's broader denigration of rural life in favor of the urban (Driessen 2018). Tsengel had once been a relatively bustling place, populated by Han Chinese farmers and a local government staffed by Mongol cadres with kinship ties to people in Bayantal. Sarna, Batbagana's wife, reminisced about the times when they had regularly gone there to buy vegetables and the delicious watermelons that thrive in Alasha's hot summers. "It was great when it was full of people" (M. *yostoi saikhan baisan, khün olon, düüren*), she sighed.

A bumpy dirt road connected Tsengel and the center of Bayantal *gatsaa*. In 2013 this consisted of a few dilapidated buildings, which had been the headquarters of the production brigade in the collective period, and some abandoned fields once tilled by Han Chinese farmers, remnants of the aggressive agricultural expansion of the 1960s. Meetings were now only very occasionally held at the Bayantal administrative center. These constituted the rare occasions on which most members of the *gatsaa* were gathered together in the same space. At one such meeting in 2013, which I was not permitted to attend, *gatsaa* members, many of whom had come from Bayanhot especially for the meeting, were told about the state's compulsory purchase of a tract of marginal land in the far south of Bayantal, on the fringes of the desert, the proceeds of which had still not been divided among households. This area was going to be part of a flood diversion zone (C. *fenhong qu*) for the Yellow River, but local officials also hoped that diverted water would enable the creation of a development zone (C. *kaifa qu*). This land had once been a collective hayfield and, unlike the rest of the *gatsaa*, had not been contracted out to individual households, though after years of drought it no longer provided the grasses and reeds that had once fed the livestock of the production brigade over the winter.

Over the next few months, herders frequently returned to the topic of the "desert money" (M. *elsnii zoos*), as they called it. Sümbür, a young herder in his twenties who lived nearby with his parents, planned to buy a secondhand black Chinese-made Volkswagen Passat, a model preferred by officials but singularly unsuited to the dirt tracks of Bayantal and useless for transporting livestock and fodder. Batbagana's son Mönkhbayar and his wife, Odonchimeg, decided to put it toward the purchase of an apartment in Bayanhot. The sale of collectively managed rural land would thus provide the capital for local households' anticipated urban futures.

However, despite policies that designated the individual household as the basic unit of rural resource management and others that pushed people toward the city, certain forms of rural cooperation and sociality were nevertheless present in Bayantal at the start of the Xi era. Though officially the conservation of the Alasha Bactrian camel was imagined to take place at the level of the household, in fact the camel's wide-ranging movements conflicted with the policy of land privatization and were enabled by an informal sense of the commons among camel herders, as well as the opportunistic use of unfenced land abandoned by rural-to-urban migrants.

While much of the literature on pastoral regions analyzes rural resource management with reference to notions of an enduring, spatially bounded community that regulates resource access (e.g., Gongbuzeren, Huntsinger, and Li 2018), it is more productive in the case of Alasha to think in terms of the *sociality of husbandry*. To invoke sociality is to emphasize that social life is not simply the product of prior social relations (Nicholas Long and Henrietta Moore 2012). Rather than established administrative or social units, such as production brigades, communities, or kinship groups, determining the cooperation involved in herding, different kinds of livestock can give rise to different degrees and forms of interhousehold cooperation and accompanying sociality. Though in 2013 the community of Bayantal appeared to come together only to abrogate its right to collectively manage grassland resources, informal interhousehold cooperation was still to be found among camel herders, in contrast to the predominantly household scale of sheep and goat husbandry. Under these conditions, the sociality of camel husbandry could also blur ethnic distinctions that have long been thought to characterize rural Inner Mongolia.

A Brief History of Grassland Management and Property Rights

Contemporary cooperation and conflict over land and livestock in rural Alasha have been shaped by the recent history of pastoral production in the region (table 1). In the first decade following the establishment of the PRC, the socialist reform of the pastoral economy was implemented gradually in accordance with Ulanhu's policy of Three Nos and Two Benefits. In 1952, mutual aid teams (C. *huzhuzu*; M. *khavsarchlakh duguilang*) were established (Shi Jifa 2001, 242), and herders were subsequently encouraged to establish cooperatives (Sneath 2000, 71). These initial socialist reforms of pastoral production in Alasha built on existing traditions of mutual aid and cooperation between households. For example, the practice of long-distance migration in response to localized drought, known in Mongolian as *otor*, involved reciprocal relations between households (Shi Jifa 2001, 241). Herders also made use of economies of scale, so that one household might arrange for its sheep and goats to be herded by another that specialized in these animals, while they concentrated on herding camels. Such cooperative herding arrangements were normally established between kin, or among those who shared the same water source at their summer camp (Shi Jifa 2001, 241). In addition, ordinary pastoralists herded livestock belonging to the banner prince or to the various monasteries in exchange for a small share of their produce, an arrangement known as *süreg tavikh*, common in Mongolian regions (Sneath 2003; Upton 2005).

However, in contrast to stereotypical images of nomads wandering freely over the steppe, in the prerevolutionary era a variety of rights over land were recognized.[5] Land officially belonged to the banner prince, and herders were not allowed to sell or rent out land.[6] The best pastures were reserved for the use of the prince and his relatives, with trespassers punished. Herders claimed use rights over the remaining pastures by digging wells, erecting sheepfolds, or most durably, building houses. Given the cost of building a house, such claims tended to be the preserve of richer herders (Shi Jifa 2001, 213) and were more prevalent in the south and east of the banner (IMAR EG 2009, 44).

TABLE I Rights over livestock and land in Bayantal, 1958–2013

1958 Collectivization of livestock and pastureland

1984 Collective herds distributed among individual households and pastureland divided among groups of households

1997 Most pastureland contracted out to households on thirty-year leases, but funding not provided for fencing, so most household pastures remain unfenced until 2013

2003– RLRG begins to be applied unevenly across Alasha. Total grazing bans implemented in some parts of Alasha, including in a *gatsaa* to the east of Bayantal, but not in Bayantal itself

2008 Bayantal becomes part of one of Alasha Left Banner's three Alasha Bactrian Camel Genetic Resource Conservation Zones

2011 PES program initiated across China's pastoral areas, including Bayantal, providing subsidies for herd reduction

2013 Bayantal herders agree to sell last significant portion of collectively held land. Herders told they can keep up to sixty camels without their PES being affected

This situation obtained until collectivization began in 1958. Across Inner Mongolia, livestock now became the property of the collectives, though households were normally allowed a small number of animals for their own use (Sneath 2000, 89). Production brigades assumed responsibility for coordinating pastoral production and the division of labor, with large single-species herds becoming the norm. Land was now owned collectively, and *otor* was coordinated by the brigades and communes (Dalintai et al. 2012, 93). This coordinated mobility helped mitigate the effects of periodic droughts in the banner (Shi Jifa 2001, 189). Brigade members were assigned to particular work tasks. Apart from the labor of herding itself, these tasks could take the form of auxiliary work (C. *fuye*), such as erecting sheepfolds or transporting salt by camel caravan. Over a third of Bayantal residents were engaged in such work. In return for their labor, brigade members received work points (C. *gongfen*), which were exchanged for cash at the end of the year, at a rate that varied according to the brigade's total production.

In 1978, two years after Mao's death, Deng Xiaoping assumed power and ushered in the reform era. Reforms began in agriculture with the formalization of the household responsibility system (C. *jiating lianchan chengbao zerenzhi*), which involved contracting out land and other resources to individual households.[7] In the early 1980s, banners in Inner Mongolia began to adopt a responsibility system for pastoralists (C. *xumuye chengbao zeren zhi*), which involved contracting out pastures to groups on a long-term basis (C. *caochang changqi chengbao dao qun*) and granting responsibility for livestock pricing to individual households (C. *xumu zuojia gui hu zi ying*; ALBG 2000, 60). In addition to the economic rationale that justified the reform in the case of agricultural regions, Mongol leaders apparently hoped that securing land titles for Mongol households would help prevent the land from being distributed to Han Chinese settlers in the future (Bulag 2004b).

In Alasha, pastureland was not contracted out to individual households until 1997; instead, the process of decollectivization began with the distribution of collective livestock to individual households in 1984 and of pastureland to groups of households. According to local officials, each of the 369 people in Bayantal received twenty sheep and goats along with five camels. This included even those who had been engaged in auxiliary work during the collective era, as well as commune officials, such as Batbagana, who had worked as an accountant for Bayantal Brigade. While some of the famine refugees from Minqin County were assigned agricultural land near the border with Dengkou County, across Alasha many of them received livestock along with other commune members.[8] The situation in Alasha thus differed from eastern Inner Mongolia, where Han Chinese settlers converted pastureland to farmland, eventually forcing many Mongols to adopt farming themselves (Borjigin 2017).

Herders in Bayantal remember the first few years following decollectivization as the time when household herds were at their most diverse. This was before the cashmere boom, which began in the late 1980s, encouraged herders to concentrate on goats, and before prolonged drought made herding cattle and horses unviable. One reason locals gave for the dramatic decline in the number of camels that followed decollectivization was that camels had been distributed to people with no experience of herding these animals, who then sold all of them for slaughter.[9] By 2013 the number of camels in Bayantal had declined to 400, from 1,660 thirty years earlier. However, those who kept herds of camels following decollectivization were not necessarily those who had herded them during the collective era. According to Batbagana, those who held on to their camels did so because they loved these animals (M. *temeend khairtai*).

Before 1997, land in Bayantal was divided up among groups of multiple households (C. *zu*; M. *duguilang*), of which there were five in Bayantal.[10] The boundaries between the pastures of these groups do not seem to have been strictly enforced, and there was no fencing. "We didn't even know what fencing was in those days" (M. *tor gej medekhgüi baisan*), said Batbagana. According to official sources, however, there were significant problems with this system. In 2000 the official *Alasha Left Banner Gazetteer* wrote that "grassland use rights [C. *caoyuan shiyong quan*] were not properly implemented [C. *luoshi bu daowei*]," and households rich in livestock benefited disproportionately (ALBG 2000, 279). In 1997 pastureland began to be contracted out to individual households on thirty-year leases (ALBG 2000, 78). By 1999, 92 percent of the rangeland in Alasha had been privatized in this manner, with the other 8 percent made up of areas of marginal land or hay fields, the use rights to which remained collective.

The policy of pastureland allocation has had a significant effect on residence patterns and labor-sharing arrangements in the *gatsaa*, as can be seen in the case of Batbagana's family. Batbagana's younger son, Daichin, married and registered a new household just before the division of the pastureland in 1997. As a result, he and his wife received a two-person portion of pastureland, where they built a new house. Mönkhbayar, however, had not yet married in 1997, so he was registered to his parents' household when pastureland was allocated. This three-person portion of pastureland had an area of roughly 10,000 *mu* (1,650 acres) and remained this size even after Mönkhbayar married Odonchimeg and officially registered a new *de jure* household.[11] Mönkhbayar continued to live with his parents as one de facto household even after his marriage, herding his sheep and goats together with theirs. He was largely responsible for pasturing the combined herd of sheep and goats, while Batbagana looked after his camels. Mönkhbayar, like many others in Alasha, had sold his camels in the early 2000s.

Since pastureland had been contracted to households on a thirty-year lease, 2027 would supposedly bring a redivision of *gatsaa* land, with households such as Mönkhbayar's now receiving their own land. However, in light of the tumultuous changes of recent years, including construction of an industrial park on the eastern edge of Bayantal, no one seemed clear about what would happen. Given that the number of registered households in Bayantal had increased since 1997, including those who now lived elsewhere but were still entitled to land, each household was likely to receive a smaller proportion.[12]

From the early 1990s, many herders in the south of Alasha had become ecological migrants when they were moved to the new settlement of

Luanjingtan. Yet state environmentalism in China does not always take such dramatic forms. In much of northern Alasha, herders had not been resettled in this way. Instead, they were subject to a complex system of subsidies that incentivized them to reduce their herds or get rid of them entirely. Building on the Removing Livestock and Restoring Grassland policy initiated in 2003, in 2011 the world's largest grassland payments for ecosystem services (PES) program was rolled out across pastoral regions of China (Hou et al. 2021). This has generally involved classifying grassland as a grazing ban (C. *jinmu*) zone or a grass-livestock balance (C. *cao xu pingheng*) zone, according to the condition of the pastures. Herders in the former zone are provided with subsidies to cease herding completely, while in the latter payments are provided to herders who reduce their herds to a certain level (Ministry of Agriculture 2011). These payments were thus part of a "cluster of governmental techniques that aimed to induce families to opt out of grazing, as if by choice" (Zee 2019, 69).

The implementation of the PES policies varied widely across pastoral regions and even within Alasha itself, as local officials sought to balance the need to reach targets set by higher levels of government with the desire to avoid confrontation and possible unrest (Kolås 2014). In Bayantal, households were allowed to choose between a grazing ban and grass-livestock balance.[13] Ninety of the 109 households registered in Bayantal opted for the grazing ban, sometimes because the allotted carrying capacity of their household pastures would not allow them to maintain an economically viable herd but also occasionally reasoning that the payments were preferable to the uncertain living provided by herding in these years of ongoing drought. In addition, it initially appeared that the limits would not be strictly enforced. Since a significant number of households (around twenty) had already left the *gatsaa*, however, this still meant that over a quarter of the herders who remained in Bayantal had opted for livestock over cash. The elective element of this policy opened a new fissure in the *gatsaa*.

Even two years into the contract, local officials were still softening the blow of the grazing ban option by allowing one goat for every 100 *mu* of pasture, though in this case the subsidy was slightly less. I was told that each working-age adult received a subsidy of ¥12,000 a year, while for older people this was ¥10,000. This amount decreased by ¥2,000 for those who still herded animals. Those who signed the contract to limit livestock according to grass received only ¥3,000 a year. Some of those who had chosen this option thought it was unfair that those who had chosen the grazing ban option were still able to herd some animals. They told me they had chosen the grass-livestock balance option because they thought it safer to have live-stock, as they were not convinced the state would actually pay the PES. This included those with kin who worked in local government, who had apparently learned that the public finances of Alasha were in a parlous state. Such concerns were substantiated by occasional complaints on the part of herders in various parts of Alasha over delays in receiving the payments, published on WeChat. In other parts of Inner Mongolia, herders have organized public protests in response to the government's failure to provide PES as promised (Qiao Long 2017).

Conservation Policies and the Camel Commons

Payments for ecosystem services are based on an assumption of exclusive household use rights over land. However, in practice, exclusion in this vast, depopulated landscape could be difficult, especially since in 2013 much of Bayantal remained unfenced. In many cases this was due to the prohibitive costs involved in fencing these large pastures, as the government had yet to provide funding for this (see also Banks 2003, 2134), though camel herders had additional reasons for not wanting fencing.[14] Sarna explained that camels were animals that "moved around to eat" (M. *yavaj iddeg amitan*). In Bayantal, as in other parts of Alasha, camels are left to roam freely year round, though in the winter they return to the household of their own accord every few days to drink from the trough, since water sources in the mountains to the north are frozen. The range of sheep and goats, however, is much smaller, and they return (or are made to return) to the sheepfold next to the house in the early evening. Batbagana told me that the Mongolian word *khariulakh* (to round up) properly refers to sheep and goats but not camels. Barbed-wire fences cause problems for camel herders not only because they restrict the area available for camels to browse but also because if not properly maintained they are liable to collapse, potentially ensnaring and injuring any camel that treads on them.

So while several households in the *gatsaa* had already decided to move to the city and collect the full grazing ban payment, meaning that no livestock could officially be herded on their pastures, in the absence of fencing there was little way of preventing access by livestock, particularly the wide-ranging camels, belonging to other households. The herding of camels, and therefore the conservation of this national genetic resource, thus partially relied on glitches in the PES system. While some analyses portray China's state environmentalism as a sophisticated machine (Zee 2020), on the ground it can instead appear as a jumble of heterogenous mechanisms that often pull in different directions, occasionally synchronizing as much by chance as by design. PES assumed household use rights over land, but it also induced households to move away from that land, making exclusive use rights harder to enforce. The rural emptiness induced by conservation policies, by rendering certain areas de facto open access, in turn unexpectedly facilitated conservation of the Alasha Bactrian camel, which was threatened by generalized pastureland enclosure.

The state's establishment in 2008 of Alasha Bactrian camel genetic resource conservation zones (C. *Alashan Shuangfengtuo pinzhong yichuan ziyuan baohu qu*) in several parts of Alasha, including Bayantal, made no legal arrangements for the extensive browsing range of these animals, which exceeded the area of individual household pastures. Instead, conservation in these zones was officially imagined to take place at the scale of individual households. Several, but not all, of the camel-herding households had been declared "core households for the breeding and conservation of the Alasha Bactrian camel" (C. *Alashan Shuangfengtuo xuanyu baohu hexin hu*) by the Left Banner Bureau of Agriculture and Animal Husbandry. Beyond a metal plaque fixed to herders' houses, this status did not appear to confer any material benefits, but it demonstrated the state's privileging of the household scale when it came to managing resources.

Over the course of 2013, herders learned of several plans to price camels within the household-based PES framework. According to one version, a single camel would be deemed equal to seven sheep for the purposes of calculating carrying capacity and PES. If implemented, this would probably have spelled the end of camel husbandry, as herders would have had to choose between a very small herd of camels and a more substantial, economically viable herd of sheep and goats. Eventually, however, it was decided that, due to the protected status of this animal and the advocacy of the Alasha Camel Society, herders would be allowed up to sixty camels without any deduction from their grazing ban payments. Alasha Bactrian camels would thus constitute a local exception to the incentivization of destocking through PES.

But despite this exception and the empty pastureland, the contracting out of land to individual households still made herding camels difficult. Even where fences had not been installed, which was most of the *gatsaa*, some herders chased camels away (M. *khöökh*) from their pastures. Sometimes this involved motorbikes, but I also saw elderly herders attempting to shoo camels away by simply shaking a stick at them. Given the size of pastures in northern Alasha and the labor shortages attendant upon rural depopulation, chasing away camels was no substitute for fencing. To camel herders, however, such acts constituted a significant example of moral decline. People were selfish now, complained Sarna. "They say, 'This is my land, that's yours.' In the past it wasn't like that. People now have bad characters [M. *muu zangtai*] and only think about what is theirs." Proximity often bred contempt rather than any sense of community solidarity: "People here [in Bayantal] are really bad" (M. *Manai endkhiin khün yostoi muu*), muttered Batbagana on occasion.

In the case of errant sheep and goats, of which the camel herders also possessed small flocks, it was expected that their owner would be alerted to any trespass and would quickly fetch them. It was in the owner's interest to do this, since these smaller animals could easily be incorporated into a neighbor's herd by being quickly daubed with the paint color employed by that herder to distinguish their animals. Even when one's animals weren't stolen, separating herds could be tiresome work. In general, sheep and goats were kept under much closer watch than camels (fig. 5). Every afternoon, for example, Mönkhbayar would set off on his motorbike to bring home the herd and secure it in the sheepfold (M. *khashaa*) for the night.

Before collectivization, these different degrees of control and mobility were recognized in the informal rules governing pastureland access. Pasture

FIG. 5. Goats and sheep spend more time in close proximity to herder households than wide-ranging camels.

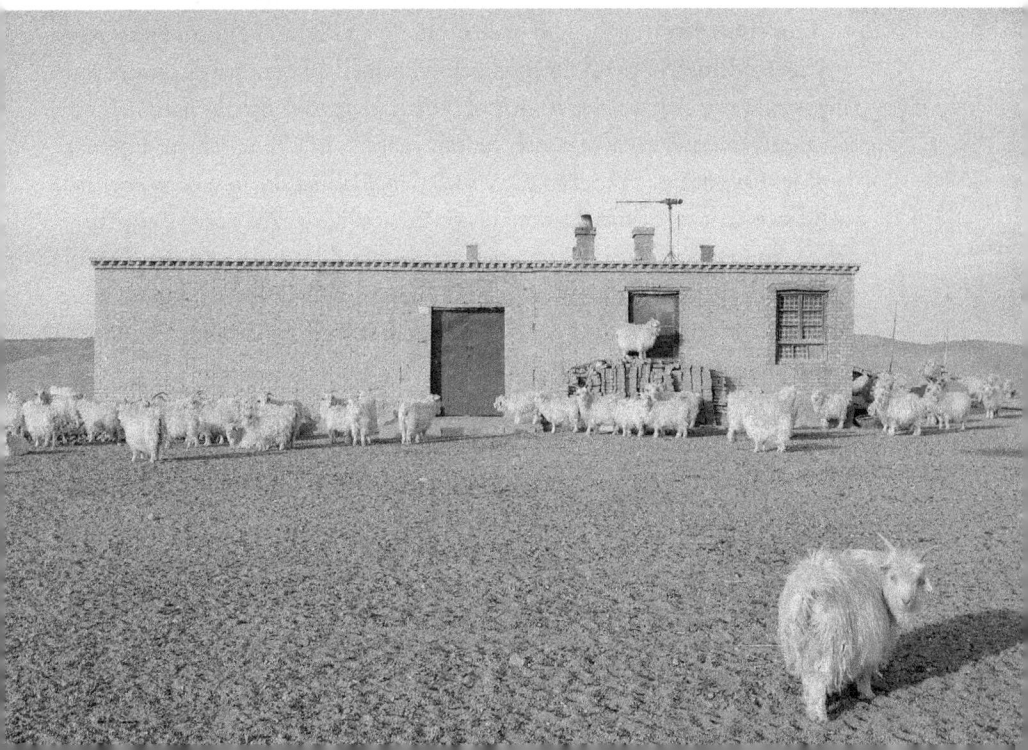

boundaries were only approximate, determined by the extent that a flock of sheep or goats would graze in a single day. Larger animals (camels, horses, and cattle), known collectively as *bod* in Mongolian, were left to roam and were not chased off pastures over which another household claimed use rights, in the expectation that this tolerance would be reciprocated (IMAR EG 2009, 43).[15] But while camel herders still adhered to these rules, many herders no longer felt bound by them, because few households in Bayantal now kept larger animals.

However, there is more to this than simply a contradiction between market-oriented subjectivities and customary rules. The central state's recent designation of the Alasha Bactrian camel as an object of conservation has also fed into moral evaluations of pastureland access. Conceptions of the commons have thus been unexpectedly reinforced by state conservation categories. In the summer, Batbagana's camels would roam the mountains to the north, which was part of another administrative district. He claimed that herders there did not chase away his camels because they understood that these animals needed to be protected (M. *khamgaalakh*) and that Alasha was the world's camel homeland (M. *delkhiin temeen nutag*). Ochir, a middle-school teacher from a family of prerevolutionary aristocrats who lived in Bayanhot but kept a herd of camels on the grasslands to the north of the city, said that some herders there chased his camels away because they were selfish and had a "low [level of] culture" (M. *soyol door baina*). They cared only about their own pastures and not about the planet, he said.

Camel herders, then, could scale up these interhousehold conflicts over pastureland, meaning that those who drove camels off their pastures were going against not only a residual sense of the commons but also the national and even global imperatives of conservation. Scholars of China's environmental policies have debated the extent to which they produce docile environmental subjects oriented to official visions of conservation (e.g., Yeh 2009; Zee 2019). Here, however, we can see how environmental subjectivity, and the alleged absence of such in others, is used to buttress conceptions of land that differ from the privatized model promoted by the state as an integral part of its grassland conservation policies.

So was the camel herders' use of conservationist discourse an attempt by the wealthier to mask their own economic interests and justify access to the land of poorer herders? In other parts of Inner Mongolia in the late 1990s, wealthier herders seem to have benefited disproportionately from privatization of the grasslands, since they were able to fence off their own pastureland while continuing to graze that of herders who could not afford fencing (Williams 2002). It would certainly be possible to argue that Ochir occupied a more privileged class position than other local herders, given both his urban employment and his membership in a former aristocratic family. However, in Bayantal camel herding was not seen as the preserve of wealthy herders, given that camels had until recently been far less economically valuable than goats. Some households with a dozen or so camels, such as Sükh's, were regarded as poor, while herders such as Batbagana's Han Chinese near neighbor Fang Guoyi, who had a relatively large herd of goats but no camels, as well as a daughter with a job in the city, were seen as wealthy. What is more, Fang, who turned up at gatherings in an expensive car and wearing a smart leather jacket, was a member of the Bayantal CCP Committee and brandished his political connections during pastureland disputes with camel herders.

Some scholars have argued that the resilience of herders in Inner Mongolia has been compromised by the community failure engendered by privatization policies, which has led to a dissolution of social bonds and collapse of the trust that had enabled cooperation in resource management (Wenjun Li and Lynn Huntsinger 2011; Conte and Tilt 2014). However, others have recently argued that in certain areas, despite the contracting of pastureland to individual households, communities have continued to manage rangelands collectively (Gongbuzeren, Li, and Lai 2021), sometimes developing innovative management systems that combine market elements with customary institutions (Gongbuzeren, Zhuang, and Li 2016), which often appear to be scaled to the level of the village. In 2007 China implemented the Law on Specialized Farmer Cooperatives, requiring local governments to encourage the creation of cooperatives, and in some pastoral areas of Inner Mongolia these have involved pooling land and livestock and reviving certain elements of mobile pastoralism (Rufei Tang and Michael Gavin 2015).

In Bayantal land privatization had not fully taken hold. But there were no formal communal institutions that might manage access to land, and Bayantal's status as a village seemed to be largely a figment of the administrative imagination. When herders did come together as a *gatsaa* in the dilapidated headquarters in late 2013, it was to sell collective land, not to manage it. In 2013, cooperatives had not been established in Bayantal. However, camel herders did practice a provisional form of commoning among themselves, facilitated by the presence of empty pastures. Referring to the official conservation status of this animal, they criticized the selfishness of neighbors without camels who sought to maintain exclusive rights over their allotted pastures. State resource conservation policies thus unintentionally bolstered conceptions of rights over land that contrasted with its privatization as household property, thus exacerbating interhousehold tensions in Bayantal, with a significant schism developing between people with camels (M. *temeetei khün*) and those without. However, camel husbandry also produced more positive forms of rural sociality that distinguished it from the herding of sheep and goats.

The Sociality of Husbandry

Some scholars have questioned the applicability to Mongolian pastoralism of the voluminous literature on rural resource management, which tends to assume that cooperation is something that happens among members of spatially bounded communities. Instead, these scholars prefer to conceptualize cooperative relations in terms of networks that are flexible and spatially extensive, often transcending the rural-urban divide (Sneath 1993; Ichinkhorloo and Yeh 2016). This could also be seen in Alasha, where herders often called on kin or schoolmates from Bayanhot to assist in shearing sheep and goats. For younger herders such as Mönkhbayar, who were educated at least partly in the city, their social networks, in which classmates figured prominently, were often oriented around Bayanhot. These networks precede and organize the cooperative work of husbandry. But in the case of camel husbandry in Bayantal, cooperative relations often did not so much derive from preexisting social connections (of kinship or education, for example), but rather emerged through the work of managing and caring for these animals and the sociality that accompanied this.

Similar socialities of husbandry are evident in other analyses of pastoralism, even if they have not been identified as such. In 1950s, for example, one anthropologist described milking mares in Mongolia as "something of a rodeo event, since mares did not submit to milking like other animals" (Vreeland 1953, 40). Those with large herds required extra help and would "send out a call for any able-bodied men in the vicinity who were anxious to drop their more humdrum herding tasks for a few days of sport." The sociality of camel husbandry in contemporary Alasha was similarly conditioned by the physiology of the animals, as well as their distinctive mobility.

Whereas goat shearing involved kinship networks that spanned the rural-urban divide, the work of camel husbandry tended to rely on fellow people with camels in Bayantal. In part, this reflected the extensive mobility required by the labor of camel herding, necessitating the use of motorbikes, and urban visitors did not arrive with their own motorbikes.[16] In the early spring of 2014, Batbagana had to locate two pregnant camels who had separated from the

FIG. 6. Camels as infrastructure of sociality

herd. Just before they give birth, pregnant camels wander off on their own far from the rest of the herd. One of these animals was eventually discovered on the slopes of a mountain about ten kilometers south of Batbagana's house, on pastureland belonging to another household. The delivery was difficult, and Batbagana was assisted by Fang San, the brother of Fang Guoyi and himself a camel herder. They returned home on their motorbikes in the early hours of the morning after the calf had been born. Batbagana would later be called out to help Fang San with the delivery of one of his camel calves. Similar forms of cooperation among people with camels in the *gatsaa* were also evident in the laborious seasonal work of removing fleas from the camels. The broad bodies of camels could even serve as a kind of improvised infrastructure of sociality: on more than one occasion I noticed herders lounging against the side of a recumbent camel as they chatted with fellow herders (fig. 6).

In Mongolian regions, herding work out on the pastures is normally conducted by men, while women remain closer to the household (Ahearn 2018). In the early 2010s camels in Bayantal spent most of their time far from the household and were no longer milked, so the cooperative labor involved in camel husbandry tended to be masculine, though women participated in the annual shearing, which took place at the household.

The cooperative labor of camel husbandry was sometimes accompanied by distinctive forms of ritualized sociality. Gelding took place in the spring, and the size of the animals made this a more complicated procedure than in the case of sheep and goats, whose castration could be performed by Mönkhbayar alone, with a little help from his father. On the appointed day, three fellow camel herders from Bayantal, riding motorbikes, helped drive Batbagana's camels into the pen next to his house. From among these, three ungelded males (M. *tailag*) were lassoed, hobbled, and pushed onto their sides in preparation for the operation. This was hard, dangerous work, as the herders had to dodge kicks from the frightened animals. The excision was performed by one of these neighbors before each camel was fed its own testicle, so that the strength contained in it was not lost, while Sarna walked round the camels with incense to purify (M. *ariusgakh*) them. She then toasted each of the camel herders in turn with Chinese spirit (C. *baijiu*). Once the bleeding had been stanched, Batbagana ushered everyone into his kitchen, explaining that it was customary to have a celebration (M. *nair*) on such an occasion. In the kitchen, he presented each of the herders with a hundred-yuan note and a silk scarf; when they refused, he insisted that this was not payment but the camel gelding's "gift" or "best portion" (M. *atanii deej*). On this rare occasion when money was seemingly exchanged for services among camel herders, it was done in a way that in fact re-embedded the exchange within a ritualized economy that sought to circulate the "merit-fortune" of the camels among fellow camel herders.

Camel riding was also bound up with interhousehold sociality. During the weeks that followed the beginning of the new year (M. Tsagaan Sar), households in Bayantal took turns hosting gatherings (M. *tsai*) to which they invited selected neighbors and kin.[17] For Sümbür, this was a chance to show off the new car he had bought with his share of the proceeds from the sale of the collective hay field. Batbagana donned his Mongolian robe and saddled his favorite riding camel before setting off at a brisk pace for his neighbor's home. In previous years Sarna had joined him, but her arthritic knee had begun to make it difficult for her to ride. This camel ride harked back to a tradition of informal racing that took place during these New Year visits between households, in which both men and women participated. Such informal races no longer take place in Bayantal, but people remember them fondly for their lively atmosphere and the good feeling among neighbors they fostered.

Through these races, then, camels connected the disparate households of Bayantal in space while facilitating the celebratory, lively sociality that is supposed to mark the New Year holiday. This desired form of sociality was often referred to in Alasha using the Chinese word *honghuo*. This word, literally "red and fiery," is translated by the anthropologist Adam Chau (2006) as "red hot sociality" and refers to the pleasing bustle and energy produced when people gather together to enjoy themselves.[18] For many in Bayantal, even those who no longer herd camels, the animals remain associated with red hot sociality among households, at a time when the *gatsaa* is widely perceived to lack unity and when crumbling buildings index an emptiness common to rural areas in postsocialist contexts (Dzenovska 2020).

Masculine red hot sociality also characterized the occasions at which camels were still raced in rural Alasha, particularly backstage, before the camels were raced in front of officials, photographers, and tourists. Camel herders from Bayantal traveled together to races several times a year, taking turns hosting a party (M. *nair*) on the evening before setting off. The herders normally spent the night at that household and then loaded the camels onto a truck early the next morning. Despite the truculence of the animals, who were reluctant to board the vehicle, spirits remained high, possibly because for some the effects of the previous evening's drinking had yet to wear off. After setting off, the truck stereo blasted loud Chinese dance music, and raucous laughter echoed round the crowded cab.

Even though camels were left to their own devices for much of the year, their extensive mobility could also produce sociality. In the autumn I accompanied Batbagana to a mosque for the celebration of Eid al-Adha (M. Ikh Mörgöl). Since this mosque lies over sixty kilometers from Batbagana's house and traveling there involves a slow journey over dirt roads, today normally by car, we arrived the night before and lodged with the caretaker of the mosque, the Hui camel herder Guo Xingjian. Guo spoke fluent Mongolian, and he and Batbagana chatted for several hours, comparing the situation facing camel herders in their respective *gatsaa*. Later, when I asked Batbagana how he came to be acquainted with Guo and how the Hui herder was able to speak such good Mongolian, he told me that Guo used to go everywhere in pursuit of his camels, and thus had contact (M. *khariltsakh*) with Mongols. Baigal of the ACS told me about other parts of Alasha where camels still moved between different districts every year, which had the effect of establishing warm relations (C. *peiyang ganqing*) between distant households, who also took turns hosting one another and serving boiled sheep's back.

Literature on pastoralism in Mongolian regions often discusses the technique of *otor*, whereby herding families and their livestock travel long distances in search of good grazing in response to local drought or excessive snowfall (Upton 2005; Dalintai et al. 2012). *Otor* is characteristically seen as a customary institution that relies on a sense of reciprocity, according to which herders in one place tolerate *otor* families grazing their livestock on pastures over which they normally maintain exclusive use rights on the understanding that they will receive similar treatment if forced to go on *otor* themselves. In the literature, *otor* appears as an adaptive human strategy for managing uncertainty and risk, "by which livestock *are rapidly moved* over long distances" (Upton 2005, 595, italics added). But according to herders in Alasha, it was the camels (or horses) that initiated such long-distance movements and thus precipitated these relations between households at a distance.

In recent years scholarship on pastoral systems, particularly in North Asia, has begun to emphasize the importance of animal agency and autonomy, in contrast to earlier theories that saw pastoralism as characterized by human domination of domestic animals (e.g., Ingold 2000). Nomadic movement is now seen not simply as a result of the decisions of herders but also as shaped by the behavior of the animals, which is not always controlled by herders (Dwyer and Istomin 2008). In North and Inner Asia, pastoralism can be thought of in terms of different modes of herding characterized by varying degrees of animal autonomy and human control. Each herding community alternates between these modes, according to the season, species, age of the animals, and environmental context (Stépanoff et al. 2017, 60).

While such analyses have helped reconceptualize human-animal relations in pastoral systems and demonstrate the importance of animals' behavior and desires to herding practices, the role played by the agency and autonomy of certain livestock in the creation of connections among humans remains less explored, as suggested by the vague reference to a herding community. The examples from rural Alasha reveal that modes of herding entail different degrees and kinds of human sociality. Camels' autonomy in Alasha makes their capacity to foster sociality across distance greater than in the case of sheep and goats, while their mobility and physical size require particular kinds of cooperation among neighbors. The distinctive sociality of husbandry afforded by the camel is of particular significance when considering the dynamics of ethnicity in this part of Inner Mongolia.

Rural Conviviality

Han settler colonization of Inner Mongolia has often taken the form of agricultural expansion at the expense of Mongol grazing lands (Yi Wang 2021). Ethnic tensions in the region have thus characteristically been bound up with conflicts over land use, and pastoralism has come to be seen as a bastion of Mongol identity in the face of Han encroachment (Bulag 2004b). Influential Western studies of Inner Mongolia have sometimes essentialized these ethnic differences, as when a stark contrast is drawn between Han Chinese and Mongol spatial identities, which correspond to these two modes of land use (Williams 2002). Such neat distinctions, however, are harder to make in the context of ethnically and religiously diverse rural Alasha; in 2013 twenty-three Han households were registered in Bayantal, fourteen of them permanently resident. Here, after all, the positive sociality produced by camel husbandry could take the form of the red hot sociality that is a central feature of *Han* social life, suggesting how modes of rural sociality could transcend ethnic divides.

The first generation of anthropological analysis of the *minzu* system in reform-era China emphasized the role of this project of state classification in shaping ethnic identity; *minzu* categories were thus seen not to describe a preexisting social reality but rather to act upon it (e.g., Gladney 1990). However, more recent analyses show how official *minzu* identities exist alongside mundane processes of ethnicity, with the boundaries between *minzu* becoming blurred in certain situations, as in the case of the Uyghurized Han of Xinjiang, who have adopted Uyghur linguistic and dietary practices (Joniak-Lüthi 2016). *Minzu* identities can be emphasized or deemphasized depending on context (Harrell 2002).

Foodways in Inner Mongolia reveal how ethnic boundaries are more fluid than suggested by rigid *minzu* classification, as Han Chinese settlers in Inner Mongolia are hybridized by adopting dietary practices conventionally marked as Mongolian (Billé 2009). In Gansu, the permeability of ethnic boundaries is evident in the way competence in the Amdo dialect of Tibetan has become a sign of *local* identity (Vasantkumar 2012). In thinking beyond the *minzu* paradigm, the notion of conviviality can be useful. Paul Gilroy (2004, xii) defines this as "the ordinary experiences of contact, cooperation, and conflict across the supposedly impermeable boundaries of race, culture, identity and ethnicity." While literature on conviviality has tended to focus on urban spaces, scholars working in other parts of Asia have recently drawn attention to the forging of relations across difference in sites beyond the urban (Marsden and Reeves 2019). The sociality of camel husbandry constitutes an example of rural conviviality across *minzu* boundaries.

Shortly before I left Alasha, I was invited to a dinner by Ochir, the teacher at Bayanhot's Mongolian school who kept a small herd of camels in the countryside. He described the event as a *tsai* (tea), using the local Mongolian term for a celebratory gathering, though it emerged that our host was in fact

Han Chinese. I asked Ochir how they knew each other, and he replied that they were "brother herders" (M. *malchid akh düü*) who both kept camels, and that in such cases it "didn't matter whether they were Mongol or Han Chinese" (M. *Khyatad khamaagüi, Mongol khamaagüi*). Ethnicity was thus situational, downplayed in favor of the shared interests of camel herders and the affinities produced through the sociality of camel husbandry.

In fact, Han Chinese camel herders were by no means uncommon in rural Alasha. Out on the grasslands of Bayantal, several households of Han Chinese herders remained, the children and grandchildren of pre-1949 migrants from Minqin County. Local Mongols clearly distinguished these families from those famine refugees who arrived in the 1960s, even if they often casually lumped all Minqin people together by using the derogatory term Sogoo.[19] Altanuul, who grew up in Bayantal, had detailed knowledge of these families. He remembered fondly that the Fang brothers' father had come to work as a hired hand (C. *changgong*) for local Mongols and was an excellent camel herder (M. *temee sain malladag baisan*). He was, said Altanuul, just like a Mongol (M. *Mongol khüntei adilkhan*).

Ethnic boundaries could, however, be reasserted in the context of interhousehold conflict. Sarna told me that we would not be attending Fang Guoyi's gathering because they might serve pork and scavenged meat (M. *ükhsen yum*). "Han eat everything," she said, derisively. The two households were on bad terms because of disputes over Batbagana's camels entering land Fang Guoyi had tried to fence, which Batbagana claimed in fact belonged to a relative of his who had moved to the city. Food taboos could thus be deployed to reassert ethnic difference and prevent commensality.

However, several days later Batbagana set off for a gathering hosted by Peng Shuyi, a Han Chinese herder who possessed the largest number of camels in Bayantal. When I asked Sarna about the event, she initially said scathingly that it would be full of Minqin Chinese (M. Sogoo). She then qualified this, saying that Namar and Tsetsenbilig, two Muslim Mongol camel herders, would also be going, because they, like Peng Shuyi, were people with camels. Here we can see how the sociality of camel husbandry, which crosscut ethnic difference, inflected other modes of ritualized sociality. Not only did the Pengs serve characteristically Mongolian mutton along with the traditional Han Chinese pork and fish dishes, but this mutton was *halal*. New Year's gatherings in Bayantal could thus be occasions of conviviality, at which Han Chinese herders, members of the national majority but in the minority locally, had to adapt to local customs. Sarna, mixing Chinese and Mongolian, said that Peng Shuyi was a wonderful neighbor (M-C. *yostoi sain linju*).

BATBAGANA COULD SOMETIMES BE HEARD lamenting that there was no longer any unity (M. *bülkhümdel baikhgüi*) in what he still referred to as Bayantal Brigade. The disciplined coordination invoked by this name offered a stark contrast to the atomized present. On languid afternoons in the summer, Sarna remembered fondly the comparative bustle of Tsengel, before it became largely a ghost settlement. Their nostalgia speaks to some of the unhappy effects of privatization and urbanization on rural Alasha and the ways they are felt to have unwoven the social fabric.

Literature on decollectivization in pastoral areas of Inner Asia has often pointed to a decline in trust and solidarity among former collective members. But this chapter has shown that species of livestock and the different socialities of husbandry they entail are important variables. For camel herders, these animals were still associated with the spatially extensive but still rural sociality they once fostered through their movement, as well as the practices of cooperative labor and accompanying sociality required by their large bodies.

Rather than appearing in response to deliberate policy initiatives such as the 2007 law on cooperatives, the cooperation involved in camel husbandry, necessitated by the materiality and mobility of these animals, was unintentionally fostered through apparently unrelated policies. For example, PES, which had partially emptied the grasslands, had the effect of allowing camel herders access to the unmanaged, unfenced pastureland of absentee households, without which camel herding might have been unviable. Urbanization, then, paradoxically enabled the rural sociality that was a distinctive part of camel husbandry. This sociality and cooperative labor were unintentionally fostered by cultural heritage policies, which induced camel herders to cooperate in the management of animals for racing. Finally, camel herders defended conceptions of the commons in their disputes with non–camel herding neighbors by referring to state conservation categories, according to which the camel was protected at the national level.

Notions of enduring rural community are hard to maintain in the context of Khöövör, a frontier region marked not only by the reordering of social life during the collective period but also by the migration of Han and Hui from neighboring regions. While conventional representations of Inner Mongolia cleave to a dichotomy between pastoralist Mongols and agricultural Han, the arid ecology of much of Alasha has meant that many Han and Hui settlers have had to take up pastoralism. Camel husbandry, which depends on cooperation among neighbors, is a site of conviviality at which neighborliness can take precedence over ethnic difference.

But the sociality of camel husbandry in Alasha also offers a counterpoint to the state's narratives of modernization in that it involves some Han Chinese taking up a form of land use stigmatized as backward rather than replacing it with agriculture. In addition, the linguistic medium of this sociality in Bayantal is generally Mongolian, in which some Han Chinese and Hui are fluent. Such trajectories of cultural influence run counter to the dominant narratives of civilization that have long oriented the Chinese state (Harrell 1995). In the 2010s, when Mongols were increasingly called on to assimilate into a Han-dominated Chinese nation, in Alasha they could also look to camel herding as a site of counterassimilation, a flickering remnant of the incorporative capacities of the pastoral frontier.

4

Techno-Pastoralism
and Memories
of Animal Labor

BAIGAL'S OFFICE is on the fifth floor of the Bureau of Agriculture and Animal Husbandry (C. Nong Mu Ju), where he works as a livestock technician in the livestock improvement work station (C. *jiachu gailiang gongzuo zhan*). We ignore the commanding view over the arid rangeland to which this suburb of Bayanhot quickly gives way and focus instead on a computer screen. He pulls up a map of the area to the north of the city. The red dots indicate the locations of herds of domestic camels; the signal is sent from a tracking device worn around a camel's neck. Baigal is working on a plan to introduce watering troughs that can be operated remotely via mobile phone. Soon herders will no longer need to live in the countryside, he tells me proudly.

Since Alasha's pastureland is now divided up among individual households, I wonder out loud how herders will control the movement of these animals and prevent trespass. "They won't!" explains Baigal happily. "You shouldn't control camels; controlling them is like putting a human in prison! You should let them wander freely [C. *ziyou zou*]." The rationale for affording such license to livestock is more ecological than ethical, Baigal makes clear. "They know when to eat what kind of grass. Camels won't choose to browse degraded grassland," he tells me. Camels in this region, he explains, are now "semiwild" (C. *ban yesheng de*). Baigal will go on to describe a scheme that seeks to embrace this wildness in the interest of defending extensive animal husbandry on unenclosed rangeland, a scheme he calls "the nomadism of livestock."

However, while Baigal saw value in the semiwildness of camels, for others in Alasha it was tractability that was prized. Several months earlier, I had attended the Camel Naadam on the outskirts of Bayanhot. Even at this event, there were signs that Alasha's camels were becoming more difficult to control. During the final race, one of the camels suddenly stopped and began to run in the opposite direction around the track, ignoring its rider's desperate attempts to get it to revert to its original course. The man sitting next to me, a herder from northern Alasha, sighed and explained that camels were now increasingly wild (M. *zerleg*). In the past, he explained, camels had been allowed to roam freely during the summer before being corralled and used for transportation and riding in the autumn and winter. While the ability of camels to live independently of humans during the summer was respected, it was their willingness to cooperate with humans during the colder months that made them valuable.

As a result of urbanization and the decreasing pool of rural labor, as well as the availability of motorized transportation, such forms of interspecies cooperation were becoming less common. Younger herders were increasingly moving to the city to find work, as the degraded pastures, now subject to grazing bans and stocking limits, no longer provided much of a living. Urbanites who keep camels in the countryside, such as Ochir (see chapter 3), admitted that their animals were now impossible to ride since they were not trained. My neighbor at the Camel Naadam explained how, before they were sheared for their hair, many camels had to be pursued on motorbike, lassoed, and pinned down by several men, all the while protesting with angry bellowing. Such camels were impossible to tame (M. *nomkhruulaj diilekhgüi*). Unlike Baigal, this man looked back fondly to the collective period when camels had been truly tame (M. *yostoi nomkhon*) and would patiently stand tethered while they were sheared or loaded with sacks; now such camels no longer existed, he lamented.

Divergent perceptions of the changing behavior and capacities of domestic animals reveal contradictory responses to the transformation of rural Alasha in the reform era. In reframing pastoralism as conservation, some Mongol intellectuals and officials, such as Baigal, embraced the increasing wildness of Alasha's camels, arguing that these animals could perform vital ecosystem services if their movements were not restricted. They proposed a vision of camel husbandry as a kind of techno-pastoralism, in which new technologies and semiwild livestock would function as a part of a techno-ecological system.

Such proposals depended on a devaluing of rural labor, now seen as something to be reduced with the aid of technical devices to the point that herders would no longer need to live in the countryside. By contrast, the remaking of camel husbandry as heritage fostered memories of the coordination of interspecies labor involved in camel caravans during the early socialist period.

The continued presence and changing habits of these animals' bodies in rural spaces thus engendered contradictory imaginings of China's political-economic transformation and the role of rural people in it.

Techno-Pastoralism

The Nomadism of Livestock

Despite warm words of support for camel conservation from the local government and the exemption of this animal from the most strict stocking limits, the division of pastureland among individual households and the erection of fencing posed significant challenges for camel herders. Advocates of camel conservation in Alasha, such as Baigal, thus joined a growing number of Chinese intellectuals criticizing the household responsibility system instituted in the early reform era, particularly the parceling of land among individual households. Elsewhere in China such critiques were mounted by leftist scholars who sought to defend elements of the collective period, disagreeing with the dominant idea that decollectivization had been a boon for agricultural production (Schmalzer 2016). In Inner Mongolia, however, such criticism was bound up with a defense of what was referred to as nomadism (C. *youmu*) and was leveled in the language of ecology. These critics, both Mongol and Han Chinese, stressed that nomadism should not be thought of as backward, since the ecology of the grasslands required mobility; they lamented that unsuitable foreign models of ranching were being imposed in a very different Chinese context, and they stressed that grasslands needed to be understood as an integrated grass-livestock system (C. *cao chu xitong*; e.g., Niantong Han 2011b, 56–65).

These ideas were echoed in Alasha, though here the distinctive ecology of the region was foregrounded, focusing on the camel as a vital part of Alasha's grassland ecosystem. Texts by Mongols working in the CPPCC, for example, emphasized the autonomy herders granted to camels, describing this in terms of a semiwild mode of camel herding (C. *ban yesheng mutuo fangshi*; Wuricaihu 2017). To varying degrees, they minimized the role of herders themselves in directing the movement of these animals. This is most evident in an article by one Alasha official involved in camel conservation, published in *The Journal of Original Ecological National Culture*.[1] "The Continuation and Development of Nomadic Culture: On the Relationship between Camels and the Grassland Ecology" (C. Youmu wenhua de chuancheng yu fazhan: Lun luotuo yu caoyuan shengtai de guanxi) argues that nomadic culture (C. *youmu wenhua*) should not be thought of as backward, as it has been according to the evolutionist ideology of the modern Chinese state (Wunimenghe 2015). Instead, the author argues, "there is no contradiction between modernization and nomadism." But this is nomadism with a twist: "There is no contradiction between the sedentarization of herders and the nomadism of livestock [C. *shengchu de youmu*]." The article thus appears to accept the conflation of sedentarization with modernization that has been characteristic of twentieth-century developmentalist states (Scott 1998), even as it also argues for the benefits of mobile livestock.

In its frequent reference to ecological pastoralism (C. *shengtai xumuye*), the article echoes Chinese writings on the concept of ecological agriculture (C. *shengtai nongye*) proposed by the agricultural economist Ye Qianji (1988). Rather than championing small-scale agroecology, this work on ecological agriculture reflected the emphasis on engineering and systems thinking characteristic of the technocratic age initiated by Deng Xiaoping (Schmalzer 2022) and envisaged the modernization of agriculture through socioenvironmental management and the dissolution of the peasantry (Rodenbiker 2021).

In a similar way, ecological pastoralism conceptualizes herding as part of a system of flows and material transfers. It argues against the erection of fencing, on the grounds that this restricts the mobility of these animals and prevents them from acting according to the laws of nature (C. *ziran guilü*). These laws "dictate when [the camel] moves to a particular piece of pasture." Allowing the camels to follow these laws, the author claims, is the best method for restoring the degraded grasslands. In moving long distances across the grasslands, camels exercise benign ecological agency by spreading their dung, which acts as fertilizer for the grasses, while their broad flat hooves crush the rats that damage desert shrubs.

In such descriptions camels appear to be merely acting according to instinct as elements of an ecosystem, but in conversation officials and intellectuals involved in camel conservation frequently ascribed intentionality to camels. One of them, for example, told me that camels were the most environmentally friendly animal (C. *dui huanjing zui youhao de dongwu*), because they deliberately selected grassless areas in which to lie down. According to Baigal, camels not only moved over a large distance every day; in certain seasons they also migrated of their own accord. This movement was not instigated by herders, according to Baigal, but was instead a conscious decision by the camels themselves. "They know when to eat what grass," he emphasized.

Such conceptions of camels as ecological actors can be contrasted with the understanding of these animals evidenced in a 1986 document that promoted camel husbandry as central to Alasha's reform-era development (see chapter 1). This document is shot through with Maoist themes of conquering nature (Shapiro 2001), as the two senior officials write that the development of camel husbandry in Alasha requires engaging in a "war on the desert" (C. *shamo da zhan*) by planting grass and trees. Rather than being an integral part of the grassland ecosystem, the camel is figured as a "faithful helper in the struggle against nature" (C. *xiang da ziran kaizhan douzheng de deli zhushou*; Liu and Wulunsai 2017 [1986], 103).

Back in his office, in between checking camels on his screen and answering phone calls from camel herders, Baigal drew an economic analogy to help me understand the ecological role of these animals. "If camels are allowed to act according to their own will [M. *sanaa*], they go wherever the grass is good. It's the same with people. They go wherever there is money to be made, of their own free will." Here Baigal linked the movement of camels to the economic migration that has characterized China's reform era and modeled the behavior of camels on the market agency of humans.

In similar fashion, the article compares the removal of controls on animal movement to the relaxation of controls on cross-border trade: "Every country in the world has developed economically by respecting the fact that the laws of the market economy [C. *shichang jingji guilü*] transcend national boundaries; likewise, the management of livestock must respect the fact that the laws of nature transcend the boundaries of enclosed pastureland." Allowing camels to move freely is thus understood as akin to the opening up (C. *kaifang*) of socialist China to global markets. Ecology and economy are seen as systems that function best when actors are left to pursue their own interests. This modeling of ecology in economic terms has a long history in ecological thought: Ernst Haeckel, who coined the term *ecology* in 1866, defined it as "the body of knowledge concerning the economy of nature" (Worster 1994, 192), and today "commercial economics and ecology are closely intertwined in Chinese thinking" (Schmalzer 2022, 126).

The proposal for the nomadism of livestock invites comparisons with recent rewilding experiments in Europe. These involve free-roaming, "de-domesticated" herbivores, which are valued for their role as "ecological engineers" (Lorimer and Driessen 2016). The geographer Jamie Lorimer (2017) argues that the popularity of rewilding is part of a broader turn to "probiotic environmentalities" at scales ranging from the human microbiome to nature reserves. These have emerged in response to a widespread sense that the Enlightenment emphasis on human mastery and control of nature has produced its own pathologies rather than securing human life. Analyzing similar modes of governing that have arisen in response to the threats posed by climate change, Bruce Braun (2014, 59) writes of "a doubling of neoliberal forms of government," whereby both the naturalness of society and that of nature are to be let alone. We can see an analogous doubling in Baigal's desire to grant freedom (C. *ziyou*) to animals so that they can contribute to the healthy functioning of ecosystems.

However, this conceptualization of the nomadism of livestock using certain market logics coexists with a critique of the division of the rangeland among individual households. Together with recent incentives for (fenced-off) plantations of saxaul bushes, which are designed to act as a form of windbreak (Zee 2019), this has led to fragmentation of the open range. Proponents of camel husbandry emphasize the need to combine individual plots of pastureland and remove fencing to allow camels to move freely. In addition, the author of the article on the nomadism of livestock argues that camels should be allowed to browse freely in shrub plantations, where they can simulate wild animals (C. *mosi yesheng dongwu*) and prune (C. *xiujian*) these windbreaks to assist their healthy growth. They claim that shrubs not browsed by camels soon wither and die.

Camels' increasing wildness is thus embraced as a sign of the naturalness of these animals and of them following their own will, with the positive effects that follow from this. The natural movements of the camel become a means of challenging the privatization of pastureland and the fencing of shrub plantations. The nomadism of livestock proposal thus combines market rationalities with the defense of nomadic, open-range grazing in the face of the state's attempt to manage the ecology of the grassland through enclosure. Instead of rural Mongols being incentivized to abandon herding and tend to windbreak shrubs, the proposal argues that herders should be subsidized *not* to sell off their camels and suggests that removing fences will allow the camels to prune windbreak shrubs and crush the rats that damage them.

The proposal thus draws on forms of governmentality characteristic of reform-era China (Ong and Zhang 2008; Yeh and Gaerrang 2011) in that it addresses herders as market-oriented actors. At the same time, it exemplifies the kind of "socio-natural governance" (Zee 2020) through which the state has sought to transform Alasha into windbreak infrastructure, in which the propensities of nonhumans and humans are simultaneously enrolled in transforming Alasha's pasturelands into windbreak infrastructure to quell the dust storms. The local state, for example, deploys tax breaks to attract buyers of medicinal plants that grow on the roots of the desert-fixing saxaul shrubs;

these medicinal plants are in turn supposed to act as an economic incentive for herders to give up their animals and engage in afforestation (Zee 2019).

In his work on cash payments to the poor in Southern Africa, James Ferguson (2011) argues that market mechanisms conventionally associated with neoliberalism are being put to "pro-poor" uses. Rather than merely critiquing government, then, he encourages us to attend to Foucauldian politics, which involves turning the arts of government to new political ends. These Mongol officials and intellectuals were engaged in an analogous form of political experimentation as they framed the camel as a vital actor in the ecosystems of Alasha's arid rangelands.

A Smart Herding System

While this governmentality as politics seeks to maintain a nomadic form of land use, it does so not by foregrounding herders' traditional ecological knowledge but instead by transforming these herders into sedentary urbanites by means of an array of technical devices, according to a vision of techno-pastoralism. This was evident in a local news report circulating on social media in Alasha in 2015, which contained a boosterist description of new herding technology, such as the tracking devices and automatic watering troughs: "Times change, technology advances. Today you can laze around at home [C. *zhai*] and order takeaway online. But did you know you can now also herd animals from home?" Herding animals was thus imagined as part of an internet-enabled urban lifestyle. Baigal told me that herders, who could now live in the city, would no longer have to waste time (C. *langfei shijian*) on the labor of animal husbandry. They could choose to become entrepreneurs, for example by selling precious stones from the Gobi, which are much sought after in eastern China. Or they could just stay at home. It was their choice.[2]

Instead of celebrating the traditional ecological knowledge of rural herders or even seeking to transform them into environmental subjects (Agrawal 2005), the proposal is complicit in a feature of Chinese state environmentalism that the environmental sociologist John Zinda (2019) refers to as "labor removal." While Zinda is primarily concerned with highlighting the unnoticed, poorly remunerated labor that goes into environmental protection (as in the case of those employed to guard "public benefit forests"), he also mentions the removal of labor from rural areas deemed ecologically fragile as farmers and herders are resettled in urban areas. In Alasha, the idea of the nomadism of livestock involves both labor removal and labor reduction. Herders are to become modern urbanized subjects and no longer labor in the countryside with their camels, whose resultant increasingly wild condition is to be welcomed as a sign of their naturalness and provision of ecological services.

Baigal had recently traveled to the Zhongguancun District of Beijing, known as China's Silicon Valley, where he arranged for a small company to produce the tracking collars for camels. In a document promoting this technology, he referred to the "smart herding system" (C. *zhineng fangmu xitong*) and the "ecological pastoralism" that would enable a more fine-tuned (C. *jingxihua*), virtual (C. *xunihua*), long-distance (C. *yuanchenghua*), and automatic (C. *zidonghua*) style of herding. In the context of the Chinese state's increasing emphasis on "indigenous innovation" (C. *zizhu chuangxin*) as it seeks to move away from reliance on imported technologies (Amy Zhang 2020), recent years have witnessed a proliferation of new technologies in China's countryside. While scholarship on this phenomenon has hitherto focused on agricultural, Han Chinese contexts (Xiaowei Wang 2020), the proposals for smart herding systems show how Mongol traditions of extensive pastoralism were being reframed as a site of technological innovation, channeling an "affect of anticipation" (Lindtner 2020, 12) from eastern metropolises toward this borderland.

With the introduction of these technologies, the labor of herding would be not only dramatically reduced but also fundamentally transformed. The article setting forth proposals for the nomadism of livestock argues that while the term *nomadism* conjures up an image of the arduous (C. *jianku*) work involved in following after livestock, in fact nomadism is perfectly compatible with the fruits of modern industrial civilization (C. *xiandai gongye wenming*) such as motorbikes, mobile phones, satellite navigation systems, and computers. This echoes Ulanhu's arguments defending pastoralism during the early socialist period, which emphasized the complementarity of pastoralism, agriculture, and industry as interdependent elements of socialist modernity. The article suggests that herders will now be able to "observe the movements of camels from a computer in the city." The term *observe* (C. *guance*) suggests monitoring natural phenomena using scientific instruments; what little remains of the labor of herding thus allows herders to perform their scientific modernity. In an inversion of the dominant domestication narratives (Swanson et al. 2018) at China's margins, in which both animals and herders are seen to require improvement (Christmas 2017; Frank 2018), the wildness of camels here correlates not with the backwardness of minorities but rather with their modernity.

This vision is notably different from that which orients many regenerative agriculture schemes in European contexts. While these schemes also champion the benign ecological effects of livestock, they do so by emphasizing the "moral virtue of working human and animal bodies" in rural settings (Cusworth et al. 2022, 1020). Techno-pastoralism, however, imagines the ecological agency of camels in terms not of labor but rather of freedom and profit-seeking, envisioning herders liberated from rural drudgery.

Techno-pastoralism is a form of technopolitics, "the strategic practice of designing or using technology to constitute, embody, or enact political goals" (Hecht 2009, 15). On the one hand these technologies performed a politics of time, embodying the claim that pastoralism is not a backward mode of production but instead coeval with industrial modernity. In addition, built into tracking devices and automatic watering troughs was the idea that camels could move without herders having to, thereby countering a long-standing denigratory Chinese stereotype of minority herders as wandering nomads, condemned by their primitive existence to be constantly on the move "in search of grass and water" (C. *zhu shui cao er ju*; Salimjan 2021, 114). Finally, these devices were inscribed with certain "ethico-political projects" (von Schnitzler 2013), namely the transformation of herders into urbanized subjects.

However, in celebrating new technologies, labor reduction, and the increasing wildness of camels, this conception of nomadism as a technoecological system was in tension with the idea of camel husbandry as cultural heritage. Two of the three camel husbandry customs listed in 2008—camel racing and the craft of camel tack—concerned the skilled exercise of human control over animals. It was noticeable that on meeting another camel herder for the first time, people often asked, "Do you tether and ride them?" (M. *Uyaj uralddag uu?*). On one occasion the name of a herder to the south of Khöövör came up in a conversation among camel herders in Bayantal. They spoke enviously of the large herd he was able to keep without difficulty in the sparsely populated desert, but someone pointed out that he did not tether or ride his camels. A consensus soon emerged that he was lazy (M. *zalkhuu*). With its foregrounding of the skills involved in controlling camels, pastoral heritage in Alasha thus instantiates a particular vision of the rural (masculine) hardworking subject. For rural herders, understandings of camels as subjects were bound up not with their freedom to choose where to browse but with their capacity to work alongside humans.

Animal Labor

The Nose Peg

According to Batbagana, camels that had not been tamed (M. *nomkhruulsan-güi* and thus could not be put to use in riding or transportation were just meat camels (M. *makhnii temee*), fit only to be sold for slaughter. In Alasha, great emphasis is placed on the insertion of the nose peg (M. *buil*), which allows the animal to be tethered and to have its movement directed (fig. 7).[3] In addition to basic verbal commands, it serves as a vector of communication between herder and animal. Rather than an instrument of domination (Ingold 2000), herders regard the nose peg as a kind of "social infrastructure" (David Anderson et al. 2017), which affords the possibility for herder and animal to work together.[4]

Mongols have a hierarchical understanding of the five kinds of livestock, with the horse traditionally held in highest esteem (Meserve 2000). Some in Alasha still compared the horse favorably to the camel. For example, Jargal, the Khöövör official who originally hailed from the south of Alasha, where horses have traditionally been more prevalent, told me that the horse was obviously superior to the camel because the latter was only used for carrying things (M. *yum achikh*). Here the labor characteristic of a beast of burden was seen to confer on the animal an undignified status, in contrast to the noble horse.

FIG. 7. Camels with the nose pegs used to direct their movement. The bridle here is merely decorative.

However, it was this very labor that camel herders emphasized when asked what was special about these animals. Batbagana insisted that they had a particularly high degree of "merit-fortune" (M. *buyan*) because of their willingness to carry heavy loads for humans. "Horses don't carry things, you can only ride them," he told me. Intriguingly, Batbagana suggested that camels were not merely vessels that contained or exemplified the merit-fortune accumulated by the household, as livestock have often been characterized in the Inner Asian context (Empson 2011), but intentional producers of merit-fortune by virtue of the work they did. Intentionality in this instance was conceived of not in terms of self-interest, as it was for Baigal, but in terms of willing participation in collective labor. Here Batbagana drew on another sense of *buyan*, which referred to doing a good deed for someone (M. *buyan khiih*). The word was commonly used by herders when they requested help from neighbors without the promise of remuneration. The particular use of this word to apply to the camel portrayed this animal as a participant in social relations based on cooperation in work.[5]

It is not only humans that labor: "Animals are working subjects, not just worked objects" (Haraway 2008, 80; see also Barua 2017; Porcher and Estebanez 2020). In rural Alasha, camels were subjects by virtue of their capacity to work with humans, indexed by a particular material object, the *buil*. As the proportion of semiwild camels without nose pegs increased, this conception of proper human-animal relations was emphasized through certain heritage practices. At the same time, it was shaped by memories of camel caravans during the first decades of socialist construction. These memories valorized coordinated rural interspecies labor in a way that was markedly different from the smart herding system of nomadic livestock and urbanized herders.

Caravans and Socialist Construction

If camel caravans were not officially itemized as part of Alasha's intangible cultural heritage, heritage-making had nevertheless led to the prominence in public culture of this now obsolete mode of transport. For example, the front cover of the 2008 edition of *Man and the Biosphere* dedicated to Alasha, published by the Chinese committee of this UNESCO initative, showed a reenactment of an archetypal scene: surrounded by sand dunes, a few caravan men sit around a fire while dozens of camels loaded with canvas sacks and connected to each other by ropes stand patiently next to them. Similar strings of camels, arranged in caravan formation, can often be seen at camel culture events such as the Camel Naadam in Bayanhot (fig. 8). In a private museum

FIG. 8. Historical reenactment: camels arranged in caravan formation and decked out with caravan equipment

of camel culture outside Bayanhot that I visited in 2017, beneath a large map showing various parts of the Silk Road emanating from Alasha, the owner had proudly displayed numerous examples of the pack cushions (M. *zaas*) that had once helped camels to carry their heavy loads.

Memories of camel caravans have also been elicited in recent years by the Belt and Road Initiative and its attendant Silk Road imaginary. In Alasha, books have been published recently with titles like *The Silk Road Camel Bell*. But if the mists of time seem to swirl around the notion of the Silk Road, the renewed interest in caravans has also stirred up memories of the more recent past, as experienced by many older people who are still alive. Recently published oral histories, collected by an official from the Alasha League CPPCC, as well as my own interviews, show how local accounts are inflected by memories of the incorporation of camel caravans into the economy of the early socialist state. Camels are seen to have played an important role in the transformation of Alasha from an imperial frontier into a national borderland.[6]

The selective framing of camel husbandry as heritage appears to obscure this socialist history of the caravans. As historian Sigrid Schmalzer (2019, 430) argues in her discussion of agricultural heritage in contemporary China, "The heritage paradigm does not appear to accommodate recent history.

Indeed it establishes a binary between tradition and modernity." In relation to China's ethnic minorities, heritage has a particular folklorizing thrust (Lee 2020), counterposing endangered ethnic tradition to the forces of modernity. In publications dedicated to Alasha's intangible cultural heritage, for example, the craft of camel tack is today said to be endangered and under threat from modern civilization (C. *xiandai wenming*; Huqun 2010, 51).

Such formulations of heritage as vanishing tradition ignore the ways camel caravans were for a time central to the project of socialist modernity in rural Alasha and the reordering of labor it involved. The camel veneration rituals listed as part of China's intangible cultural heritage in 2008 could be straightforwardly cast as heritage that had disappeared during the Cultural Revolution, only to be revived thanks to the more tolerant policies of the reform era. Indeed, official interpretations of them were couched in a primitivist vision of the ecologically noble herder. The temporality of caravans, however, was more ambiguous. Despite recent associations with a distant Silk Road past, many older people in Alasha had themselves worked on caravans or been responsible for coordinating them during the early socialist period.

China's countryside was powered largely by human and animal labor until at least the end of the 1960s, when oil became more readily available (Smil 2003). In a speech in 1960, Ulanhu exhorted cadres responsible for pastoral production to increase the number of larger livestock (cattle, horses, donkeys, and camels), since these could be used as draft animals in agriculture, thereby demonstrating once more the integration of agriculture and pastoralism as elements of the national economy. Citing a nationwide shortage of oil, he also encouraged the use of camels for transportation, claiming that one camel could carry as much as a small truck (Wulanfu 1990, 202). Bayannuur League, of which Alasha was then a part, was singled out for praise as the only part of the IMAR where the number of larger livestock had increased by 10 percent. In 1960, the year the Soviet Union recalled its 1,390 oil technicians and ended all oil assistance programs in China (Klinghoffer 1976) as the Sino-Soviet split took effect, Ulanhu called for the rest of region to follow the example of western Inner Mongolia and make greater use of camels and donkeys for transportation. In doing so, Inner Mongolia would demonstrate its commitment to the Maoist virtue of self-reliance.

In Alasha, the use of camels for salt transportation had been expanding since 1949 (Shi Youtian 1998, 40). This was accompanied by rationalization, with the establishment of the Alasha camel transport station (C. *tuo yun zhan*) in 1953, which was responsible for drawing up yearly plans for salt transport, coordinating the timing of convoys and the rates of pay, and digging wells and providing fodder along the various routes, in order to avoid competition for resources with local herders (Shi Youtian 1998, 40–41).[7] Official histories remark that socialism brought about the end of the long-established tradition of uncoordinated pack transport (C. *ziyou tuoyun*), where individual herder households decided whether to participate based on economic and ecological conditions, and installed in its place a system of regulated (C. *guizhang*) pack transport. The word *ziyou*, which I have translated as "uncoordinated," also has the sense of "free" when used approvingly, as it was by Baigal when describing semiwild camels. The shifting semantics are significant, indexing alternative visions of the state's proper role in relation to the economy.

When people recounted their memories of the caravans, they described this system of state-coordinated pack transport in great detail. In the autumn, after the camels had been put out to pasture to fatten on summer grasses, the people's communes, established in 1958, would issue instructions to the various brigades under their authority; each brigade secretary would then call a meeting and assign (C. *anpai*) transport work to brigade members. Some brigades even had their own dedicated transport teams (C. *yunshu zu*; Mandoula 2019, 64) and craftsmen to prepare camel tack (Liu Yuelian 2017, 31). Today, official heritage publications ignore this history of socialist coordination of camel tack production.

Oral histories dwell on the bureaucratic intricacies through which pack animal transportation was organized and remunerated. For example, camels were used to transport saxaul, a source of fuel, from the rural brigades to the headquarters of the banner government, as well as hospitals and schools. Upon delivering the wood, the caravan men would receive a receipt from the particular work unit (C. *danwei*) that had requested it, which had to be given to the accountant of the brigade, who was responsible for ensuring that the brigade was paid by these work units (Liu Yuelian 2017, 30–31). This form of labor was thus a way rural people came to experience the spatial and institutional relations that made up the high modernist socialist state beyond their own commune.

Mongol officials who were involved in caravan transportation during the socialist period also emphasized the way it harmonized the interests of ordinary people (M. *ard*) with the state (M. *ulus*). Tömör, a retired official in his seventies who had been responsible for the coordination of salt transportation in Right Banner, told me that it served two purposes (M. *hoyor ashigtei*). On the one hand, through a long-established form of labor, ordinary people earned income for the collective and, via the work point system, for themselves; at the same time, the state benefited by having salt transported from the depths of the desert to railheads on the fringes of Alasha, and thence to various factories around the country. Camels were also used to transport dried animal dung to the railheads, where it was taken by train to agricultural areas of China and used as fertilizer. Work on the caravans thus gave people in Alasha a sense of contributing to the national economy, despite Alasha's remoteness (Liu Yuelian 2017, 43).[8]

Tömör's words suggest how the relationship between rural people in Alasha and the new socialist state was experienced through caravan work. Indeed, in the 1950s, the government in Alasha clearly regarded this work as important in establishing its legitimacy in the eyes of herders. Even after it became possible to use trucks to transport salt from the lakes in the middle of Alasha's deserts, the state for some years still reserved three to four thousand tons a year for transport by camel, to "show consideration" (C. *zhaogu*) for herders and for the established practice of salt transportation (Shi Youtian 1998, 42). Today herders lament that the state no longer shows this kind of consideration, as they are expected to find employment for themselves in the city in low-status jobs such as taxi driving.

Laboring Subjects

In the prerevolutionary period, not only were the caravans uncoordinated by the state; they were also structured by class dynamics. Richer herders who possessed large herds of camels were unwilling to work on the caravans themselves and so would hire poorer herders (Shi Jifa 2001, 183). Caravan work was low status, with negative connotations as heavy labor (M. *khar ajil*). In Mongolia, many of the first generation of revolutionaries had worked on caravans (Lattimore 1962, 77). In Alasha, this work was performed not only by the poorer stratum of local Mongols but also by impoverished Han Chinese migrants from Minqin County (ALBG 2000).

Under socialism, these class dynamics led to a revalorization of caravan labor. This is clear in the Chinese title of a song from Alasha that in 1964 received a prize at the IMAR level: "The Caravan Man's Heart Yearns for the CCP" (C. Tuo yun de ren xin'er xiang dang; ALBG 2000, 865). During the collective era, labor was remunerated through a system of work points. The importance and difficulty of caravan work was reflected in the amount of work points that accrued to those involved in this work, among the most given for any task (Liu Yuelian 2017, 29). Before caravan workers departed for the salt lakes, they were given a send-off at which they were toasted by officials, who wished them a safe return (Liu Yuelian 2017, 75). The status of this work was also reflected in the quality of the food provided for the caravan teams (Liu Yuelian 2017, 43).

Since the salt convoys traveled during the autumn and winter, caravaneers (M. *ayanchid*) had to cope with extreme cold. Night watches were posted to guard against wolf attacks. Those who worked on the caravans remember that the ability to endure hardships, or to "eat bitterness" (C. *chi ku*) as the Chinese idiom has it, was required. "Eating bitterness," it should be noted, was central to CCP revolutionary narratives of heroism and self-sacrifice (Griffiths and Zeuthen 2014). Herders remember that through this hard work they earned money for their brigades and provided for their families. This instilled a lasting work ethic: one herder claimed that "to this day I have never relied on poverty relief funds from the state" (Liu Yuelian 2017, 43). Such subjectivities now find themselves at odds with contemporary regimes of value, especially the state's policy of payments for ecosystem services, which incentivize the reduction of pastoral labor and encourage resettlement in the city without the promise of employment.

Grassland management policies in the reform era have targeted individual households, resulting in many cases in a breakdown of relations between households and a perceived lack of unity in the *gatsaa*. Caravan work, by contrast, is remembered for the unity and cooperation (C. *tuanjie hezuo*) it required. As in other contexts in contemporary China (Xia Zhang 2020), there are fond memories of this form of socialist labor. Despite the hardships, these journeys were sites of intense camaraderie: herders remember singing songs together as they walked along with the camels (Liu Yuelian 2017, 65). Caravans had their own "miniature social organization," divided into small units known as "fires" (M. *gal*) consisting of several caravan men (Humphrey 2020, 20; Mandoula 2019). Caravans were characterized by egalitarianism: the men took turns cooking, for example (Liu Yuelian 2017, 70).

The caravans not only fostered distinct forms of sociality among the caravaneers; they also cultivated interspecies affection. Former caravaneers remembered the feelings for the camels that developed over many years of working with these animals. While mostly gelded camels (M. *ata*) were used in the caravans, occasionally it was necessary to use a few female camels. These would constantly wail as they walked, calling to offspring born the previous spring but left behind with the herd. The caravan men found this heartrending and noted that these animals were particularly tender-hearted (Liu Yuelian 2017, 45). The caravan journey itself could also be a process of animal training. While most of the camels had already been trained to carry loads, sometimes untamed animals were brought along to be trained en route. Caravan work is thus closely associated in the minds of older herders with an understanding of camels as subjects capable of emotion and with the taming of camels, a practice that has become increasingly rare in an age of semiwild camels. This kind of interspecies affective bond has no place in the vision of techno-pastoralism, which is predicated on the estrangement of herders from their camels.

Animal Exemplars

Beyond their importance to the socialist reconfiguration of labor in Alasha, camels also gained a metaphorical significance in Chinese socialist cosmology. In part this is a result of the geographical particularities of the Chinese Revolution. Following the Long March (1934–35), the remnants of the Red Army holed up in Yan'an, in the arid north of Shaanxi, not far from the Inner Mongolian border. In the context of the Sino-Japanese War (1937–45), northwestern China gained new prominence in the national imagination and in state-building efforts, as the Japanese dominated the eastern seaboard (Hsiao-Ting Lin 2007). In Chinese paintings from this time, camels came to symbolize wartime resilience and solidarity between Han and minorities (Gu 2020). In Yan'an camels provided a ready source of metaphors for CCP cadres. During the Yan'an Rectification Campaign (1942–45), one cadre apparently told Zhou Enlai, later the PRC's first foreign minister, "I've been carefully studying the character and capabilities of camels. They are particularly tenacious [C. *wanqiang jianren*], resistant to cold, disease, hunger, and thirst. They can eat bitterness and put up with great hardship [C. *chiku nailao*]. I think that Comrade Zhou Enlai is our party's and our revolutionary army's camel!" (Li Ye, Tuhong Fang, and Jingguo Pan 2019).[9]

But the most famous camel in the CCP was Ren Bishi, an important Red Army commander and Politburo member until his early death in 1950 at forty-six, which was ascribed to his extraordinary dedication to serving the people. He was memorialized in a *People's Daily* obituary: "He was our party's camel, the Chinese people's camel. Carrying a heavy load, he travelled a long and arduous [C. *jianku*] road. He never rested, never sought any enjoyment, and never looked for personal advancement." Ren was the first senior figure to be buried at the Babaoshan Revolutionary Cemetery in Beijing, following a solemn state funeral. Zhou Enlai exhorted people to "study his 30 years of ceaseless struggle and his spirit of self-sacrifice which meant that he did not rest until he was dead" (Li Ye, Tuhong Fang, and Jingguo Pan 2019). Ren thus became a model of socialist morality, one of the exemplars (Humphrey 1997; Bulag 2002b) through which the party sought to inculcate its ideology. Today the "camel spirit" (C. *luotuo jingshen*) exemplified by Ren is an established element of CCP ideology. In the wake of Xi's anticorruption campaign, CCP cadres have been subject to increasing ideological education. In this context, Ren's camel spirit has received renewed attention in party publications as an example of hard work, dedication, and probity that party members must follow (Zhou Jianguo 2015; Li Ye, Tuhong Fang, and Jingguo Pan 2019).[10]

The notion of camel spirit also provides Mongol elites in Alasha with a way of linking local culture to socialist cosmology. For example, Bayandai, one of the founders of the Alasha Camel Society, in a report on the society's progress, writes that it aims to "celebrate camel spirit and pass on camel cultural heritage" (Bayindai 2007). The eclectic volume *The Silk Road Camel Bell*, published by the Alasha League CPPCC (Batuchulu and Siqinbielige 2017), includes the poem "Camel," by the famous Han Chinese intellectual Guo Moruo, next to a Mongolian-language account of the techniques involved in training camels. This poem again uses the camel as a metaphor for the heroic struggle of the CCP in the face of hardship.

The Yan'an period quickly became prominent in the mythology of the CCP. Yan'an Spirit (C. Yan'an Jingshen) came to refer to the sense of sacrifice and hard work against all odds that characterized the experience of CCP members in this remote location (Denton 2012; Selden 1971). What has not been remarked upon is the way one of the characteristic animals of this region came to serve as a model for the socialist morality of the new state. As animal exemplars, camels no longer represented the "the exotic and the alienating," as they had done for earlier generations of Chinese artists (Gu 2020, 143); instead their ability to carry heavy loads in arduous conditions provided an ideal metaphor for the CCP's wartime struggles and its valorization of the ability "to eat bitterness."

Marginal Histories of National Incorporation

The contribution of camels to the CCP extends beyond metaphor. In recent years, the role of these animals in consolidating China's borders has been highlighted in various local newspaper articles, and these narratives have subsequently been taken up by Mongol elites in Alasha as they make the case for camel conservation. While celebrating the territorial consolidation of the contemporary PRC, these marginal histories of national incorporation implicitly challenge dominant historical narratives in which China's peripheries feature as the passive recipients of liberation and modernization. They are marginal not only in the sense of highlighting the role of China's peripheries in revolutionary history but also in reading between the lines of official narratives to foreground the role of nonhumans (White 2023).

One of these concerns the role of Alasha's camels in the "peaceful liberation" of Tibet in the early 1950s. The PLA was forbidden from requisitioning food from local Tibetans, so 27,000 camels, including many from Alasha, were used to transport supplies from other parts of China across the frozen mountain passes (Scott 2009, 45–47). According to an article published in Chinese in *Alasha Daily News* by a journalist from Ningxia (Tang 2009) and later reprinted in *The Silk Road Camel Bell*, the camels, so hardy in desert conditions, found it hard to cope with altitude sickness and freezing conditions, with the result that over four thousand of them died. The article calls for greater recognition of the "tragic heroism" (C. *beiqu yu zhuanglie*) of these animals and refers to them using the term "outstanding servants" (C. *gongchen*), a term reserved for those who have rendered especially important service to the state and nation. The language of heroism, service, and sacrifice is redolent of the early period of socialist state-building in China. These marginal histories, freighted with "socialist affects" (Schwenkel 2013), confer on camels the status of historical actors in China's territorial consolidation. In the words of one Mongol official, "Without Alasha's camels, Tibet might now be independent."

Batbagana remembered that herders in Khöövör had given five hundred camels to the PLA to assist in the "liberation" of Tibet. Though they had received money in compensation, he said that herders had donated the animals "voluntarily" (M. *sain duraaran*). A similar story, in Mongolian, of the voluntary donation of camels to the PLA by herders in Alasha Right Banner is recounted in *The Silk Road Camel Bell* (Ölziit 2017). Such memories must be understood in contrast to dominant contemporary representations of China's ethnic minority peripheries as recipients of "the gift of development" (Yeh 2013b) in the wake of the Open Up the West campaign. This has involved a partner assistance (C. *duikou zhiyuan*) program, whereby wealthy eastern provinces and municipalities provide aid to partnered areas in western minority regions (Joniak-Lüthi and Bulag 2016). Western China is thus configured as deficient, requiring the beneficent assistance of coastal Han Chinese regions. By contrast, memories of camel donation establish Alasha's herders as givers, rather than receivers, of aid. Such gifts constitute Alasha's rural Mongols as historical actors in the processes of Chinese revolution and national incorporation.

In 2014, just before I left Alasha after my initial period of fieldwork, Batbagana was struggling to find neighbors who could help him break in a gelding, as their lives increasingly orbited the city. He looked back fondly to the collective period, when Bayantal was full of camels, all of them fitted with *buil*. People and camels were becoming lazier, Batbagana complained. Others argued that the increasing wildness of the camels was indicative of moral failings on the part of herders. "With these PES people now just sit at home watching television," said one herder in his sixties. The collective period was seen to be one when people were very poor but equality was demonstrated by equal participation in labor. PES are seen as severing the connection between labor and value that was a key component of the commune system, and across Inner Mongolia people complain about the shortage of labor in the countryside (Han Niantong 2011a, 9). This shortage is a result of the privileging of urbanization and the concomitant unmaking of rural lives, not only through the grazing bans but also through the closure of schools and clinics that had made possible a rural modernity.

One frequent complaint about the environmental policies targeting herders was that the state did not arrange work for relocated herders. Such complaints revealed how expectations of state coordination of labor have persisted. There was widespread concern that herders who moved into the city attempted to live off their PES without engaging in work. I was told that these former herders now had nothing to do (M. *khiideg yum baikhgüi*), which led them to fill their days with drinking and gambling. They established "chaotic" (C. *luan*) sexual relationships and became "hooligans" (C. *liumang*). In Bayanhot, one of the residential neighborhoods where ex-herders live was popularly referred to as the alcoholic's neighborhood (C. *jiugui xiaoqu*). Rather than producing civilized urbanites, then, as the nomadism of livestock proposal hoped, the reduction of labor was here seen as leading to moral decline. The increasing wildness of camels in the countryside found its complement in the errant behavior of urbanized former herders, no longer able to control either camels or themselves.

From the beginning of the twenty-first century, Alasha's herders, like many rural people across China's western regions, have found themselves targeted by a strategy of labor removal, a central feature of Chinese state environmentalism. Such policies, however, address a rural population that still remembers an alternative ideology of labor. Writing in the context of Mongolia, anthropologist Caroline Humphrey (2020, 9–10) has suggested that "the dispositions and sentiments" nurtured by caravan work "may have been passed on among rural families and may still have some relevance." In contemporary Alasha, the dispositions and sentiments of caravan work remain alive thanks in part to the selective framing of camel husbandry as heritage, which has unintentionally stimulated memories of caravan work during the early socialist period and the valorization of hard work that accompanied it.

The anthropologist Christina Schwenkel (2020) has shown how East German architecture in a Vietnamese city, constructed during the socialist period following US bombing but since fallen into a state of disrepair, continues to convey the affects of socialist nation-building in the midst of market reforms. Rural Alasha, by contrast, contains few material traces of the early socialist period. However, for herders in Alasha, camels, in addition to their status as vessels of heritage, can appear as a kind of socialist remnant. The semiwild condition of Alasha's camels can be understood from this perspective as a form of ruination, as these animals are estranged from humans and thus no longer able to perform the labor to which they are thought to be most suited. Their continued presence in Alasha nevertheless acts as an everyday reminder not so much of mythical Silk Road antiquity but rather of more recent experiences of an alternative political-economic order and the contribution of remote rural Alasha to foundational projects of national incorporation.

THE REFORM ERA IN CHINA has witnessed the unprecedented movement of rural people to urban areas. While much literature has focused on the challenges migrants face in cities, other scholars have recently shown how households of rural-to-urban migrants also face a predicament in how to allocate labor to ensure that fields in their villages remain in cultivation (Kaufmann 2021). Pastoral regions of China have witnessed outflows of people, often as a result of environmental policies as well as the consolidation of schools in urban areas. If in agricultural regions urban migration means that fields are in danger of turning into wasteland (C. *huang*; Kaufmann 2021, 18), in Alasha the lack of rural labor means that most camels are no longer trained and are said to be more wild or fierce. China's political-economic transformation and its privileging of the urban (Driessen 2018) must thus be understood as a process that also transforms rural ecologies and nonhumans.

In Alasha, the increasingly wild condition of camels is an outcome of their obsolescence as beasts of burden. Even though the Alasha Bactrian camel was officially listed as a protected genetic resource at the national level, Mongol officials and intellectuals still had to make the case for the value of the camel now that it was no longer used for transportation, in order to convince the local government to provide support, whether in the form of changes to enclosure policies or subsidies for camel herders. Where did this value lie? One answer to this question involved foregrounding the independence of camels from humans, with the aid of technical devices, to emphasize their naturalness and portray them as integral parts of the grassland ecosystem. The nomadism that was thus defended was understood according to market logics and suggested that rural labor was backward and inefficient, something that needed to be reduced or removed.

But this novel articulation of the nomadism of livestock was in tension with heritage-making in Alasha, which involved celebrating a set of skilled practices of control over camels. While heritage often looks back to traditions that were seen to be sundered by high socialism, by foregrounding the use of camels in caravans, it also stirred up memories of the early socialist period, when camels as pack animals were central to Alasha's economy and to the region's role in the territorial consolidation of the PRC. The conservation of camels was thus also conservation of material remnants of alternative regimes of value. While the threatened extinction of the Alasha Bactrian camel had not come about, the problem of its obsolescence continued to haunt rural Alasha, prompting experiments in techno-pastoralism but also invoking memories of animal labor and the political-economic orders in which it was enrolled.

5

Commodifying Camels on an Extractive Frontier

IN 2013 THE INAUGURAL ALASHA FESTIVAL of Ethnic and Folk Cuisine was held in Bayanhot. Han Chinese tourists were treated to a range of delicacies cooked by chefs from across China's northwest, as well as more local specialties. These included roasted whole sheep (C. *kao quan yang*), a dish once reserved for the tables of aristocrats that is said to have emerged from local attempts to cater to the tastes of the Manchu princesses married to the princes of Alasha. These royal women missed the roasted duck served in the capital, which is now enjoyed in Chinese restaurants across the world in the form of Peking duck. In "Little Beijing" (M. Bag Beijing), as Bayanhot/Dingyuanying was informally known, they had to content themselves with roast sheep. In 2008, the dish was listed as part of Alasha's contribution to China's National Intangible Cultural Heritage.[1]

But on the menu at the 2013 festival was a dish that took the localization of Peking duck to new lengths. Served as part of a performance at the grandest hotel in the center of Bayanhot was roasted whole camel (C. *kao quan tuo*; M. *sharsan temee*). Photos of the event showed the roast camel being paraded past a row of women in Mongolian dress holding the blue silk scarves (M. *khadag*) whose offering to guests has become emblematic in China of Mongolian hospitality. As in other parts of China (Klein 2013), the performance of culinary heritage here was part of the broader effort to create a distinctive Alasha cultural brand, as the region sought to diversify its economy away from natural resource extraction. Alasha, as one Mongol party secretary told me, was going to leave mining behind; its future lay in "digging up cultural resources" (C. *ba wenhua ziyuan wa chulai*). What could be more appropriate than this spectacular dish, which hinted at the distinctive imperial history of Alasha while rendering Camel Country edible?

I first learned about roasted whole camel while scrolling through my social media during an idle moment at Batbagana's. Despite its remote location some two hundred kilometers north of Bayanhot, the house enjoyed fairly good mobile internet connectivity thanks to a transmitter on a nearby hill. By the time I left Alasha, all members of the household had smart phones, which they used mainly to access the Chinese social media app WeChat. In 2011 the Chinese company TenCent had launched WeChat, and when I opened an account in 2013, it already had over 500 million users in China (Harris and Isa 2019). In Alasha WeChat groups made up of kin or former schoolmates often had both urban and rural members, and the platform constituted a space that to a significant degree transcended the divide between city and countryside (see McDonald 2016). In Alasha, WeChat exposed rural Mongols to images of urban consumption, while allowing urbanites some insight into rural lives and the activities of herding (through the circulation of messages reporting lost livestock, for example).

On this app I came across the following post in Chinese, from a young Mongol woman originally from a camel herding household in rural Alasha but now living in Hohhot: "Camels are herders' pets and members of the family; they are also national protected animals [C. *Guojia ji baohu dongwu*]. But now someone has roasted a camel, served it to VIPs, and displayed it as part of a 'food festival.' Don't be taken in by the tourist propaganda! Don't violate folk customs and beliefs! Just look at the camel's eyes and listen to the feelings that herders have for their camels and then decide whether you ever want to eat camel meat again." The text was accompanied by two images, one of which showed the roasted whole camel, its now skeletal face stripped to cooked flesh, appearing fixed in a howl of pain. The other image showed an idyllic pastoral scene of a camel calf being affectionately nuzzled by its mother. Other posts expressed similar outrage at the roasted whole camel, and officials apparently told the Han Chinese chef not to repeat the stunt in the interests of preserving social harmony.

In China's pastoral regions, policies aimed at moving herders off the grasslands have been accompanied by others seeking to commercialize more thoroughly the pastoral production that remains. In Tibetan regions, herders have been encouraged to sell yaks for slaughter, with the meat branded as "green" and environmentally friendly (Gaerrang 2015). Officials in some pastoral areas, including Alasha, have criticized herders for their "traditional" reluctance to sell animals for slaughter (Levine 1999; Liu Xiaowang and

Wulunsai 2017). In an echo of Herskovits's (1926) cattle complex theory, herders are alleged to avoid the sale of animals because they regard livestock as "a symbol of wealth" (C. *caifu xiangzheng*) (Nyima 2014).

In Alasha, despite warm words of support for camels and their exemption from stocking limits, subsidies from the state for herding camels were not forthcoming.[2] As a result, those Mongols in Bayanhot concerned with camel conservation came to emphasize "orientation toward the market" and the "active development of camel products" (Batuchulu and Siqinbielige 2017, 74). With a telling use of metaphor that reflected the prevalence of resource extraction in Alasha, Mongols in the penumbra of the state talked of the need to "excavate" (C. *wajue*) the camel's economic value.

This involved representing camel meat as organic and healthy. Higher prices for products such as meat were a way to "adjust the enthusiasm of herders for camel herding" (Batuchulu and Siqinbielige 2017, 40). The superficially paradoxical dependence of conservation on slaughter and consumption can also be seen in rare breed conservation initiatives in other parts of the world; for example, in the United States livestock conservation organizations encourage consumers to eat rare breeds in order to save them, implying that "consuming diversity is a means of overcoming endangerment" (Radin 2015, 223). The FAO's (2007, 5) Global Plan of Action for Animal Genetic Resources declares that "properly managed [animal genetic resources] need never be depleted, for there is no inherent incompatibility between utilization and conservation."

However, as indicated by the angry WeChat post, for many in Alasha, conservation and consumption appeared to be in tension. While the official classification of the Alasha Bactrian camel as a protected genetic resource implied that market demand for this animal was deficient and in need of stimulation, vernacular understandings of this classification suggested instead that camels were protected animals (C. *baohu dongwu*), at risk of extinction if exposed to the excessive appetites of consumers across China. Opposition to the sale of camels for slaughter was thus not simply the result of enduring folk customs and beliefs; instead, a distinctive conservation subjectivity was being produced by the circulation of conservation discourse and the biopolitical classification of nonhuman life. Conservation or environmental subjects are those who come to understand their world and act on it in accordance with the discourses of nature deployed by the state and conservation organizations (Agrawal 2005; Yeh 2009). In Alasha, this conservation subjectivity was found particularly among urban Mongols, though its performance circulated across the urban-rural divide thanks to the new technology of WeChat.

In Alasha this subjectivity centered on the camel did not emerge straight-forwardly from the discourse of genetic resources but was shaped by local anxieties, and it opened up critical perspectives on the local state. Examining how globally circulating conservation categories were taken up in the particular context of Alasha reveals the anxieties generated by legacies of violent settler colonization but also decades of intensive resource extraction. In the early twenty-first century, rural areas of Alasha had recently witnessed several natural resource commodity booms, stimulated by the desires and purchasing power of newly wealthy Chinese in distant cities. China's rapid economic growth had transformed Alasha, like other parts of Inner Mongolia, into a resource frontier (Woodworth 2017).

While in some other minority regions of China commodity booms have generated a degree of wealth for rural people (Sulek 2019; Hathaway 2022), in Alasha it was largely outsiders who were seen to have benefited, at significant cost to the environment, raising fears that Alasha's natural resources were being depleted. These booms were not confined to mineral resources, but all shared the hallmarks of extractive economies involving "the transfer of key resources to benefit the people and economy of the destination to the detriment of the people and environment of the origin" (Shapiro and McNeish 2021, 10). Local understanding of the camel as a protected animal configured the animal as threatened by integration into an extractive economy.

In some Tibetan areas of China, a Buddhist movement urging herders to refrain from selling their livestock, in accordance with principles of compassion, has gained ground (Gaerrang 2015). Lamas transmitted their teachings on slaughter renunciation in public speeches delivered to large audiences of monastics and laypersons (Kabzung and Yeh 2016). In Alasha, despite the relative strength of Buddhism, at least compared to other regions of Inner Mongolia, there has been no comparable lama-led slaughter renunciation movement. Rather than taking the form of a coherent movement, urban and rural Mongols shared their objections to camel commodification via the new medium of WeChat. Though it would later become an instrument of surveillance and repression, particularly in Xinjiang (Byler 2021), this platform could, in the early 2010s, generate new ethnic cyber-communities, strengthening feelings of ethnic identity and awareness of unjust treatment by the Han Chinese majority (Grant 2017). In Alasha, WeChat enabled the performance of ethnicized conservation subjectivities and the emergence of digital care for camels, through which nonherders could feel for and feel responsible for these animals. However, rather than simply strengthening ethnic identity, digital care came in conflict with novel forms of entrepreneurialism on the part of some herders, for whom WeChat offered the opportunity to market camels and camel meat for sale.

Taking the Camel to Market

"They are completely natural [C. *chun tianran*] and original-ecological [C. *yuanshengtai*]. They aren't injected with anything, and they don't eat any feed. They're semiwild!" Baigal was helping me understand the healthiness of camel meat. He proudly showed me certificates from the China Quality Certification Center (C. Zhongguo Zhiliang Renzheng Zhongxin) conferring organic status on 12,571 camels in Alasha Left Banner, distributed among the banner's three Camel Conservation Zones. Almost all of Alasha's camels were in fact organic, he said, but the government did not allow them to be certified en masse, since they were not able to guarantee the organic status of so many.

A local environmental NGO had assisted with the process of gaining organic certification and provided over ¥10,000 to cover the costs of printing a small booklet highlighting the "green" nature of Alasha's animal products. The 8337 Development Strategy, announced by the party secretary of the IMAR in September 2013, called for Inner Mongolia to become "a center for the production, processing, and export of green agricultural and livestock products."[3] A few years earlier, in 2011, "Alasha Bactrian camel" had been registered as a geographical indication (C. *dili biaozhi*) for camel products by China's Ministry of Agriculture, as local governments across China sought to promote local food brands (Klein 2013).

With the organic certification, Baigal sought to target urban consumers in China who had become increasingly concerned about food safety, due to the heavy use of chemical fertilizers and pesticides and numerous scandals involving tainted food (Yunxiang Yan 2012). The popularity of the idea of *yuanshengtai*, which Baigal applied to camel meat, has emerged from these anxieties over the toxicities of urban modernity in China, and the term has become associated with the simple, pure food purportedly eaten by ethnic minorities in remote areas, which is now sought out by a new generation of tourists (Xu Wu 2014).

In 2009 members of the Alasha Camel Society founded the Alasha Desert Bactrian Camel Herders' Specialized Cooperative (C. Alashan Shamo Shuangfengtuo Zhuanye Hezuoshe). Its geographic scope extended to the whole of the banner, and it functioned as a marketing cooperative rather than a means of pooling pastureland. Baigal explained that its establishment sought to address one of the central obstacles to camel conservation in Alasha: the low price of camel products. Camel hair provided herders with some income, but given the relatively small size of camel herds, this was far less than they were accustomed to earn from the sale of cashmere.[4] The value chain for camel hair was already well established, with a small factory in Alasha producing camel hair quilts for the domestic market but also supplying some overseas companies. Instead, the energies of the Alasha Camel Society were initially directed toward making camel meat into a resource that could supply health-conscious urban consumers.

This resource-making involved collaboration with Mongol scientists at the Inner Mongolia Agriculture University. Meat from Alasha's camels was taken to the National Meat Quality Supervision and Inspection Center for tests, and the results were published in several academic articles in 2011. Baigal was listed as coauthor, along with professors and graduate students at Inner Mongolia Agricultural University, of an article declaring that camel meat is an ideal foodstuff because of its high protein and low fat content. According to Baigal, this research proved that in nutritional terms camel meat was similar to beef and in some respects even better.[5] In part as a result of this research, insisted Baigal, but also because of the increasing fears over food safety, the price of camel meat had shot up in 2012 to ¥50 per kilo, having previously been around ¥20. Indeed, in the past camel meat had been sold as beef in nearby Ningxia; now beef was apparently being sold as camel meat.

Given his enthusiasm for the promotion of camel meat, I wondered what Baigal thought about roasted whole camel. "Well, it's fine to develop that [C. *keyi kaifa*]," he told me. "They don't roast them alive, after all. But culturally people won't accept it [C. *bu jieshou*], as it's a new thing." He then corrected me when I referred to the camel as a protected animal (C. *baohu dongwu*). "It's not a *baohu dongwu*!" he said, slightly exasperated at having to make what was obviously a frequent clarification. "It's a protected livestock breed" (C. *baohu jiachu pinzhong*). Baigal's answer hints at some of the frictions that had emerged in Camel Country: for some, the market was seen to provide a solution to camel endangerment by making it more economically attractive for herders to raise these animals, while for others the protected status of the animal should have prevented its sale for slaughter.

Taboo

It was not just roasted whole camel that some Mongols in Alasha opposed. They also objected more broadly to the slaughter of camels for meat. Another

WeChat post that circulated around this time contained graphic images of slaughtered camels on a snowy street in Bayanhot with the message "Let's stop being so cold and indifferent [C. *lengmo*] and boycott camel meat! If there is no market, there will be no killing. Boycott camel meat!" Opposition was often cast in the language of taboo (M. *tseer*). One Mongol student in his twenties told me that "Mongols in Alasha didn't use to eat camel meat. For the older generation this was extremely taboo [M. *ikh tseerlene*], but now some people have been significantly assimilated [C. *tonghua*] and have been influenced by other *minzu* [i.e., Han Chinese], and so have started to eat camel."

According to state ethnographers in the 1950s, Mongol herders did not eat camel meat or slaughter these animals, preferring to let them die of natural causes on account of the "great service [C. *laogong*] they provided to people" (IMAR EG 2009, 14). A recent Mongolian-language publication, *The Taboos and Customs of the Alasha Mongols* (M. Alasha mongolchuudiin tseer yos), states plainly that "killing or eating camels is taboo" (Tsetsenbilig and Tsagatai 2013, 176). On the first day I arrived in his house in the spring of 2013, Batbagana sought to introduce me to the culture I had come to study by telling me that Alasha Mongols, including Muslim Mongols, traditionally did not slaughter or sell camels because to do so was inauspicious (M. *buyangüi*), though he said many herders now did. Sarna explained to me that slaughtering and eating camels was bad because these animals were known as "the blessing of heaven" (M. *tenggeriin khishig*) and "meritorious animals" (M. *buyantai amitan*). One woman in her twenties from a herding family, now studying at a university in Hohhot, recounted a rumor that linked the death of a Mongol entrepreneur in a car accident to his opening of a small camel meat processing plant in Right Banner. A Mongol official in the Bureau of Agriculture and Animal Husbandry who had been responsible for arranging the sale of many camels to Hui traders in Ningxia in the 1990s was said to have suffered health problems as a result, which he eventually sought to ameliorate by becoming involved in camel conservation efforts.

For some in Alasha, it was a point of pride to be able to hold camels back from the market. On a visit to a privately run camel culture museum outside Bayanhot, I listened to a famous local Mongol singer tell the proprietor that he would never sell his camels. The proprietor, who himself owned around a dozen camels that were herded by a relative, concurred, claiming that they wept if you sold them. "They're as sensitive as humans" (M. *khünii setgel adilkhan*), he insisted.

However, by no means all herders observed a taboo on camel slaughter and meat consumption: it was not a strictly observed taboo like the consumption of pork was for local Muslims. There appeared to be geographical and subethnic differences at work: it was said to be eaten quite commonly in Right Banner and Ejine and by Khalkha Mongols in the north of Left Banner but less by Khoshuud Mongols. But even in this latter group, there were many who admitted to eating it. Some herders said they ate camel meat but not from their own animals, preferring to purchase it from other herders. Batbagana's camel-herding nephew told me that he did eat camel meat, even from his own animals. He explained that an American scientist had said it was the most healthy meat because it had "no poison or fat" (M. *khor, öökh baikhgüi*). Another herder in Bayantal told me that "camel meat is a 'green' food, and scientists have discovered that it can be used to treat different kinds of illness; in the past we didn't like to eat it, but now that it has so many good qualities, it's right that it should be eaten." Despite camel meat not being served in Batbagana's house, he occasionally praised its qualities. "Camels just eat grass, so their meat is good for your body," he told me, contrasting it with meat from livestock raised on fodder (M. *tejeesen mal*). Discourses of food safety and health, then, had to some extent overridden ideas of taboo.

However, there remained a lingering association of camel meat consumption with the violence of settler colonization. For some Mongols the practice of slaughtering camels for their meat was associated with the mass immigration into the banner in 1960 of starving Han Chinese fleeing famine in neighboring Gansu (An 2009, 39), which profoundly altered the demography and ecology of Alasha. Camel meat, they said, subsequently began to be served in the collective canteens of the people's communes.[6] One elderly Mongol in Dengkou County told me that when the Production and Construction Corps (C. Bingtuan) first arrived on the eastern edges of Khöövör in the 1960s to establish military-agricultural settlements, they scandalized local Mongols by stealing, slaughtering, and eating some of their camels.[7] Forced consumption of camel meat was also deployed as part of the violent attempts to erase Mongolian culture during the Cultural Revolution. According to Danzan of the Alasha Camel Society, Mongols were made to eat camels, since their respect for the camel was regarded as superstition, one of the Four Olds that had to be destroyed.

Extractive Anxieties

If outrage at this spectacle of camel meat consumption was partly influenced by memories of settler violence and state projects of cultural elimination, objection to the slaughter of camels was also conditioned by local deployment of the state's conservation discourse. As one Mongol official working for the local Bureau of Culture (C. Wenhua Ju) told me, people disapproved of roasted whole camel because this was thought to be a protected animal, whose slaughter was forbidden. The camel's conservation status had come to be understood in this way in response to the proliferation of informal economies that transformed rural Alasha around the turn of the millennium into an extractive frontier supplying consumers in Chinese cities. By invoking the idea that the camel was protected by the central state, Mongols in Alasha voiced their opposition to the relative absence of local regulation and enforcement that had allowed outsiders to extract and deplete Alasha's resources.

Alasha's resources have long been part of extensive commodity chains, most notably in the case of salt. The region's salt lakes were once the private property of banner princes funding their lavish lifestyle in Beijing (Lixia Liang 2006). Other natural resources were also historically in high demand, including *Cistanche deserticola* (C. *rou congrong*; M. *tsagaan goyo*), a parasitic plant that grows on the roots of saxaul bushes, sought after for its medicinal properties (Zee 2019). When state ethnographers conducted their investigation of Alasha in the 1950s, they found that one third of households surveyed earned some income from the sale of cistanche; for a few households this accounted for more than half their income (IMAR EG 2009, 115). Before 1949, Han Chinese who had not become banner subjects were not allowed to enter the banner and dig cistanche, though at times the banner prince did grant licenses to certain Chinese merchants (IMAR EG 2009, 113).

Market reforms in the late twentieth century prompted the emergence of new informal economies of natural resource extraction, whose commodity chains linked Inner Mongolia with markets in China's booming eastern and southern regions. Unlike in the Qing period, there were now no restrictions on the entry of Han Chinese into Inner Mongolia. Today cistanche remains highly sought after, and some entrepreneurial herders have sought to profit by creating small saxaul plantations in their pastures (Zee 2019), though these can in turn become targets. One herder in the south of Khöövör installed a closed-circuit TV camera to monitor his plantation, which had been subject to frequent theft.

Another notorious commodity boom involved *facai* (*Nostoc flagelliforme*), an edible cyanobacterium resembling human hair, hence its Chinese name, which translates as "hair vegetable." Since the Chinese name is homophonous with the phrase "get rich" in Chinese, it is regarded as auspicious to serve *facai* at Lunar New Year, particularly in Hong Kong and Guangdong. In the 1990s, large numbers of Hui from impoverished Ningxia began to enter Inner Mongolia to collect *facai*. The manner of extraction, involving rakes, was particularly destructive to the grassland, and large conflicts often broke out between local Mongols and the Hui (Bulag 2004b). My friend Ganbold on one occasion showed me what he said had once been a wolf's lair in the mountains near his home to the west of Khöövör, where he said Hui *facai* pickers had briefly lived before they were driven out by Mongols defending their homeland (M. *nutag*).

The central government became increasingly concerned not only by the environmental degradation caused by *facai* extraction but also by the ethnic conflict to which it was giving rise. In 2000, it upgraded *facai* from the second category of protected plants to the first and forbade its collection and sale on the grounds that these led to "grassland degradation and desertification, destruction of the environment" and "negatively affected the normal livelihoods of herders and farmers, and even in some places the unity of nationalities and social stability" (Guowuyuan 2000).

Natural resources that do not enjoy this protected status have also been the subject of destructive commodity booms. These include a kind of wild onion (*Allium mongolicum*; C. *shacong*; M. *khömüül*) that grows widely in Alasha and often provides an important supplement to rural diets in the summer. In recent years, demand for this plant has increased rapidly among Chinese consumers, since it is considered to be natural and free from artificial chemicals and pollution. As a result, large numbers of Hui from Ningxia have come to Alasha to pick this wild onion. Local Mongols complain that they do so in a clumsy manner that damages the grassland. However, in many cases herders are not able to prevent the practice, because they have signed away the rights to their grassland as part of grazing ban (C. *jinmu*) or public benefit forest (C. *gongyi lin*) contracts (Han Niantong 2011b, 20). Attempts to have the local government's grassland supervision (C. *caoyuan jianli*) unit deal with the problem have often failed, leading some herders to hire local toughs to try to scare off the *facai* pickers (Han Niantong 2011b, 23). Other herders, realizing the impossibility of protecting their pastures, have decided to start extracting these resources themselves before outsiders are able to.

Across Inner Mongolia the extraction of coal has created pockets of wealth but also unmade rural livelihoods. At the beginning of the new millennium, the Open Up the West development strategy configured China's periphery as a zone of extraction that would provide natural resources to supply the cities and factories of eastern China (Woodworth 2017). This has transformed

Inner Mongolia, nowhere more so than in Alasha's neighboring region of Ordos, whose coal reserves have made it one of the richest parts of China. In Ordos the mining boom was accompanied by large-scale resettlement of farmers and herders in the urban area of Dongsheng (Woodworth 2017). In other parts of Inner Mongolia, the deleterious effects of the mining boom on the grasslands have sparked protests by Mongols, including one of the largest in decades in 2011, after a herder was run over and killed by a mining truck (Baranovitch 2016b). Images of local protests by herders against mining operations in other parts of Inner Mongolia occasionally circulated among my friends in Alasha.

The mining economy in Inner Mongolia is made up both of large mining firms as well as myriad small-scale, often illegal operations (Woodworth 2017). By the time I began to conduct fieldwork, such operations had proliferated in the mountains of northern Alasha, whose mineral deposits included coal, iron, copper, and molybdenum (Han Niantong 2011c, 77), giving a boomtown air to places like Khöövör Town. In northern Alasha, mining has not led to the mass resettlement of herders. Some herders leased portions of their land to small mining operations while continuing to herd on the remaining pastures, though there were complaints about insufficient and late payments, as well as about damage to grassland and livestock caused by the proliferation of these small-scale, low-tech operations (Han Niantong 2011c, 77).

Mongols insisted that only Han Chinese really struck it rich from mining. Few Mongols worked in the mines; lamas told them they would become ill if they did so, since it involved breaking a taboo on digging the earth.[8] Alasha's resources had apparently even attracted foreigners: I heard talk of a South Korean who had operated a mine for precious stones in the Kharuuna Mountains. These small-scale mines were widely known to be illegal but were said to enjoy the protection of senior local government officials in exchange for kickbacks. For people in Alasha, then, mines were associated with corruption and lawlessness. I once accepted a lift from Khöövör Town from a friendly man in his thirties who drove me to the nearest train station in Dengkou in an SUV with tinted windows. Later, my friend Ma Jun from the Khöövör Cultural Station warned me against any further association with this man, who he said was connected with organized crime (C. *hei shehui*) and used violence to protect the interests of mining bosses. The local government wouldn't touch him, apparently, since he had friends in powerful places.

But perhaps the most remarkable form of natural resource extraction to have gripped Alasha in recent decades centers on "strange stones" (fig. 9),

FIG. 9. A "strange stone" in the form of a camel

varieties of quartz that geological and meteorological serendipity had formed into the shape of something else—a slab of meat, a chicken emerging from an egg, a camel. One hot summer afternoon an expensive-looking SUV pulled up in front of Batbagana's. Only Mönkhbayar and I were at home, and we received the guest, a former schoolmate of Mönkhbayar's, in the kitchen. As we poured tea for him, he shook his wrist to draw attention to an expensive-looking bracelet engraved with animal figures, which he said was made with Russian jade. He explained to me that he was a dealer in precious stones, especially Alasha's strange stones. He took a quick call via his Bluetooth ear-piece. "I'm going to invest in a mall in Hohhot," he explained once he had hung up. To Mönkhbayar he said, "You need to get into stones; you can't lose money with stones," going on to describe how easy it was to pick up girls in Hohhot once you had an expensive car. "There are no stones left [M. *chuluu baikhgüi bolson*]," lamented Mönkhbayar. "Nonsense!" his friend replied. "They might be gone from the surface, but there are loads still underground."

Lithophilia has deep roots in Chinese culture, with mention in a text from the third century BCE of strange stones (C. *guai shi*) sent as a tribute to the mythical emperor Yu (Parkes 2005). Alasha's northern Gobi regions offered an abundance of such stones, but it was not until the 1990s that their extraction began in earnest, fueled by demand from newly wealthy Chinese eager to display their culture and connoisseurship. For nonlithophilic Alasha Mongols, stories of the prices paid for some stones conjured up the possibility of sudden, spectacular enrichment. In 2005, for example, the Beijing municipal government was said to have paid ¥130,000,000 for a stone from Alasha (Han Niantong 2011b, 11).

However, as Mönkhbayar's former schoolmate admitted, most of the people who became wealthy from stones were not from Alasha. Even those rural Mongols who did make some money from selling stones soon spent it; unlike Han Chinese, Mongols were not good at holding onto money, I was told. It was hard to know how much a stone was worth, and its value increased exponentially as it was sold on. One young Mongol who worked for the local Mongolian-language newspaper told me that if I wanted something interesting to research, I should look at how Alasha's stones were traded in southern China. He said that herders in Alasha were tricked into selling stones at low prices. Lacking contacts, most herders who went into the stone trade simply set up stalls in Bayanhot's old town and waited for passing tourists. Ganbold had once decided to embark on an episode of lithic entrepreneurialism, buying stones in Bayanhot that he planned to sell at the famous tourist site of Dunhuang in Gansu. However, the highway tolls were such that he started running out of money before he reached his destination and was forced to return to Alasha. Today, these large unsold stones sit outside his home, their strange forms still holding out the possibility of sudden wealth, even as their dull weight embodies the practical challenges faced by would-be entrepreneurial herders.

As valuable stones disappeared from the surface, herders' chances of striking it rich became ever slimmer. Instead, those who profited substantially were increasingly people with capital and equipment who could extract stones from deep under the ground—those already running mining operations, for example. Bosses (C. *laoban*) like this, many of whom were not local, were able to ride out the volatility of the market, holding onto stones until their price rose. The strange stone business, which once seemed accessible to herders, who could simply gather up these objects from their pastures, now increasingly resembled other capitalized forms of extraction, in which value was captured by outsiders.

As with previous commodity booms, such as *facai*, outsiders who appeared on the scene damaged the grassland with their trucks and digging equipment. Attempts were made to prevent them from accessing these areas, with some *gatsaa* hiring patrols to chase them away. However, strange stones are found across vast, sparsely populated areas of northern Alasha, and preventing access proved impossible. Some *gatsaa* began to charge access fees, until in 2006 they were told that the collection of such fees was illegal, and managing access became the responsibility of the local police, who were as ineffective as the earlier patrols (Han Niantong 2011b, 18).

By the time I arrived in Alasha, urban, well-connected locals still saw the promise of wealth in stones, but attempts to realize this promise were surrounded by a hazy illicitness. As Alasha was steadily emptied of valuable stones, they were still readily found only in very remote northern regions on the Mongolian border. Such areas are often accessible only to the military. On one occasion I was offered the chance to buy a piece of meteorite by a taxi driver whose son-in-law worked as a border guard. At one dinner a few months later a Mongol friend who worked for the local government introduced me to a member of the People's Liberation Army, a Mongol from eastern Inner Mongolia who served at the border. Gradually, through the fumes of *baijiu*, I came to understand that the purpose of the dinner was to firm up plans to dig for stones close to the Mongolian border. The next day I accompanied my friend and his hungover associates to a Buddhist temple in the center of Bayanhot to pray to the local deities (M. *sakhius*). While it was fine to purchase stones from other people, digging them up yourself contravened taboos of which all Mongols in Alasha are aware. My friend's mother had told him that only by venerating (M. *takhikh*) and praying to (M. *daatgakh*) these land spirits would he avoid illness.

There was a feeling that engaging in the stone business had corrupted some rural herders. I heard stories of people tricking relatives into selling valuable stones cheaply. This corruption was all the more noticeable because these stones were concentrated in northern Gobi regions, which, in the moral geography of Alasha, are regarded as home to more honest and simple Mongols, less exposed to the alleged cunning of the Han and Hui than those southern parts of Alasha that border Gansu and Ningxia. Some local herders were now said to be in cahoots with the outsiders who came to dig for stones, shielding them from the police by claiming they were merely working as shepherds, for example. Such concerns echo those of the Qing authorities in the nineteenth century, when some Mongols were thought to be secretly sheltering illegal Chinese mushroom pickers (Schlesinger 2017, 117). The pursuit of lithic wealth in Alasha was seen not only to have caused local Mongols to turn their back on their traditional protection of the environment but also to have made them more sly (Han Niantong 2011b, 19). Scholars have noted that rural commodity booms in other parts of China have also been accompanied by moral anxiety. In the case of caterpillar fungus in Tibetan regions, not only do some regard its collection as sinful, but the income it generates for former pastoralists has become a subject of criticism, with some lamenting the negative effects of the boom on rural Tibetans' work ethic (Yeh and Lama 2013, 327).

However, commodity booms in other peripheral regions of China provide a useful point of contrast, illuminating some of the distinct features of Alasha's informal extractive economies. In the case of caterpillar fungus, as well as matsutake mushrooms in Yunnan (Hathaway 2022), rural societies have been transformed by the wealth produced by these booms, enabling, for example, the construction of large new homes (Sulek 2019). In Alasha, however, there are far fewer stories of herders becoming rich. Instead, local discourse focuses on outsiders profiting from the region's natural resources at the expense of locals.

Crucially, herders in Alasha have been far less successful than their Tibetan counterparts in profiting from the control over access to these resources. Whereas in Tibetan regions, herders made money by collecting fees from nonlocal diggers (Sulek 2019), in Alasha this has proved much more difficult, both because of local government opposition to the collection of such fees and because the scale of Alasha's rural areas and its comparatively small population make it hard to prevent open access. The inability of rural herders to control resource extraction is then exacerbated by environmental policies that encourage herders to move off the grasslands. It would be hard to argue, as in the case of Tibetans involved in caterpillar fungus collection in Qinghai, that Alasha's Mongols were "masters of the situation" (Sulek 2019, 263).

While a few in Alasha have benefited from these informal extractive economies, the tables of ever smaller, less valuable, stones set up by former herders in the center of Bayanhot for tourist buyers contribute to a pervasive sense among Mongols in Alasha of uneven development, with the rapid depletion of Alasha's natural resources benefiting people in other parts of China. This understanding of resource depletion, evident in the frequent assertion that the strange stones had all been dug up, also distinguishes Alasha from these other peripheral regions, where commodity booms centered on renewable resources.

Protecting Camels, Upholding the Law

These anxieties about resources disappearing as a result of demand from Chinese consumers shaped how camel commodification was understood in Alasha. While Baigal was proud of the higher price camel meat now fetched thanks to the efforts of the Alasha Camel Society and its marketing cooperative, others were more ambivalent. One of the Mongol scientists with whom Baigal collaborated told me that he was less keen to promote camel meat: "There are lots of people in China; as soon as they know that it's good for you, camels will be eaten until there are none left." Another Mongol who lived in Bayanhot worried that "however many camels the Mongols have they will never be as numerous as the mouths of Han Chinese." While for Baigal, market demand was key to conservation in that higher prices would encourage herders to raise more camels, some other Mongols, by contrast, understood increasing demand in extractive terms, as a threat that could precipitate the disappearance of this resource. Here we can see how the anxieties generated by extraction in Alasha had seeped into understandings of the pastoral economy. But why did these anxieties come to surround the Alasha Bactrian camel in particular?

Significant in this respect is the distinctive physiology of the camel, particularly its slow rate of reproduction and maturation. Given the long gestation period of thirteen months, a mother gives birth to only two calves every three years, and it is five years before they reach maturity. Rather than a simple binary distinction between renewable (e.g., animals and crops) and nonrenewable resources (e.g., minerals), there are degrees of renewability; the camel is not quite as renewable a resource as sheep and goats. Citing the low replacement rate of camel herds, the scientist feared that increasing sales of the animals in response to a surge in demand would quickly lead to depletion of the resource.

Extractive anxieties surrounding the camel were also stimulated by the concurrence of camel endangerment and the informal extractive economies described above. In the early years of the twenty-first century, camels, like *facai* and strange stones, were bundled into trucks and driven out of Alasha. Because many of those who purchased camels from herders were Hui from Ningxia, the ethnic dimension of this trade was similar to informal extractive economies. Once again, value was captured by these outsiders, as camel meat was apparently sold as beef, which was then more expensive, in the restaurants of Ningxia.

The manner in which camel meat was sold in Alasha created analogies between this animal and endangered wild animals. In the early 2000s, some upmarket hotels in Alasha began to serve braised camel foot, on the model of a famous dish involving bear paw, long considered a rare delicacy in China (Dunlop 2023). According to anthropologist Magnus Fiskesjö (2017, 233), such dishes "are perceived to hold beneficial properties precisely in as much as they derive from known hard-to-access exotic and wild species and places." The sale of bear parts is now illegal in China, and the brown bear is a protected species. Officials sometimes seize large shipments of bear paws smuggled across the Russian border into Inner Mongolia (BBC 2013). In serving camel foot in Alasha, these hotels hinted at this now illegal delicacy, replacing it with an animal that for many Han Chinese consumers remains exotic. But when Mongols encountered such dishes in Bayanhot, analogies with bear paw only served to reinforce anxieties over the camel's endangerment and to configure the appetites of distant Han Chinese consumers as a threat.

As a result of the camel's physiology, the concurrence of its endangerment with the emergence of illicit extractive economies in Alasha, and analogies with endangered exotic wild animals, the Alasha Bactrian camel came to be understood as a protected animal, rather than simply a protected genetic resource. In the words of one young Mongol from a herding family in northern Alasha who now lived in Bayanhot, "I'm absolutely opposed to roasted whole camel. It's meant to be a protected animal, and they still allow roasted whole camel! The state doesn't implement laws properly [C. *guojia guanli bu xing*]. Why isn't there such a thing as roasted whole panda?"

For these Mongols, the fact that the hotel was able to make such a public spectacle of this dish was a sign that the local state was unable or unwilling to implement the law. One teacher at the Mongolian school in Bayanhot complained to me, "They are protected animals, but people are still able to slaughter them indiscriminately: there is a general problem with the implementation of law [C. *falü zhixing*]." Playfully alluding to the reform-era ideology of socialism with Chinese characteristics, he called this "law with Chinese characteristics" (C. *Zhongguo tese falü*). Such invocations of law in this context represented an attempt to contest Alasha's transformation into a resource frontier, where the local state was seen to be complicit in illegal small-scale mining ventures and powerless to stop them even if it had wanted to, since those involved also had connections with higher levels of government. The local state had also proved ineffective in preventing outsiders' environmentally destructive collection of natural resources such as wild onions, as well as strange stones.

While China's minorities have in many cases been subject to the coercive power of the state in the name of the environment, they have also been negatively affected by the state's failure to enforce environmental laws. In an attempt to counter the ecologically and socially destructive processes bound up with frontier-making (Tsing 2003; Cons and Eilenberg 2019), Mongols in Alasha did not seek to avoid the state but in this case wanted its regulatory presence. In other words, they invoked the territorializing capacity of the state, its ability to create and police spatialized systems of rights over resources (Vandergeest and Peluso 1995; Rasmussen and Lund 2018). One Mongol official, for example, told me that it was not mining itself that was the problem; instead it was the way mining trucks took illegal shortcuts across herders' pastures. Were they to stick to the roads built by the state, mining would not be so damaging. Interviews conducted by Chinese scholars sympathetic to pastoralism suggest that it was not mining per se to which herders in Alasha objected, but rather the disorderly (C. *wuxu*) proliferation of small-scale mines (Han Niantong 2011c, 77).

While existing literature on pastoral regions of China has conceptualized territorialization in terms of the restrictions placed on pastoralists by the state in the name of environmental protection (Yeh 2009), herders in Inner Mongolia have also protested against industrial pollution, for example, complaining that local officials had violated national laws and seeking compensation for pastureland fencing illegally destroyed by a factory (Otede 2019). Minority populations can thus actively desire territorialization in their opposition to frontier dispossession.

By referring to the camel as a *national* protected animal, these Mongols engaged in a politics of scale that is familiar in the Chinese context. This approach seeks to remedy the incompetence or corruption of the local state by appealing to the central authorities and has long been institutionalized in the form of petitions (O'Brien 1996; Lianjiang Li 2013). Opposition to extractivism in Alasha thus took the form not of politically impossible resource nationalism but instead of a commitment to national laws, as they have come to be understood on the ground. Mongols thus positioned themselves as loyal to the central state but aggrieved by the failure of the local state to prevent Alasha's transformation into a lawless extractive frontier.[9]

The Demands of Digital Care

The rapid uptake of WeChat in Alasha in the early 2010s allowed conservation subjectivities to be performed through the circulation of affectively charged images. Some posts, like the one protesting roasted whole camel, were directed at Han Chinese tourists. An image of camels lying dead by the side of roads was accompanied by Chinese text addressed to "[our] tourist friends" (C. *lüke pengyoumen*) that read, "Don't make an innocent life pay for your holiday," a reference to the frequent instances of roadkill. This was a period in which social media in China was enabling ethnic minorities to engage in new forms of representational politics, calling out the disrespectful actions of Han Chinese tourists at sacred sites, for example (Grant 2017).

But in Alasha the performance of conservation subjectivities was also directed at locals. One post showed a camel being winched onto a truck, apparently on its way to slaughter; the accompanying Chinese text read, "Protecting camels is the duty [C. *yiwu*] of Alasha people!" Another featured Mongolian text superimposed on a herd of camels with the exhortation, "Alasha Mongols, love your camels!" WeChat allowed local road users, who glimpsed imperiled camels from the windows of their car, to participate fleetingly in the work of husbandry. "Can the owner of this camel please come and rescue this poor [C. *kelian*] creature!" read one typical message, posted in the summer after flash floods had destabilized fence posts along a stretch of highway in central Left Banner. Digital care could be performed by both urban and rural Mongols; thus urban Mongols who did not possess any animals could come to feel responsible for the protection of Alasha's camels.

WeChat also enabled the promotion of ethical consumption. In 2014, one post urged people to purchase goods made of camel hair to increase the price of this undervalued product so that herders would not be compelled to sell their camels to survive (C. *weixi shenghuo*). The message claimed that herders were often tricked into selling their camels to outsiders (C. *waidi de*) who claimed to want to raise them themselves but then went on to wantonly slaughter (C. *siyi tusha*) the animals. With the increase in the price of camel meat, there was greater incentive to sell camels for slaughter: in 2014 a single camel could fetch over ¥10,000.

Indeed, some herders were beginning to harness the entrepreneurial affordances of WeChat to market camels and camel meat themselves, revealing themselves to be anything but the dupes of Han and Hui traders. Sümbür, the young neighbor of Batbagana who had bought a car with money from the sale of collective land, wanted to know whether, if he made dumplings from camel meat, it would be possible to export them to the UK. Just before I left he changed his WeChat name to Bayantal Camel Meat, the brand name he planned to use for his business.

Nars was a herder from Khöövör in his late thirties. In response to the RLRG policy, he had sold off his entire herd of sheep and goats a couple of years previously and begun to live some of the time in a small town between Bayanhot and Khöövör. He was an active participant in camel culture events, still owning a couple of camels that he raced enthusiastically and which were now part of the herd of one of his former neighbors in Bayantal. His wife had died in an accident, and to support his two young children, he bought camels from across the region and sold them to tourist sites or had them slaughtered and sold the meat.

In September 2014 Nars posted photos of some camels on his WeChat account with a note saying that he was selling camel meat. Several of the responses to his post contained angry-faced emojis, to which Nars replied, "They're camels, not people!" (C. *tamen shi luotuo bu shi ren*). Later, however, he deleted the entire post. Nars told me that many people thought camels were a protected animal and so could not be sold or slaughtered, but in fact owners could sell as many as they liked. But in selling camels via WeChat, Nars confronted the performances of digital care and conservation subjectivity that this platform also enabled. Rather than simply creating an ethnic cyber-community in opposition to Han Chinese outsiders (Grant 2017), WeChat revealed ethical tensions among Alasha's Mongols, with some herders caught between the commercial opportunities provided by this platform and the expectation that they should behave as proper conservation subjects.

IN THE EARLY TWENTY-FIRST CENTURY, peripheral regions of China witnessed a variety of commodity booms, with significant consequences for the livelihoods of rural people. Inner Mongolia has been transformed by intensive natural resource extraction and attendant processes of environmental degradation and dispossession. In parts of the region, large-scale extraction has severely limited the land available to pastoralists, sometimes leading to open protest. In turn-of-the-millennium Alasha, many Mongols felt as if their region's natural resources were being plundered by outsiders for the delectation of distant consumers in China's cities, a situation exacerbated by the state's environmental policies, which had encouraged herders to move off the grasslands, leaving these vast areas apparently open to small-scale extraction of natural resources, including plants and minerals.

The early Xi Jinping era brought at least a temporary halt to some of this extraction. In 2014, after a mine collapse killed three Mongols who were running a restaurant nearby, all small-scale mining in the Kharuuna Mountains ceased on the orders of the Inner Mongolian government. As officials sought postextractive possibilities for Alasha, those Mongol elites involved in camel conservation hoped that new markets for camel products might secure the future of the animal. Consumption would enable conservation. However, the case of roasted whole camel showed how, for some local Mongols, attempts to realize a postextractive future for Alasha as a destination for Han Chinese tourists could be haunted by memories of settler violence, as well as more recent resource extraction.

Opposition to the slaughter of camels was framed not only in relation to customs and beliefs but also with reference to the legal protection this animal was thought to enjoy. The discourse of genetic resource conservation thus took on new meanings in the context of Alasha's peripherality in the Chinese political economy, as analogies were created with other natural resources endangered by the demands of distant Chinese consumers. With the rapid rise of WeChat in the early 2010s, the forms of ethnicized conservation subjectivity that emerged as this discourse of genetic resources was localized in Alasha could now be performed via social media. But while WeChat bridged the urban-rural divide and enabled urban Mongols to perform acts of digital care for Alasha's camels, it was simultaneously a space of ethical tension, as conservation subjectivities rubbed up against the digital entrepreneurialism of some herders, for whom the sale of camels and camel meat could provide vital cash resources as the small ruminant economy was increasingly restricted.

6
Dairy
Frontiers

ON THE PLAIN in front of Bull Camel Monastery, gigantic steel arms turn in slow circles over the arid ground. Center pivot irrigation was patented in 1952 by a Nebraska farmer, transforming farming on the drought-prone plains of the western United States, even as it rapidly depleted the Ogallala Aquifer (Bessire 2021). Here, on the fringes of the Ulaan Bukh Desert, it enables alfalfa to be grown on the former pastures of herders who were forced to sell their animals and become ecological migrants after the local government designated the area a grazing ban zone (C. *jinmu qu*) in the early 2000s. This land has now been contracted to a large organic dairy company, Shengmu High Tech. Incorporated in the Cayman Islands in 2013, this company was listed on the Hong Kong Stock Exchange the following year. Shengmu's alfalfa fields now provide organic fodder for over thirty thousand high-yield Holstein cattle. This is a confined animal feeding operation (CAFO), with the animals housed and fed in twenty-three industrial units and milked using robotic milking machines. Shengmu's organic dairy operations straddle the border between Alasha Left Banner and Dengkou County, and a network of newly built roads links the farms, worker dormitories, and the milk processing plant. On a tour of Farm No. 13 I was introduced to several Chinese workers who spoke with the distinctive accent characteristic of China's northeast, as well as young managers who had arrived fresh from universities in southern China. Glossing over the enforced absence of minority herders, Shengmu markets its milk as pollution-free by describing the surrounding desert as "without human trace" (C. *ren ji han zhi*).

   In China, dairy is now big business. By 2018, China's citizens were consuming on average thirty-six kilograms of dairy products every year, up from eighteen kilograms in 2007 (Inouye 2019). This growth has been fueled by a discourse promoted by the state that associates milk with modernity and national rejuvenation: in 2006 Chinese premier Wen Jiabao declared, "I have a dream, a dream to provide every Chinese, especially children, one jin [500 grams] of nourishing milk a day" (China Daily 2006). However, in 2008 it emerged that milk produced by a large dairy producer, Sanlu, had been adulterated with melamine to inflate the apparent protein content, leading to the deaths of several infants and causing kidney damage in thousands more. Milk consumption in China subsequently became a site of intense anxiety over food safety (Tracy 2016).

In the wake of the Sanlu affair, the state has promoted "vertical integration" or "industrialization" of dairy production (C. *chanyehua*; DuBois and Gao 2017; Mak 2021a). In some cases, large dairy companies now produce their own milk on megafarms like Shengmu; others, however, operate according to the "dragon head" model, of which Sanlu was an example, which involves contracting out production to households. Dragon head companies (C. *longtou qiye*) connect peasant households with the market; they are thus like the performers at the head of the ceremonial dragon dance who lead coordinated lines of dancers (Schneider 2017). The relationship of dragon head company and peasant household (C. *longtou qiye* + *nonghu*) is often mediated by production contracts and the supply of inputs by the company (Qiangqiang Luo, Joel Andreas, and Yao Li 2017). Dragon heads are supposed to radiate (C. *fushe*) technology, information, and market opportunities out to rural farmers (Schneider 2017, 9). In return, the official dragon head designation affords the company access to government subsidies (Schneider 2017, 8).

Dragon head dairying has begun to transform parts of rural Alasha through a collaboration between the local state, a businessman from southern China, and Inner Mongolian scientists. This has involved the commodification of camel milk collected from local herders' cooperatives by a dragon head company. The households in these cooperatives have been encouraged to pool their land to provide adequate rangeland for the camels, which in 2019 were not being raised in stalls. While Mongol pastoralists have long consumed camel milk domestically, it has only recently become a commodity sold across China. Its commodification has relied heavily on scientific research into its purported health benefits, funded in part by the dragon head company and produced and circulated by Mongol scientists at an Inner Mongolian university. These scientists have also established the Inner Mongolia Camel Research Institute in remote Right Banner and are actively involved in attempts to intensify certain aspects of production, through selective breeding programs, for example.

China's agricultural modernization has come about through a close relationship between state and capital (Schneider 2017; Qiangqiang Luo et al. 2017). In Alasha, for example, the local state's collaboration with capital in camel dairying has come to be framed as part of a national poverty alleviation (C. *fu pin*) campaign launched by Xi Jinping in 2015. But in Alasha, the role of scientists was also crucial: they worked to transform the camel into a dairy resource by performing its potential through publications, media appearances, and international conferences. This work of resource-making helped convince the local state to support this unconventional form of dairying. Camel dairying in Alasha thus exemplifies the "hugely complex but little-understood nexus of state-market-science/technology" in contemporary China (Greenhalgh 2020, 8).

Political economy approaches to agrarian change often draw on the idea of expanding capitalist, commodity, or resource frontiers, attending to processes of commoditization and transformations in rural land and labor that occur following the making of new resources (Peluso and Lund 2011; Schneider and Coghe 2021). However, as Jason Cons and Michael Eilenberg (2019, 4–5) have recently noted, "Political economies of frontiers are always entangled with a broader array of factors that structure the transformation of marginal space into frontier zone." Thinking of *dairy frontiers* in the plural illuminates how novel forms of commodity production are in complex relation with political and ethnic frontiers and the discourses of civilization, cultural difference, and backwardness that construct them (Harrell 1995; Regassa et al. 2019). My use of *dairy frontiers* encompasses the notion of a scientific frontier (Saraf 2020; Franklin 2007), with its particular temporality and affective charge, while also foregrounding the *spatial* qualities of scientific knowledge production (Finnegan 2008; Choy 2011). By thinking of dairy frontiers in the plural and inquiring into their relations with each other, we can begin to account for the unexpected ways the remoteness of a pastoral border region is being transformed by new forms of resource-making and commodity production.

Camel Milk and the Multispecies Household

Throughout the Mongolian world, "white foods" (M. *tsagaan idee*), as dairy products are known, play a central role in social life, particularly during summer (Thrift 2014). They are an important vector of hospitality (Ruhlmann

2019), and guests visiting rural households are normally offered a bowl of milk tea. They also have numerous ritual uses. Every morning in Bayantal, Sarna skimmed off the top (M. *deej*) of the milk tea she had boiled and, standing in front of the house, tossed it into the air as a libation. In Alasha, Mongol herders traditionally refused to sell dairy products, to prevent the dispersal of household fortune (see also Empson 2012). Even today, for logistical reasons, production for the market has tended to be limited to areas close to Bayanhot. In the early 2000s resettled herders were provided with dairy cows that they then had to raise in stalls with fodder. This milk was sold locally in Bayanhot. Soon, however, the market became saturated, and the price of milk collapsed (Dalintai and Zheng 2010, 455–79).

Batbagana remembered the collective period as a time when they had plenty of dairy products because the grass was abundant and they were allowed to milk the animals outside of the ration ticket system (C. *fanpiao*). People used to be healthier, Batbagana insisted, because they lived in the countryside and subsisted mainly on milk rather than the "poisonous" (M. *khortoi*) foods now prevalent in the city. In recent decades, however, household dairy production has been severely affected by both drought and rural depopulation. Sarna sometimes milked a goat, adding the milk to our tea in the morning. More often, however, the milk used in the household for tea came from packets of UHT cow's milk produced by one of Inner Mongolia's large dairy companies. Visitors to herder households often bring boxes of this milk as gifts. Sarna was reluctant to milk their goats more often because she worried that the kids would not get enough to eat, given the effects of drought on their pastures. Milking also tends to be regarded as a female task, and now that many younger women live in Bayanhot while their children go to school, there are fewer hands left to milk. Sarna's perseverance in this task was regarded locally as evidence of her hardworking character.

Batbagana's camels were no longer milked, which Sarna explained was because the grass was not good and she did not want to deprive the calves of milk and because she suffered from chronic pain in her knees, a legacy of decades of exertion.[1] Occasionally a plastic jerry can of camel milk would turn up at the household, brought from across the Mongolian border by a relative who worked at a customs post in northern Alasha. Camel milk was held to be particularly nutritious (M. *shimtei*) and was said to have been used in the past to feed infants whose mothers had died in childbirth.

Milking was seen to rely on affective bonds between human and camel, and it was said that camels would refuse to be milked by people they did not know. When I discussed the possible intensification of camel milk production with herders in Bayantal, they expressed skepticism that camels would allow themselves to be milked by a machine. The fact that camels produced much less milk than cows was also seen as rendering them unsuitable for large-scale production. In 2014, a single cooperative in Alasha Right Banner produced camel milk for sale to the Mongolian hospital in Bayanhot, where it was used in treating diabetes. All this was soon to change, however, as a collaboration between the Alasha Right Banner government, southern Chinese capital, and Inner Mongolian scientists planned to turn camel milk into a commodity sought after by health-conscious Chinese consumers.

Making a Dairy Resource

In August 2018, the main Chinese-language news program on Inner Mongolia Television featured a segment titled "Sprouting a New Industry from the Desert: Relying on Science and Technology to Dance with Camels." A representative from Desert God Biotechnology dressed in a lab coat and hair net informed viewers that the company would transform camel milk into "products with a high science and technology content [C. *gao keji hanliang*] and with high added value," which would benefit both the company and herders. As technicians pipetted in the background, the party secretary of Alasha Right Banner appeared, explaining that "with science and technology showing the way, through genetic research, the value of the Alasha Bactrian camel to biotechnology and healthcare will be excavated." Such performances of science and technology have been central to the transformation of camels into a dairy resource and the commodification of camel milk.

In 2014, Xinjiang Wangyuan, the parent company of Desert God, and the government of Alasha Right Banner signed an agreement to establish a camel industrial park (C. *luotuo chanyeyuan*) in the banner. Desert God would purchase camel milk from local herders at a price subsidized by the local government. In 2017 Desert God paid ¥40, and the local government ¥10 on top of this, per liter of milk supplied. The company collected fresh milk from herder cooperatives using its refrigerated trucks, and the local government was building a network of milk collection points around the banner. The camels, however, were owned by the herders.

In 2017, even the highest-yielding camel still produced only around 1.5 liters of milk a day: selective breeding to increase milk yield was still in its infancy.[2] Indeed, camels sometimes appeared to be unwilling to collaborate in commodification. At one cooperative I visited, Mongolian folk music was played from speakers in the milking parlor to try to induce the cow camel, accompanied by her calf, to let down her milk. She failed to do so on this occasion, which her owner ascribed to the presence of strangers. Given the low level of intensification, Desert God's business model relied on state support and on the high prices it was able to charge for camel milk: processed camel milk sold for ¥45 for a 180-milliliter can and could be purchased through various online retailers in China.

The support of the local state was secured thanks to the resource-making work of ethnic Mongol scientists, who were central to the model of camel milk production in Alasha Right Banner. This model was said to comprise industry (C. *chanye*) + herder households (C. *muhu*) + cooperatives (C. *hezuoshe*) + science (C. *kexue*). In 2005, the Dairy Biotechnology and Engineering Laboratory, designated a key laboratory (C. *zhongdian shiyanshi*) by China's Ministry of Education, was founded at Inner Mongolia Agricultural University. In 2014, scientists from this laboratory published several books proclaiming the potential value of the camel, including *Camel Products and Biotechnology* (C. Luotuo chanpin yu shengwu jishu; Jirimutu and Chen 2014) and *The Mysterious Camel and Diabetes* (C. Shenmi de luotuo yu tangniaobing; Jirimutu et al. 2014), funded by Xinjiang Wangyuan, whose CEO was listed as a coauthor. Replete with cartoon graphics, the latter book in particular was apparently aimed at a general audience. Wangyuan would later go on to fund a project to map the camel genome, headed by a scientist at the same university. This is typical of trends in reform-era China, where laboratories have become integrated with commercial activities and scientists are encouraged to become entrepreneurs (Nancy Chen 2010).

These books suggest that camel milk can be used to treat a range of health problems, including type 2 diabetes. Such diseases of prosperity have proliferated in contemporary China, where 11 percent of the population now suffers from type 2 diabetes (Economist 2019). Some scientists attribute such therapeutic effects of camel milk to the high concentration of insulin and insulin-like proteins in camel milk (Ayoub et al. 2018). In recent years the lead scientist from this laboratory, an ethnic Mongol who speaks Mongolian as his first language, has appeared on numerous national television shows, often dressed in a white lab coat, to extoll the health benefits of camel milk. China has a long history of medicinal foods, which are often used to respond to novel health crises (Nancy Chen 2020). However, while camel milk is mentioned in the famous Ming dynasty *Compendium of Materia Medica* (C. Bencao gangmu), it has not, until recently, been commonly used as medicinal food in China. Instead, its commodification shows how the dairy industry collaborates with experts, particularly academics and medical professionals, to produce nutritional knowledge (Mak 2021b). As state support for health care has declined in China and in the context of low patient trust in doctors (Yunxiang Yan 2017), practices of self-medication have proliferated, providing a receptive audience for such expertise.

As with some other exotic products from China's western regions, such as the medicinal caterpillar fungus (Yeh and Lama 2013), the commodification of camel milk has involved adopting scientistic discourse and imagery, which makes little reference to any *terroir*-like qualities of place (cf. Tracy 2013). A store selling camel milk in a mall in the southern Chinese city of Wuhan, for example, gave particular prominence to the lead scientist at Inner Mongolia Agricultural University, including a list of his scientific publications on its walls.[3] This deployment of science serves to authorize the status of camel milk as a medicinal food in the eyes of both consumers and regulators, in a context in which these consumers have no tradition of consuming this product. However, it is not simply the case that products from the periphery are being redescribed in technoscientific language; instead, dairying is bound up with the reconfiguration of Alasha itself—and its camels—into a frontier of scientific knowledge production.

A Scientific Frontier

The Inner Mongolia Camel Research Institute sits on the main road of Badain Jarain, the dusty small town that is the administrative center of Alasha Right Banner, in comparison to which Bayanhot seems a pulsing metropolis. The institute occupies a large three-story building, formerly the local court, which was given to the institute by the banner government when it was established in 2014. Unlike some of the buildings in Badan Jarain, its beige stone facade features no markers of Mongolian identity; instead, it is built according to a standardized design found all over China (Kipnis 2012). If it was unusual to find an IMAR-level institution headquartered in a remote banner rather than in Hohhot, it later emerged that even more impressive scale jumping was planned for the institute, as it applied to become the *National* Camel Research Institute (Wang Xiaochun 2021).

This institute has become central to the resource-making work of Inner Mongolian scientists. When I visited in the summer of 2015, I was shown around by a scientist in a white lab coat, Li Rui, an ethnic Mongol from eastern Inner Mongolia. He told me that the institute had been established by scientists from Inner Mongolia Agricultural University in Hohhot, and that scientists from Beijing and the UK were also involved. Several graduate students were now based at the institute. On the wall in the entrance hall was a map of the world that traced the international connections of the Inner Mongolian camel scientists, with photos of them meeting colleagues in Dubai, Kazakhstan, and Australia. I asked Li Rui why Alasha Right Banner was chosen as the site of this research institute. He explained that the Right Banner government was very supportive of them because there were lots of camel herders in the banner. "This is a remote place, and in terms of development it is rather backward [C. *fazhan bijiao luohou*], so people traditionally used camels for transport and the necessities of life," he added.

Guests of the research institute are shown around a large exhibition room, which features various camel products in spot-lit display cases, including tins of camel milk powder as well as camel milk cosmetics. Some of these, Li Rui explained, were still at the prototype stage. On the way out he showed me a large display board in front of the building. This featured a computer-generated image of a planned camel industry and science park (C. *luotuo chanye kexue yuan*), featuring a series of identical low white buildings arranged in neat rows in front of a glass-fronted main building. This was described as a collaboration between the institute, Desert God, and the local government. The imagined site was interspersed with elegant greenery and water features, and the image itself had been superimposed on top of a photo of a dense rainforest, such that the camel industry and science park seemed to be floating amid tree canopy in the tropics, having been successfully unmoored from Alasha's harsh desert surroundings.

A description broke down the project into various stages over the coming years: phase 2, beginning in 2016, would involve production of a health food that could help treat diabetes; phase 3 involved developing edible camel milk cosmetics; phase 4 would consist of research into the development of biopharmaceuticals (C. *shengwuzhi yaopin*). The display hall and board revealed that the research institute was not simply engaged in producing scientific research; instead it exemplified the work of resource-making by performing the potential value of the camel to an audience that could occasionally include visiting anthropologists and camel scientists but more regularly consisted of state officials. Indeed, in 2019 the then governor of the Inner Mongolia Autonomous Region and granddaughter of Ulanhu, Bu Xiaolin, visited the institute and expressed her support for its vision of camel-based development (Neimenggu Ribao 2019).

Dominant representations in China portray the country's eastern coastal regions as the home of scientific modernity and progress, while the country's western periphery is regarded as backward and lacking these qualities (Yeh

2013b, 116). Here, Chinese rule is legitimated by the state's promise to bestow the blessings of science and technology. According to this imagined geography of expertise, scientific knowledge is *conveyed* to these remote regions from elsewhere. However, China's biotech fever has begun to reconfigure these established ethnicized geographies.

In recent decades, the Chinese state has put particular emphasis on biotechnology (Nancy Chen 2010), and it features prominently in five-year plans, including the 2016 goal for biotech to make up 4 percent of China's GDP by 2020. The most recent five-year plan (2021–25) prioritizes modernization of the rural economy by deploying biotech in agriculture. The biotech revolution appears to offer Asian states a chance to catch up with and even overtake the West (Ong 2010). Scholars have situated China's scientific ambitions in relation to a national concern with challenging the global hierarchy of science (Greenhalgh 2020, 12), but how such concern can challenge domestic ethnic and spatial hierarchies remains more obscure. Inner Mongolian universities, for example, with their strength in traditionally unglamorous livestock sciences, have recently become sites of important breakthroughs in the life sciences.

The biography of the ethnic Mongol biologist Shorgan is instructive here. Born in eastern Inner Mongolia in 1940, he studied and taught at Inner Mongolia University in Hohhot before going to Japan in 1982 to study for his PhD. In an interview with Chinese television late in life, echoing the impressions of several generations of Chinese intellectuals and scientists, he remembered being astonished at the difference between Japan and China in the early 1980s and considering it his responsibility to transform his country's "backward condition" and help it to "catch up" (C. *ganshang*) with this developed country (Kexue Piyao 2021). In Japan he successfully performed the world's first in vitro fertilization of a goat, and he is referred to in China as the "father of the test tube goat." Upon returning to Inner Mongolia, he established the Experimental Animal Research Center at Inner Mongolia University and later became president of the university. In the late 1990s, he started a biotech company that engaged in industrial production of in vitro cattle. He would later go on to become vice president of the prestigious Chinese Academy of Engineering (C. Zhongguo Gongcheng Yuan).

Like Shorgan, the senior scientists who established the Inner Mongolia Camel Research Institute are ethnic Mongols who studied in Japan before returning to take up positions in universities in Hohhot. According to one of them, camel science had lagged behind because these animals were found only in remote parts of China, which meant it was harder to attract the interest of scientists. The dispersed nature of camel herds also made them harder to study. But despite the late start, this scientist averred, camel science had developed quickly and was now having a big impact, though there was still much to do. Scientifically, the frontier camel was an exciting "zone of not yet" (Tsing 2003).

What was particularly striking about the institute and the billboard's "traces of the future" (Braester 2016) in the form of the anticipated biotechnology park was the way they overturned some of the fundamental spatiotemporal hierarchies that undergird modern China (Clarke-Sather 2020). Alasha Right Banner, remote even by the standards of Alasha, was to become a hub of biotech research and commodity production. While global peripheries have long been the site of bioprospecting, this has normally been understood merely as an extractive process bound up with colonial exploration, with specimens "transported 'home' in the service of empire" (Parry 2004, 12). Locating the institute in remote Right Banner, however, unsettles the relationship between periphery and metropole, as this pastoral banner performs an act of developmental leapfrogging thanks to the biotech revolution.

Camel Country was being reconfigured as a space of anticipation. At the Camel Research Institute, fears for the extinction of the Alasha Bactrian camel, so prevalent in the early years of the twenty-first century, had given way to imaginings of the bright future that camel science would apparently make possible. The very building that housed the research institute was material evidence of the state support that this performance of potential could yield. The local state could be convinced to help save camel husbandry from the ruins of the pastoral economy because of the promise that was now thought to be contained in the relatively uncharted bodies of these animals.

Indigenous Innovation

The anticipation that surrounded camel dairying was also evident in local technological innovation. In Bayanhot I came to know Tömör, a wealthy ex-herder in his fifties who was also a delegate to the local CPPCC. He had founded a company, Polaris Agro-Pastoral Machinery, in 2014. Two years earlier, he had sold off most of his livestock, but he told me that he did not want to just sit around at home living off the PES. "Humans can't just sit around doing nothing," he said. "If you just sit there playing mahjong and gambling you're done for!" He had decided to establish this company and had also registered the brand Agwangdander, the name of a famous Qing-era scholar from Alasha who happened to be one of his ancestors. His WeChat profile picture showed him in full Mongolian dress seated behind an imposing desk, engaged in an important business call. He combined entrepreneurialism with a revalorization of pastoralism in a way that has been noted in other minority areas of China (Yeh 2022).

Tömör had invented a camel milking machine featured on national television. The show *I Love Inventing* (C. Wo ai faming), broadcast on CCTV 10, China's national science education channel, consists of short documentaries featuring the inventions of ordinary people; its stated mission is to "encourage everyone to use their intelligence to establish a business."[4] This particular segment began with a discussion of camel milk's health properties, especially its use in treating diabetes. This was accompanied by shots of scientists in white coats performing tests in a laboratory, reproducing the technoscientific associations of the camel milk health discourse. The segment emphasized the difficulty of milking camels, with herders expressing some skepticism about the milking machine, since, they explained, camels have to be familiar with those who are milking. The voiceover noted that the degree of domestication (C. *xunhua chengdu*) is less in camels than in other livestock.

Eventually, after some alterations to make the process more comfortable for the camel, the machine proved successful. Tömör told me that he had sold dozens of these machines to herders across Alasha. Toward the end of the show one of the camel scientists from Inner Mongolia Agricultural University appears on screen and declares that the camel milking machine will provide benefits in terms of reducing human labor and because of the cleanliness and hygiene (C. *ganjing weisheng*) it affords. The segment concludes by looking forward to a near future when camel dairying will be industrialized (C. *gongyehua*) and milking parlors will contain up to eight machines.

As Tömör and I chatted over dinner, he revealed that the *I Love Inventing* segment was produced with extensive funding from the Alasha League CCP Propaganda Bureau (C. Xuanchuan Bu). Furthermore, herders' purchase of milking machines has been heavily subsidized by both the local state and the Inner Mongolia Autonomous Region.[5] The adoption of this technology by herders in Alasha thus cannot be understood merely in terms of the productivity gains enjoyed by increasingly market-oriented herders. Indeed, such gains are limited, since the machine can milk only one camel at a time. Instead, herders' use of these machines represents a performance of technological innovation and rural modernity underwritten by the local state, designed to attract capital and impress senior officials. The milking machines I saw in herders' houses had been plastered with labels on which "milking machine" was written in large Mongolian and Chinese scripts, while the company name appeared in tiny characters at the bottom of the label, in an inversion of the conventional semiotics of branding. Such labeling was obviously redundant for the herders in question, but it rendered the device easily legible to visiting officials or those viewing subsequent reports on the visit who might not recognize this unfamiliar piece of technology.

Tömör's invention was even deployed as a tool of international diplomacy. When a delegation from Ömnö Govi, the Mongolian province bordering Left Banner to the north, visited to discuss the opening of a new border crossing as part of the Belt and Road Initiative, they were taken to view one of Tömör's milking machines. This visit was aimed at convincing the Mongolians of the benefits of opening this border crossing, which, it was suggested, would provide access to this kind of technology. Milking machine diplomacy exemplifies the way camel dairying, far from simply involving the production of commodities for a market, could also become a *spectacle* (Stone 2018), deployed to political ends by a variety of actors at different scales, all of whom were concerned to demonstrate the modernity and potential of Alasha and its camels.

I Love Inventing describes itself as a program dedicated to "indigenous research and development" (C. *zizhu yanfa*). The Chinese state's recent emphasis on indigenous innovation builds on the emphasis on self-reliance in science that characterized the Maoist period, when the agricultural innovations of ordinary peasants were often publicly celebrated (Schmalzer 2016), but it is now accompanied by emphasis on mass entrepreneurship (C. *dazhong chuangye*) in response to a slowing Chinese economy (Lindtner 2020).

In the case of Shengmu, expansion of the dairy frontier into the Ulaan Bukh Desert relied on technology transfer from the United States and Europe, in the form of center-pivot irrigation systems, robotic milking machines, and Holstein dairy cows. But Alasha's camels have enabled an alternative trajectory of technology to emerge, as a remote borderland becomes a site of technological innovation, which can then be displayed across national borders in a performance of Chinese modernity. If China's emergence as a site of tech entrepreneurialism manifests the "displacement of technological promise" away from centers such as Silicon Valley (Lindtner 2020), this displacement also works at other scales, shifting to rural areas of China, which are increasingly the site of experiments in agrotechnology innovation

(Xiaowei Wang 2020), but also to ethnic borderlands, thereby reconfiguring the characteristic peripherality and "backwardness" of these regions as opportunity and anticipation.

Transnational Science along the New Silk Road

In September 2017 scientists from Inner Mongolia Agricultural University hosted an international conference, "The Belt and Road Initiative: Camel Science, Industry, and Culture," in tiny Badain Jarain with support from the Right Banner government. Attended by local officials and some herders, as well as international scientists, and widely reported in the local media, this conference was saturated with an affect of anticipation and became an important site for performing the camel's potential as a resource. In referencing the Belt and Road Initiative, the organizers were able to access funding from the central government. Over fifty international scientists from more than twenty countries attended the conference. Indeed, it was said to be the largest number of foreigners ever seen on the streets of Badain Jarain. Many of the delegates did not even visit China's capital, instead flying from Dubai to Yinchuan, the capital of the Ningxia Hui Autonomous Region, on a route opened in 2016 by the airline Emirates, before traveling by car to Badain Jarain.

By connecting a global city to China's remote peripheries and bypassing Beijing, the itinerary of these international scientists disrupted the strict vertical encompassment (Gupta and Ferguson 2002) that characterizes the political geography of China, according to which the banner/county is nested within the league/municipality, which is in turn encompassed by the autonomous region/province, and so on. In their discussion of emergent translocal social formations in China, geographer Tim Oakes and anthropologist Louisa Schein (2006, 27) describe the various "switching points" in contemporary China, which "serve as the connection between the domestic and the transnational." In Oakes and Schein's account, these switching points are concentrated in southern China, long known for its economic vibrancy and connections with overseas Chinese communities. In the era of the "New Silk Road," however, the camel has allowed once archetypally remote, western, frontier Alasha to become a switching point for transnational scientific knowledge exchange. If Alasha was once classified as a "remote, purely pastoral banner," this international conference dedicated to the camel worked to undo the association of pastoralism with remoteness and backwardness.

The Inner Mongolia Camel Research Institute in Badain Jarain has solidified this status, in 2018 hosting a ceremony to mark an agreement between the institute and King Faisal University in Saudi Arabia. In their reports, the Inner Mongolian scientists describe this kind of collaboration as "exchanging cutting-edge achievements in camel science with countries along the Belt and Road" (C. *yidai yilu yanxi guojia*). The institute, notwithstanding its distance from centers of political power, can thus be scaled up to become part of the state's grand vision of a global China.

If science in China has often been understood as lagging behind the West and Japan (Greenhalgh 2020), camel science maps out an alternative geography of expertise. Global livestock geographies are intimately connected to colonial histories, from the Columbian Exchange (Crosby 1972) through which European livestock entered the Americas to the "waves of white sheep and settlers" that crashed upon the shores of Australia (Franklin 2007, 126). Dolly the cloned sheep, for example, was the "offspring of more than two centuries of continuous trade between Britain and Australia based on sheep experimentation, sheep breeding, sheep products, and exchanges of actual sheep" (Franklin 2007, 154).

Camels, however, existed largely outside these colonial circuits of scientific and genetic exchange. Until very recently, they had not been subjected to the kinds of technoscientific interventions that have transformed other species of domestic animals. At the 2017 conference in Badain Jarain, however, scientists and veterinarians based in Dubai shared their research into embryo transfer techniques for camels, which would allow breeders to work around the camel's long gestation period, which poses challenges for the selective breeding necessary to produce high-yield dairy animals.

The conference thus revealed Dubai to be at the cutting edge of camel dairy science. This complicates standard accounts of the global hierarchies of science (Greenhalgh 2020) and of the transnational nature of science in contemporary China, which emphasize ties with the United States (Zuoyue Wang 2014). Instead, it shows the importance of attending to the multiplicity of geographies that are opened up by different kinds of scientific knowledge exchange, some of which, for historical and ecological reasons, might provincialize the West and link frontier spaces such as Alasha Right Banner to alternative imagined geographies of expertise and scientific knowledge production along the Belt and Road.

In Situ Poverty Alleviation

The theme of the conference harmonized camel dairying with the central state's Belt and Road Initiative. But camel dairying could also be reimagined in line with the state's increasing domestic emphasis on poverty alleviation. In 2015, Xi Jinping announced an ambitious goal of eliminating poverty by 2020. While poverty alleviation is nothing new, this new goal operated at a novel scale: rather than merely identifying impoverished counties, Targeted Poverty Alleviation (TPA; C. Jingzhun Fupin) would involve local cadres registering poor households to create a poverty database (C. *jiandang lika*) and adapting interventions to those individual households. Scholars of development in China have argued that TPA relies heavily on a strategy of resettling poorer households, or "resettlement *as* development" (Rogers 2019). In this view, TPA should be understood within the broader context of the conflation of modernity with urbanization in China (Rogers et al. 2020, 547). In pastoral regions of China, some scholars have suggested that TPA is designed to bring an end to the pastoral way of life (Ptackova 2019).

In Alasha Right Banner, however, TPA has been implemented in a way that does not involve resettlement but instead mobilizes the dragon head + scientific research + coooperative camel milk production-circulation network, in a kind of in situ poverty alleviation. Rather than abolishing pastoralism, the local government talks of "combining traditional husbandry methods with modern scientific assistance and management" (Alashan Youqi Rong Meiti Zhongxin 2020). One of the institute's senior scientists told me they were not planning to scale up to large dairy farms, but instead would focus on cooperatives and households, partly because large-scale operations were bad for the environment, would require significant amounts of water, and would increase the risk of animal disease, but also because one of the primary aims, he said, of developing the camel industry in the banner was to increase herders' income. Indeed, on the walls of the Desert God dairy hung a red banner with white characters, the kind used to convey government messages, that read, "Develop the camel industry! Enrich the herders of the borderlands!" Rather than agribusiness leasing land directly, as had happened in the case of Shengmu in Left Banner, here herders would be encouraged to pool their land in cooperatives.

The local scale features prominently in Right Banner's strategy of TPA through camel dairying. Officials in the banner regard nurturing specialized industry (C. *peiyu tese chanye*) as central to poverty alleviation and cite Xi Jinping's assertion that the key to development lies in promoting specialization (C. *tuchu tese*). In interviews, local officials told me that Right Banner was "the camel country within Camel Country" (C. *tuoxiang zhong de tuoxiang*), pointing to the fact that the majority of Alasha camels were to be found in Right Banner. "Sheep and goats are not our speciality [C.

tese]," another official told me. "Other places can do them better." They also contrasted Right Banner with Left Banner, which had a larger population and a more diverse economy: "We have to rely on camels." A similar strategy of specializing on particular livestock species has been noted in the case of local governments in Tibetan regions of China, where some townships are encouraged to raise sheep, while others focus on yaks (Gaerrang 2019), mirroring processes of regional specialization seen across agricultural regions of China in recent years (Zinda and He 2020).

In justifying their reliance on camel dairying to alleviate poverty in the banner, officials also draw on the Mao-era idea of suiting local conditions (C. *yindi zhiyi*; Yiletu 2019), referring to the fact that the banner comprises a vast area of arid rangeland in which camels alone can flourish. Rather than merely applying models from farming areas to this pastoral region (cf. Yeh and Wharton 2016; Ptackova 2019), these officials have pursued a locally specific initiative, a form of experimentation that has deep roots in the CCP. To varying degrees in the course of the PRC's history, local cadres have been encouraged to "try out new ways of problem-solving and then feed the local experiences back into national policy formation" (Heilmann 2008, 1). Indeed, there are indications that Right Banner might achieve this kind of national prominence. Its model of poverty alleviation has been featured on national television, and in 2020 it was selected as one of the thirty-four best global poverty reduction practices in an initiative cosponsored by China's International Poverty Reduction Center and global development partners including the World Bank, the FAO, and the Asian Development Bank (Alasha Right Banner Media Center 2020). In assessing how TPA has transformed China's rural regions, it is thus important to attend to how the local scale is mobilized.

However, there is more at stake here than merely the enrichment of borderland herders. Over breakfast on the final day of the conference, one of the institute's senior scientists emphasized to me the intensity of feeling Mongol herders had for their camels. He told me that he and others involved in promoting dairying had hinted darkly to local officials that such were the depths of this emotion that if the herders were forced to give up their camels to conform with strict stocking limits, it would have severe consequences for the social stability (C. *shehui wending*) of this border region. Similar ideas can be seen in a 2013 policy proposal uploaded to the national E-Polity Square website, which contrasts agriculture to pastoralism in that the former involves engaging with an "artificial environment, livestock in pens, and emotionless [C. *wu ganqing*] crops," while pastoralism requires few material inputs but a significant input of emotion (C. *touru ganqing*). Animals are not only an economic resource but a "source of psychological [C. *jingshen*] and emotional sustenance."

Emotion and affect play an important role in state projects of governance (Jie Yang 2014). In Tibet, for example, Chinese rule is legitimated through a pervasive discourse of Tibetan happiness (Lama 2018). In militarized, ethnically diverse border regions such as Alasha, the management of affect in the interests of preventing unrest is particularly important, but the forms it takes draw on local ecological conditions, as well as deeply rooted understandings of cultural difference. The idea that the peoples of northern frontier regions are particularly attached to their animals can be seen as far back as the Tang dynasty (618–907), when "barbarians" were held to have a "profound understanding of animals, particularly the animals of their homelands" (Abramson 2003, 138). Such stereotypes were accompanied by a derogatory conception of barbarians as closer to animals and thus in need of civilizing by the Chinese state, a form of racialization that lingers in contemporary China despite the official rhetoric of the equality of nationalities (Fiskesjö 2011).

However, these associations of frontier alterity and animality can also be spun into new political arguments, such as in Right Banner, where Mongol scientists link the importance of dairying to borderland security. States often see the presence of extensive pastoralism and other mobile forms of land use in border regions as a security issue (Eilenberg 2014; Korf et al. 2015). However, in the context of the Chinese state's preoccupation with "affective governance" (Sorace 2021), the attachment to animals seen as characteristic of pastoralism is apparently being factored into the local government's concern for borderland security as well as economic development. As scholars of agrarian change in China remind us, state agents have other priorities besides merely pursuing growth and acting in the interests of capital (Zinda and He 2020, 3). In addition to poverty alleviation, the local state was also enrolling camels in a form of more-than-human affective governance, as these animals were imagined as themselves taming the potentially unruly frontier.

Give a Man a Camel

What, then, does TPA in a pastoral region look like when it does not involve resettlement? One way TPA is localized is by the Right Banner government providing two pregnant camels to targeted poor households (Ji 2020). These camels must then be contracted for three years to a cooperative supplying Desert God. The household in turn receives proportionate shares in the cooperative; after three years the household can continue to leave the four camels with the cooperative or decide to look after the animals themselves. In this way, the future reproduction of the camel functions as a kind of interest accruing to poor households.

In China's western regions, poverty alleviation has often taken the form of direct cash subsidies, grain, or housing (Ptackova 2019). In some cases, payments for ecosystem services have even been translated by local officials as "subsidies for poverty alleviation" (Bum 2018). However, TPA involves a shift from direct subsidies toward helping poor households engage with the market through their own initiative (Boullenois 2020). The provision of free training courses (C. *peixunban*) has become central to this shift. In one Tibetan area, resettled pastoralists were provided with a course training them to become cooks, though since the course was in Chinese and included no training in restaurant management, it was of little practical use (Ptackova 2019).

In Alasha Right Banner, however, training courses have been incorporated into the model of in situ poverty alleviation. Rather than retraining pastoralists to become cooks, for example, this training is designed to make pastoralists better at animal husbandry. If the discourse of camel culture imagines Alasha's herders as possessing distinctive skills in camel husbandry, poverty alleviation now targets them as deficient in the knowledge and skills necessary to participate in the production of camel milk. One official complains that herders suffer from a "traditional mentality" and are used to "taking it easy" (C. *anyi shenghuo*); even when they have camels, they are not willing to train them (C. *xunhua*) so that they can be milked (Yiletu 2019). However, given the semiwild nature of many of Alasha's camels, such training is not straightforward. This kind of discourse on the part of officials disregards the various reasons herders might be unwilling to milk camels—including lack of labor power in the household and conceptions of interspecies care that involve leaving milk for calves—and instead blames herders for their own poverty. Herders, then, must be trained to train camels, in order to lift themselves out of poverty.

Even if camel dairying in Right Banner does not involve resettlement, the importance of wage labor to TPA in other parts of China finds its echo here (Rogers et al. 2019; Byler 2021). If the vision of techno-pastoralism with semiwild camels was predicated on labor removal, by contrast, as camels become a dairy resource, herders are being reimagined as wage laborers. Officials in Right Banner have sought to raise incomes through a hybrid model of "shares + salary" (C. *chanye fenhong + jiuye gongzi*): in addition to earning money by contracting their two camels to the cooperative, it is expected that poor households will undertake wage labor for the cooperative, working on tasks such as milking and herding. In 2017, some of this work appeared to be conducted by migrants from Mongolia, but recent party publications show that cooperatives are being tasked with actively recruiting local poor households as laborers (Ji 2020). Herders will thus be transformed into industrial workers (C. *chanye gongren*), this document avers with satisfaction. The distinctive feature of in situ poverty alleviation is that creating opportunities for wage labor involves not new, urban occupations but rather restructuring the relations of rural production.

Poverty alleviation thus differs significantly from the socialist transformation of rural China that characterized the early years of the CCP. Whereas in the 1940s and '50s the CCP had approached pastoralism through the lens of class struggle, attacking "herd lords" and redistributing herds, TPA produces new hierarchies of class, with poorer households owning a very limited stake in the means of production, necessitating their simultaneous proletarianization. At the same time, poverty alleviation funds act as an indirect subsidy for agribusiness.

Officials in Right Banner have noted the problems of inequality that have begun to emerge from this model of poverty alleviation through agribusiness. Reports suggest they are concerned that TPA funds are ending up in the wrong hands (e.g., Yiletu 2019). Some cooperatives enroll poor households and claim TPA funds but then do not engage with these households. The Right Banner model also clearly benefits those who already possess large herds of camels, who thus dominate the cooperatives, and officials note that a few households are now able to earn over ¥1,000 a day. In 2017, the head of one cooperative selling camel milk to Desert God was a young Han Chinese university graduate, the son of local herders. When the conference party toured his milking parlor, local party officials referred to him as "boss" (C. *laoban*); when I mentioned this cooperative to a Mongol friend, he claimed that this was in fact not a cooperative but a private business (M. *huviin bizniz*). China has indeed seen a proliferation of fake cooperatives following passage of the law on cooperatives in 2007, since cooperative status enables access to preferential policies and subsidies (Yan and Chen 2013).

Those households that sold off their camel herds in the early 2000s in accordance with the state's environmental policies are now at a disadvantage. Concerned officials note that households without camels that want to join the cooperatives by transferring their grassland usufruct rights in return for a stake are legally unable to do so because of the grazing ban contracts they signed. Understanding processes of agrarian change in China, particularly in its western regions, involves reckoning with this kind of situated contradiction between state environmentalism and poverty alleviation.

Finally, it is worth noting the vulnerabilities of this model of poverty alleviation through specialization. The boom in camel milk in China has encouraged several brands to enter the market, and in 2020 China granted import licenses to three camel dairies in Kazakhstan, which can now store their products in a bonded warehouse in Gansu for sale on the Chinese market (Song 2020). This trade in camel milk clearly has a (geo)political function, as it can be portrayed as exemplifying the opportunities provided by the Belt and Road Initiative. Some of the tins of milk powder are themselves emblazoned in English with "One Belt One Road."[6] At the same time, the camel milk boom has been accompanied by concerns over fake products. With increasing competition, including from imports, as well as concerns of product safety, market fluctuations could cause problems for herders in Right Banner, as has been noted in the case of commodity booms and busts in other parts of rural China (Zinda and He 2019). While officials in the banner are attempting to adopt a similar dragon head model for camel meat and hair, at the moment these products are described as "low grade" (C. *dangci di*; Yiletu 2019). The overlapping effects of specialization and state environmentalism have resulted in monostocking, with many herders in the banner now lacking the diversity of livestock that might enable them to pursue other opportunities.

Beyond the Dragon's Head

In recent years the Chinese government has increasingly promoted entrepreneurship as a solution to slowing economic growth (Yeh 2022) and as an integral part of poverty alleviation efforts (Naminse et al. 2019). In Alasha, this focus on entrepreneurship is less evident in Right Banner, where, as we have seen, a dragon head company is channeling camel herders' participation in the market. In Left Banner, however, greater emphasis is placed on entrepreneurship, presumably because the city of Bayanhot and proximity to the much larger cities of Yinchuan and Wuhai provide readily accessible markets. This emphasis can be seen in the proliferation of training courses in recent years. Tömör, the CEO of Polaris Agro-Pastoral Machinery, for example, offered courses for herders in Left Banner that taught them how to make their own dairy products for sale.

In the summer of 2019, I accompanied Tömör to visit a friend of his son, a herder in his twenties who lived on the edge of the Ulaan Bukh Desert in the east of Left Banner. He used to work in the Left Banner government, but a couple of years previously his father died, leaving his mother and grandmother alone in the countryside. Nandin thought about bringing them to the city but decided it would be too expensive. He noticed that the price of camel milk had increased markedly and decided this might allow him to support his family with their camel herd while living with them in the countryside. Literature on reform-era China paints a picture of a mass exodus of young people from hollowed-out rural areas to booming cities in search of opportunity (Hairong Yan 2003; Driessen 2018). Nandin's story, however, confounds teleological narratives of urbanization, revealing how young people are sometimes pulled back to the countryside, with the transformation of rural livelihoods that this involves.

Nandin's family had around a hundred camels; almost all of their sheep and goats had been sold to comply with the grazing bans. Since keeping a herd of camels, unlike sheep and goats, did not affect one's entitlement to PES, Nandin's family had a small guaranteed income. Unlike in Right Banner, however, the production of camel milk was not subsidized. In 2017 they hired an itinerant herd hand from Mongolia to train the humans and camels of the household in how to milk and be milked.

Nandin had around forty regular customers, all of them Han Chinese in the city of Wuhai, less than an hour's drive away. Fluent in Chinese like most Mongols of his generation, Nandin had been put in touch with these customers via friends in this city. He used his WeChat account to advertise his products, then delivered them in Wuhai in his pickup, which had no refrigerated storage. Unlike Mongols, Nandin said, Chinese prefer fresh camel milk to yogurt. His WeChat account featured numerous photos of his family's camels being milked by hand, and Nandin also regularly reposted articles about the health benefits of camel milk, which often had their source in the Camel Research Institute in Right Banner. His customers were willing to pay ¥80 per liter of camel milk because they used it to treat or prevent various illnesses, particularly diabetes.

I asked why they didn't use medicines prescribed by doctors. Nandin said his customers believed that "natural things don't harm the body" (M. *baigaliin yum biyend khorgüi*). Nandin explained that they preferred to buy their milk directly from him rather than purchasing Desert God's products, because the latter were processed (C. *jiagong*) and contained preservatives. This desire for the natural apparently extended even to the labor of milking.

Over dinner, Tömör extolled the benefits of his milking machine. It was cleaner (C. *ganjing*) and more hygienic (C. *weisheng*), he said, using the Chinese words in the midst of an otherwise Mongolian conversation. It prevented germs from the milker's hands from getting into the milk. Nandin interrupted, however, saying that his customers explicitly requested that the camels be milked by hand rather than machine.

Nandin's engagement with the market was thus mediated by science and technology in a fundamentally ambivalent way. On the one hand, demand for camel milk was stimulated by the production of a scientistic discourse on the health benefits of camel milk, which emerged from the distinctive process of camel milk commodification through the state-agribusiness-science nexus centered on Right Banner. Nandin actively reproduced this discourse by circulating reports from the institute on WeChat. However, his customers sought out his products in preference to Desert God's, which were associated negatively with the health problems that come with an industrialized food system. Concerns over hygiene and pasteurization did not appear to loom large for Nandin's customers, who explicitly desired a nonmechanized process of production (cf. Tracy 2013). This was not about a preference for craft or artisanal products on the grounds of taste or an ethical desire to support rural livelihoods; instead it was about the trust that Nandin and his production methods inspired by virtue of personal recommendations, as well as a desire for the natural and the uncontaminated, a desire that is immediately comprehensible as soon as one enters the suburbs of Wuhai and begins to breathe in the noxious clouds emitted from its coking plants.

Others had been drawn back to these deserts by the entrepreneurial promise of camel milk. Enkhbat had been working as a trader across the China-Mongolian border but decided there was more potential in camel dairying. He spent ¥10,000 on a lucky phone number that ended in three eights and began selling camel milk using WeChat to reach customers. He told me he had not received any support from the Left Banner government; instead, he relied completely on his own strengths (C. *quan kao ziji de liliang*).

Nandin was happy with how business was going. The sale of camel milk provided his family with around ¥100,000 in income per year. He was formally a member of a local camel milk cooperative, but there had been some disputes, and he felt he did not need this cooperative to access the market. Nandin thus appeared to be an entrepreneurial subject who fashioned market opportunities out of livestock capital (the existing family herd) as well as the cultural and social capital that had come from living in a city and being exposed to the Chinese language.

However, Nandin complained that more and more residents of the *gatsaa*, encouraged by subsidies from the state, were erecting barbed-wire fences around their pastureland, thus preventing camels from browsing there. He resented the way people put up fences to "take control of the land" (M. *gazarig ezlekh*). People have become selfish, he said. I learned from him that pastureland in this part of Alasha had been allotted to individual households only in the last five years; before that it was still divided among large groups of households (M. *duguilan*), though in effect the entire *gatsaa* was treated as commons. Today camel herders still allow camels from other households onto their putatively private pastureland, but camel movement is increasingly obstructed by barbed-wire fences. Nandin's dairy entrepreneurialism thus coexisted with opposition to the enclosure of land and a commitment to the camel commons.

THE MONGOLIAN PLATEAU has long been the site of indigenous dairying practices (Yimin Yang 2020). Indeed, today the marketing practices of Inner Mongolian dairy companies make much of this association between Mongols and milk (Tracy 2018). However, thinking in terms of expanding *dairy frontiers* is illuminating precisely because it denaturalizes such associations, which can be used to mask the processes of dispossession at work in intensified dairy production in Inner Mongolia. This lens helps us look beyond mining to the kinds of primitive accumulation involved in other forms of frontier commodity production.

In the case of Shengmu, producing organic milk has nothing to do with the existing dairying practices of local herders. Instead, it has relied on processes of "green grabbing" (Fairhead et al. 2012): herders first had their use rights to land restricted on environmental grounds before being asked to sign over these rights to this agribusiness company. The relationship between state environmentalist green grabbing and dairy frontiers is also evident in other parts of Inner Mongolia. Reasoning that too much cash might exercise a corrupting influence on resettled herders, the state in Inner Mongolia has sometimes redirected money for environmental protection toward dairy companies, who then contract out production to these relocated herders, who are given nonnative dairy cows to be raised in barns with fodder (Dalintai and Zheng 2010, 455–79). To grow this fodder, grassland must be turned to cropland, representing the renewed expansion of the agricultural frontier, this time in the name of ecology (Han Niantong 2011a).

However, while it is important to contextualize Inner Mongolia within a global context of expanding livestock frontiers (Schneider and Cöghe 2021), we must also attend to the distinctiveness of the political-economic experiments with livestock production that are currently transforming peripheral regions of China. In Alasha Right Banner, agribusiness has benefited from the use of state poverty alleviation funds to supply poorer herders with camels. But the novel commodification of camel milk has not yet involved frontier processes of land grabbing and resettlement of ethnic minority herders. Instead, camel dairying is premised on these herders remaining on the grasslands with native camels, thereby constituting an exception to the logics of destocking and ecological migration that have characterized state environmentalism in the region. Where use rights to land have been signed away, this has been to small cooperatives rather than agribusiness. Consumer concerns about industrial food production have also enabled some individual household producers to access urban markets directly.

In Alasha, camel dairying serves ends besides merely those of capital, as borderland stability in this region is portrayed as a more-than-human achievement dependent on the continuation of rural interspecies relations enabled by dairying. Mongol officials and scientists have emphasized the affective bonds between herders and camels, suggesting that resettlement away from these sources of emotional support could result in ethnic unrest in this strategic borderland. Thus long-standing ideas of frontier alterity and animality are tactically redeployed in this context to defend camel husbandry.

At the same time, however, the transformation of camels into a dairy resource has challenged long-standing spatial and ethnic hierarchies. In contrast to dominant representations of ethnic minority regions as grateful recipients of modern scientific knowledge conveyed to these regions by Han Chinese, the Inner Mongolia Camel Research Institute is an exercise in scale-jumping, positioning Right Banner as a site of cutting-edge scientific knowledge production and transnational exchange, mediated by ethnic Mongol scientists; in addition, local Mongol inventors have been featured on national television with their camel dairying technology, and mediatized events such as the 2017 international conference have played a vital role in producing an affect of anticipation around camel dairying, relaying promises from Dubai that science and technology would soon overcome the limits of camel physiology. Resource-making depended on these promises of future

165

Dairy Frontiers

intensification and new product development, so that the power of the local state could be harnessed to restructure the rural economy around camel husbandry. The emergent scales and geographies of expertise that have accompanied the development of camel dairying in Alasha reveal how China's borderlands are being transformed in unexpected ways by novel forms of resource-making and commodity production.

Conclusion

IN EARLY SPRING 2017 two miraculous creatures appeared in Alasha. At one of the cooperatives in Right Banner that supplied Desert God with milk, a pair of camel twins was born. Their Han Chinese owner followed Mongolian custom and consecrated (M. *seterlekh*) the mother, tying a blue *khadag* around her neck and vowing never again to milk or sell her, and promising to let her die a natural death. The birth of camel twins is extremely rare. In the prerevolutionary era the banner prince would mark this auspicious event by presenting a silver nose peg to the herder before the consecration of the animal. In the reform era, this ritual has been revived, with party secretaries taking the place of banner princes: in 2017 the silver nose peg was presented jointly by the Right Banner and Alasha League party secretaries. When delegates to the international conference in late summer of that year were taken on a tour of the cooperative, they noticed the consecrated camel with the silver nose peg next to her two calves in a specially constructed pen. A placard had been attached to the pen with Chinese text explaining that these were "twin Alasha Bactrian camels from Camel Country" (fig. 10). The placard displayed images of two sheets of paper, franked with the seal of an official institution. On closer inspection these turned out to be the results of genetic testing conducted by scientists at the Camel Research Institute, which confirmed that these two creatures were indeed twins.

Pastoralism and the State

If China's pastoral regions are known at all outside the country, it is as places where nomads are being resettled by the state: "China's campaign to force

FIG. 10. A sign reading "Twin Alasha Bactrian camels from Camel Country" and displaying the results of genetic testing

its millions of nomadic herders into static lives of grim social engineering is proceeding rapidly," declared a *New York Times* editorial in 2015, the first year I returned to Batbagana's house on the rangelands of northern Alasha after my initial period of fieldwork. Resettlement has undoubtedly transformed many of China's pastoral regions, often against the will of pastoralists. This coercive environmentalism (Yifei Li and Judith Shapiro 2020) represents the kind of high modernist state power famously described by James Scott (1998), which rides roughshod over local knowledge in favor of a one-size-fits-all plan, with unexpected deleterious consequences.

This book has sought to show that this is not the only way state power manifests itself on the grasslands of China. In Alasha in the 2010s, pastoral traditions were not only subjected to environmental governance in the form of stocking limits and grazing bans; they could also provide resources for "cultural governance," or "the deployment of symbolic resources as an instrument of political authority" (Perry 2017, 29). Local officials participated in pastoral rituals of livestock fertility and abundance, even as national policies called for the rapid reduction of livestock numbers. As officials presented the silver nose peg, state power took on the mantle of an indigenous Inner Asian biopower inherited from the prerevolutionary period.

Even as national-level policies blamed extensive animal husbandry for grassland degradation, the state proudly listed certain localized forms of pastoralism in Inner Mongolia as items of national intangible cultural heritage. Some herders became "cultural transmitters" and hosted revived pastoral rituals at their households, actively seeking state officials as their guests. It was not suppression of culture by the state that they resented so much as the state's eventual co-opting of rituals as commodities and its rescripting of cultural forms according to the diktats of an anticorruption drive. Discourses of camel husbandry as valuable local heritage enabled intellectuals to articulate ideas of herders' traditional ecological knowledge. This remaking of pastoralism as heritage has continued in China in recent years. In 2022, the UN's Food and Agriculture Organization included the Ar Khorchin Grassland Nomadic System on its list of Globally Important Agricultural Heritage Systems, the first time a nomadic "agricultural heritage system" from China had been included.

At the turn of the millennium, as the effects of years of drought were compounded by grazing bans, Alasha's dwindling camel population became a proxy for fears over the disappearance of pastoralism, so central to Mongolian identity. Concern about the extinction of these charismatic animals of China's west provided a new analogy for cultural vanishing, a recurrent fear among China's Mongols. It also enabled a new form of issue framing (Mertha 2009). Actors in the local state, or in its penumbra, deployed discourses of extinction and conservation so that the Alasha Bactrian camel became a "national genetic resource," thus framing pastoralism such that it appeared no longer as a backward mode of land use responsible for the degradation of the grasslands but as a means of conserving resources (and heritage) of national importance. These advocates of pastoralism were characterized by their intimacy with the state and their facility with its discourses, complicating state/pastoralist binaries.

By the early 2010s, when I began to conduct fieldwork, it was widely known in Alasha that the camel was a protected animal, granted this status by the central state, though exactly what this entailed was less clear. Local conceptions of taboo were articulated alongside vernacular understandings of the state's biopolitical discourse. It was important to people that the state had recognized this animal as needing protection. The distinctive physiology and mobility of this protected animal in turn afforded a defense of extensive animal husbandry, in the face of grassland enclosure and the architecture of PES that had been built on it.

The politics of Camel Country are complex; they trouble established ways of thinking about minority-state relations in China. If framing camel husbandry as a question of local heritage in Alasha was part of a history of attempts by generations of Mongol elites in Inner Mongolia to defend Mongolian pastoralism in the context of settler colonization and, more recently, state environmentalism, it nevertheless also opened up a discursive space amenable to the assimilatory nation-building narratives of the Xi era. Recent publications by Han Chinese anthropologists (e.g., He 2020), for example, now celebrate camel culture as an example of the "contact, exchange, and mingling" between nationalities that is promulgated as part of "second-generation" nationality policies. In formulating a distinctive *local* camel culture, this framing of pastoralism participated in ascendant narratives of frontier contact and mixing, as well as the foregrounding of place over nationality. The defense of pastoralism in Alasha was also a project of cultural rescaling. This is evident in the recent listing of the Ar Khorchin Grassland Nomadic System as agricultural heritage: nomadic movement becomes the specialty of a particular place rather than a nationality, and Chinese media can report on the listing while making no reference to Mongols (*Zhongguo Xinwen Wang* 2023).

In 2020, after the fieldwork for this book was completed, Inner Mongolia witnessed large protests against education reforms in the region that downgraded the status of Mongolian language in Mongolian-medium schools. Mongol cadres were pressured to implement the reforms, and their intermediary role became harder to occupy. In Alasha, one party cadre committed suicide, which her family described as an act of protest against the reforms (Qiao Long 2020). The following year, Bu Xiaolin, the granddaughter of Ulanhu, once governor and party secretary of Alasha League, was replaced as chair of the IMAR, apparently because of her perceived lack of enthusiasm for the education reforms. These reforms have left pastoralism as the remaining bastion of Mongolian identity and anxiety. In 2021, culture workers in Beijing and Hohhot raised funds on social media to support herders affected by coronavirus lockdowns (Baioud 2022). It remains to be seen how urban Mongols' intensified interest in pastoralism as the locus of Mongolian identity articulates with attempts to preserve pastoralism as local heritage or to develop it as in situ poverty alleviation.

Silver nose pegs had been awarded in the past, but 2017 was the first time camel twins had their extraordinary status confirmed by genetic testing. This is characteristic of the role science and technology have come to play in the creation of Camel Country. While the politics of pastoralism is normally understood as a politics of land, in early twenty-first-century Alasha it came to be conducted in the idiom of nonhuman life. This livestock biopolitics shifted from a focus on camel extinction around the turn of the millennium to anticipation in the 2010s, as Inner Mongolian biologists and indigenous innovators in Alasha reconfigured camel bodies—and associated technical devices—as sites of future value.

Camels had once been emblematic of the remoteness of Alasha. Their replacement by trucks and trains was heralded as an example of the modernization brought about by the CCP. By the late twentieth century, in the eyes of some unsympathetic officials in Alasha, they exemplified the backwardness of pastoralism: low yield and entailing extensive husbandry. Far preferable would be imported dairy cows raised on fodder in barns. But in the first decades of the twenty-first century, this began to change. The relative lack of human intervention in camel bodies was recoded as something positive: semiwild camels could be cast as benign ecological engineers, their extensive mobility subjected to GPS monitoring by computer-equipped herders in the city. Pastoralism could thus be represented as coeval with industrial modernity rather than superseded by it.

With the involvement of Inner Mongolian biologists, the very primitivity of camel bodies began to generate anticipation, framed in articles, reports, and meetings as a frontier of biotechnology, holding out the promise of potential biopharmaceutical value. This novel conjoining of primitivity and futurity is part of a broader transformation of the human relationship to nonhuman life brought about by biotechnology. Extremely thermophilic archaea, for example, known as "living fossils," are said to "offer intriguing opportunities for biotechnology [that] are directly related to their proposed primitive beginnings: the ability to inhabit at extreme temperature and pH" (Straub et al. 2018. 543).

But this rescripting of the relationship of nonhuman life, time, and value takes on particular significance in the context of China's ethnic margins, where both humans and the animals they keep have been targeted by a state that seeks to improve them out of their backwardness. The changing meaning of camels in Alasha emerged through the articulation of discourses of bio-technological potential with a shift in the discursive production of China's peripheries in the early twenty-first century, such that qualities once associated negatively with backwardness, such as remoteness, become valuable resources, whether for tourism (Yu Luo et al. 2019) or data centers (Darcy Pan 2022). These novel discourses of value nourished speculative visions of a future in which Alasha's primitive, semiwild camels roamed the open grasslands providing ecosystem services, to be occasionally rounded up by techno-pastoralists so that their genetic resources could be mined by scientists for biotechnological secrets.

However, as the local state, Inner Mongolian scientists, and southern Chinese capital came together to restructure rural Right Banner around camel dairying, new demands were placed on camel bodies. If milk yields were to increase, improvement would be required. Alasha's semiwild camels would have to be trained and subjected to new breeding regimes. This reorientation of camel bodies in Alasha has further unsettled established geographies of science and technology. As a frontier of camel science research, Alasha has become a node in an international network of scientific knowledge production and collaboration that is taking shape around the improvement of the bodies of camels. Camel science is an "open field," as one European attendee at the 2017 conference told me, and Inner Mongolian scientists have seized the opportunity to become pioneers.

A growing literature has analyzed the role of livestock in shaping the economies and ecologies of our globalized world. Cattle in particular played a part in settler colonial projects, transforming New World ecologies and enabling the dispossession of indigenous peoples (Virginia Anderson 2004; Ficek 2019). Today, historical connections between colony and metropole are recapitulated in the transoceanic movement of livestock biomatter, livestock products, and scientific knowledge about livestock (Franklin 2007), including, for example, emerging ideas about livestock sustainability (Cusworth et al. 2022).

However, the transcontinental Old World geography of camels and the spatialized networks of scientific knowledge production and exchange it still shapes today tell a rather different story of historical and contemporary global connections. These networks are exemplified by the arrival in Alasha Right Banner in 2019 of an Iranian scientist from the University of Tehran to perform the world's first Bactrian camel embryo transfer. This scientific knowledge transfer was significant enough to merit an article in the English-language *China Daily* (Jiang and Wang 2019). Embryo transfer would help overcome the barrier to selective breeding for high milk yield posed by the camel's slow rate of reproduction. The fact that the scientist hailed from Iran was characteristic of the way camel science involves alternative forms of global connectivity, outside the transoceanic circuits that are the legacy of livestock-assisted settler colonialism.

In the same year the Northern China Camel Training and Education Base was established in Right Banner. The first training session held there was presided over by not only the head of the institute, an ethnic Mongol from Inner Mongolia, but also four experts and scholars from Mongolia (Neimenggu Luotuo Yanjiuyuan 2019). Rather than knowledge flowing from eastern China and Han Chinese experts, here it was being transmitted to herders not only by ethnic Mongol scientists based in Inner Mongolia but also from across the international border in Mongolia, a country widely understood in Inner Mongolia as poorer and less developed than China (Bayar 2014b). The creation of Camel Country thus challenges long-standing hierarchies of knowledge and expertise.

In the context of China's going out into the world, the cultural and religious competency of some of China's ethnic minorities, such as the Hui, facilitates their role as mediators, helping to broker relationships between China and its Belt and Road partners (Yuting Wang 2018). But the example of the camel shows that transnational relationships are also mediated by the biological specificity of nonhumans and the distinctive knowledge and techniques this requires of humans.

Inner Mongolian scientists now make explicit connections between camel genetics and the Silk Road narratives through which the Chinese state seeks to legitimize its Belt and Road Initiative. Recent analysis of genome sequencing by Inner Mongolian scientists and international colleagues has indicated that camels were initially domesticated in western Asia around 4,500 years ago, arriving at the eastern end of their contemporary range in China and Mongolia around 2,400 years ago "with the increasing economic exchange and cooperation between West and East" (Ming et al. 2020, 6). This language is redolent of the Chinese state's vision of the Silk Road as an archetype of peaceful transcontinental exchange, in contrast to the violence of European imperialism. Instead of cattle colonialism (Fischer 2015), here we are presented with a vision of continental camel cooperation.

Such interpretations of genome sequences are thus grounded in the kind of politics typical of minority elites in the penumbra of the state, who seek to reframe pastoralism in the light of national policies and goals. Camel bodies are no longer simply unimproved and backward; instead, through genetic knowledge, they become *historical*, manifesting the ancient, peaceful forms of connectivity that China now claims to be reviving with the Belt and Road Initiative. Here we can see the multifaceted nature of the resource-making project in Alasha: as genetic resources, camels can also become narrative resources, used to bolster contemporary state imaginaries and projects of cultural rescaling. Through these new forms of resource-making, Mongol scientists and those in the penumbra of the state seek to secure the support of the state for camel husbandry, while also reimagining the position of this borderland within China.

With the introduction of new breeding technologies, Alasha's camels are on the cusp of transformation. Some international camel scientists portray intensified camel dairy production as an important global adaptation to climate change, allowing for the continued production of animal foods in increasingly arid environments (Nagy et al. 2022). Other scientists have sounded a note of caution with regard to new breeding technologies required to intensify production, emphasizing the importance of "keep[ing] a balance between conserving the genetic integrity, diversity and traditional management of the species, while responding to the constantly growing needs for intensification of breeding and selection using modern genomic tools" (Burger, Ciani, and Faye 2019, 598). Some involved in the international pastoralists' rights movement are more forthright, declaring that "we don't want the camel to become a cow" (Köhler-Rollefson 2023).

While improved milk yields are said to promise greater returns for herders, it remains to be seen what other transformations selective breeding will entail in Alasha. Who will be able to access improved dairy camels, and what forms of husbandry would these new animals require? Will new forms of stratification based on access to improved animals emerge? Will the proliferation of these new animals finally bring about extinction of the Alasha Bactrian camel? Will they be compatible with traditions of extensive husbandry, or will further forms of intensification be set in motion? Local media in Alasha have recently begun to feature stories of wealthy camel herders scaling up dairy production, investing in large barns and fodder (Meili Alashan Youqi 2023). New breeding technologies are already transforming frontier livestock elsewhere in China, in line with the demands of an intensive production system that makes less use of open-range grazing: a new breed of yak has recently been developed with "no horns and a mild temperament" such that they are easier to raise in stalls (Yu Fei 2019).

The Limits of Camel Culture

If technoscience-assisted camel dairying was the future in Alasha Right Banner, the situation in the north of Khöövör, once the heartland of camel culture, had become much more uncertain. In 2017 I returned to Bayantal briefly, this time in the company of an Inner Mongolian film crew making a documentary about Alasha's camels. Batbagana, dressed in his Mongolian robe, rode out on his favorite camel to greet our car. I noticed how much had changed since my last visit two years ago. Lines of transmission towers now stretched over the hill and continued on to the industrial zone. The director complained that they were ugly and wondered how to keep them out of shot.

Back at his house, Batbagana told me happily that there had been numerous camel culture events recently, and the state had provided half of the money for a new pen for his growing herd of camels. Enthusiasm for camel racing among the herders of Bayantal appeared undimmed. Indeed, novel breeding practices were being deployed locally to ends quite different from those envisaged by the Camel Research Institute. One herder had apparently purchased a captured wild camel (M. *khavthai*) from Xinjiang and was attempting to create a cross-breed with local domestic camels that would be particularly fast.[1] In the 1980s, the state had encouraged camel racing as a way of facilitating selective breeding for uses other than transportation; now camel racing had become an end of breeding itself. As in other examples of livestock conservation (Cassidy 2009), the conservation of genetic resources and the conservation of cultural heritage seemed here to be pulling in different directions.

As our conversation progressed, the mood darkened. Batbagana and Sarna complained that they were now poor (M. *yaduu*). They had been forced to sell all their sheep and goats to comply with the grazing ban (fig. 11). Batbagana had offered to raise them on fodder in a pen instead of letting them graze, but this request was denied. They could no longer depend on their own animals for subsistence and from now on would have to rely on the market. The sheep and goat meat from the north of Alasha that they wanted to eat was expensive, at least ¥60 per kilo, since it was highly sought after by urban consumers. Meat from animals raised in pens in the environs of Bayanhot was cheaper, but they did not want to eat that, since they thought it unhealthy. How could they afford to eat healthy meat when their only income was ¥10,000 a year each in grazing ban subsidies? It seemed likely that camels would have to be sold to purchase meat. While camel culture appeared to be thriving for now, they complained that the grazing bans were "destroying Mongolian culture" (M. *Mongol soyol ugüi khiij baina*) in this pastoral region.

The remaking of pastoralism as heritage in Alasha was inevitably a partial process: being a Mongol herder in rural Alasha involved more than camel husbandry. Herders looked back with "eco-nostalgia" (Angé and Berliner 2021) to times when they had been able to raise all five kinds of Mongolian livestock, when they had raced horses in the summer in Bayantal, and when cattle got lost in grass so high it obscured the animals. Now, they were being made to get rid of the sheep and goats on which they depended for healthy subsistence but also for their ability to host the celebrations (M. *nair*) that Batbagana insisted were a central part of what it meant to be Mongol.

In 2019 I returned to Bayantal for the final time before COVID lockdowns made visits impossible. This time I approached from the mountains to the north and had to pass under a new highway bisecting the *gatsaa*. This road now connected Beijing with Ürümqi in Xinjiang, having opened to much fanfare in 2017. Mönkhbayar and several local herders had worked on construction of the road; others had opened small shops to cater to the migrant workers from all over China who lived in temporary accommodations at the construction site.

Our car was able to squeeze through a passageway underneath the road designed to facilitate the movement of livestock, but on reaching the other side, I was forced to get out and open a barbed-wire gate. The *gatsaa* was now crisscrossed by fencing, and we had to open several more gates before we finally arrived at Batbagana's. He told me that the local government had begun to provide fencing to local herders for free, as it sought to reinforce the privatized tenure of land on which the payments for ecosystem services depended. Given the recurrent droughts and now these restrictions on camel mobility, Batbagana was uncertain how much longer they would be able to herd camels. Some of the key participants in camel culture no longer remained in Bayantal. The Han Chinese herder and enthusiastic camel racer Fang San had sold his animals after his pastures were purchased to make way for the road and had bought an apartment in Bayanhot.

However, there was some pushback against this new round of fencing from those involved in camel conservation. Baigal was asking herders to send him photographic evidence of camels that had been injured by fences; he would then submit these to the local government in an attempt to persuade them to rethink their policies. Once again, animal bodies were central to the way the situated politics of pastoralism in Alasha was conducted. More recently, the IMAR government has solicited comments and suggestions on a

FIG. 11. Goats sold off to comply with grazing bans are transported to market

document published online that acknowledges some of the problems caused by fencing and calls for an end to excessive fencing in the region (Guojia Linye he Caoyuan Ju 2021). This draft document calls on local officials to respect the wishes of herders and scientifically assess (C. *kexue panduan*) the necessity and practicality of fencing in particular locations. It also suggests that in cases where there is no conflict between households, herders should be encouraged to remove fences between pastures and enter into cooperative herding arrangements. It seems that critiques of the division of the pastureland into privatized household plots are gaining more purchase; Chinese media reports covering the Ar Horchin Nomadic Agricultural Heritage System, for example, referred to the ecological benefits of moving flocks seasonally (*Zhongguo Xinwen Wang* 2023), an argument that critics of grassland enclosure had, of course, long been making.

However, it was hard to see how this awareness could be reconciled with the latest round of fencing in rural Alasha. Indeed, in the last few years, state power had begun to assume a more arbitrary, destructive form on Alasha's grasslands. A recent rural infrastructure modernization campaign in the IMAR, known as the Ten Complete Coverages (C. Shi ge Quan Fugai), had been applied particularly aggressively, with herders' homes and traditional sheepfolds destroyed. Batbagana's was only spared because it was far from any road and thus not visible to higher-up officials making an inspection tour.

This campaign had now subsided, but people were profoundly uncertain about the future and what the continuing development of infrastructure, for example, would mean. There was talk of constructing an off-ramp from the highway that might pave over some of Batbagana's pastures, but they were not sure if or when this would happen. Batbagana wanted to believe that Xi Jinping was sincere when he talked about the need to protect minority cultures (this was before the reforms to Mongolian-language education were announced in the summer of 2020). But with his characteristic cynicism, Jargal, the official from Khöövör, told me that nothing was fixed in China (M. *togtmol gesen yum baikhgüi*). Now they were applying the stocking limits to sheep and goats, but tomorrow they might say you could herd as many as you like; camels were currently exempted from the stocking limits, but if Xi Jinping suddenly changed course, "all of Alasha's camels would be killed tomorrow."

Batbagana and Sarna remained in Bayantal with their camels, but these animals required little day-to-day labor, and the couple was growing too old to ride them or train them to be milked. An atmosphere of quiet listlessness now hung about their rural home. Unlike many herders in China's pastoral regions over the last few decades, they had not been resettled away from the grasslands. They were still herders, but there was little herding left to do. "Now that our sheep and goats have gone," said Sarna, "we just spend our time cooking and sleeping." Batbagana's cultural energies seemed to have been redirected toward running a Khöövör folk song society, many of whose members now lived in Bayanhot. Unlike camel culture, this form of heritage did not require access to land. The large old sheepfold where they had once kept hundreds of sheep and goats was now silent and empty. The mixed media of its walls remained a testament to the mundane synergies of multispecies pastoralism: clumps of sheep wool still clung to bricks made from compacted camel dung, and I recalled the churning huddle of sheep and goats packed inside.

Notes

Introduction

1. For discussion of the accident see 52 Hezi Shiyanshi 2021; Yu Yuan and Li Xiancheng 2021.

2. According to official statistics, while in 2003 there were only 55,900 camels in the whole of Alasha League, by 2012 this had risen to 78,300 and in 2016 stood at 100,260 (Batuchulu and Siqinbielige 2017, 321).

3. Definitions of *pastoralism* and *pastoralists* vary considerably. Perhaps the simplest way of dealing with this problem is to treat these categories as *emic* rather than *etic*—in other words, to define pastoralists as those who identify themselves as such (Koster and Chang 1994; Tan 2018). Seen in this light, the rural people described in this book would all be pastoralists (M. *malchin*). However, for many scholars pastoralism remains an important analytic category that allows questions to be asked about the transition from pastoralism to ranching, understood in its most basic terms as the commodification of both livestock and land, where both become exclusively held property (Ingold 1980; Sayre 2009). Schareika, Brown, and Moritz (2021, 54) have recently distinguished between "cattle logic" and "capital logic," arguing that "in pastoral systems, the everyday interactions and decisions of a cattle owner follow the logic of cattle and are aimed at ensuring the long-term continuity of the lineages of humans and animals," whereas "in capitalist ranching systems, by contrast, a cattle owner follows the logic of capital and makes decisions with the aim of increasing monetary returns on investments." But the example of Alasha, as this book makes clear, shows that such neat analytic distinctions are harder to maintain in the face of ethnographic realities. In Alasha, land is supposedly privatized but still not always treated as such, and herders are integrated into the market but are also concerned with the long-term continuity of herds and do not engage with livestock merely as potential commodities. Crucially, their attitudes are not simply some kind of residue of tradition but are supported by an official discourse of conservation, which exists alongside, and sometimes in tension with, an emphasis on commodification.

In this book I have avoided referring to "nomads," since this word is analytically unhelpful, carrying with it certain stereotypical notions of freedom, egalitarianism, and low technological capacity (Humphrey and Sneath 1999, 1). I have thus preferred the terms *pastoralists* and *herders*, though I have occasionally used *nomadism* or *nomadic* as ethnographic terms, where the equivalents of this word were used by people in Alasha.

4. In 1988 the price for cashmere increased from ¥70 per kilo to ¥130, while

between 1993 and 1995 the price rose to ¥360, before peaking at around ¥400–500 per kilo (Bulag 2002a, 221).

5. In this context, the concept of carrying capacity refers to the number of livestock a particular piece of land is considered able to support, based on the assessment of scientists. While central to China's grassland management policies, the concept has been subject to considerable criticism (Sayre 2008).

6. This is not the same as *The Story of the Weeping Camel*, a 2003 German docudrama set in Mongolia.

7. Inner Mongolia's cities are overwhelmingly majority Han Chinese, meaning that Chinese is the language of everyday life (Jankowiak 2013).

8. The prevalence of this practice is suggested by a joke that circulated on social media among Mongols in Alasha in 2013. A lamb asks its mother, "Why do we have to come out to graze at night and spend our days in the sheepfold?" The mother replies, "Because the higher-ups have issued a grazing ban order so we're not allowed to eat grass during the day." The lamb then asks, "But what happens if a wolf comes along? I'm scared!" To which its mother responds, "Stop talking and eat! If the police come you'll be even more scared!"

9. Throughout the book I have used pseudonyms for the names of my interlocutors.

10. The question of how to translate *minzu* (M. *Ündesten*) is complex. The conventional English translation "nationality" can sometimes sound unwieldy, but I have tended to adopt it here because of its association with the constitutional rights that are guaranteed to China's minorities. More familiar alternatives, such as "ethnic group," now have certain connotations in China's political discourse, as they are promoted over *minzu* or nationality as a way of depoliticizing the status of China's minorities, on the alleged model of the US melting pot of ethnicities (Bulag 2021). Occasionally I have employed "ethnic" as a translation of *minzu* in adjectival form.

11. Vernacular understandings of phenotypical difference among Alasha's camels do not accord with notions of a singular breed of Alasha Bactrian camel. Herders distinguish, for example, between the smaller, lighter-colored animals found around the Khöövör region and the larger, darker camels of Gobi regions to the north. What is more, across the border in Bayannuur Municipality, Gobi camels are themselves now regarded as a distinct breed, the Gobi Red, demonstrating the arbitrary nature of breed designation, which is often based on political-administrative distinctions.

12. In the forests of northeastern Inner Mongolia, reindeer have become exceptions due to their inconsistent classification by different branches of state bureaucracy as both domestic and wild (Kolås 2011). Similar classificatory confusion was at work on the ground in the case of the camel in Alasha, as I discuss in chapter 5.

13. Tensions between Mongolia and China over the UNESCO registration of Mongolian heritage forms have emerged in recent years (Sarina Wu 2020). Some

recently developed forms of camel culture have been brought across the border from Mongolia, including camel polo, though this is more popular in Urad Rear Banner, to the east of Alasha in Bayannuur Municipality.

14. Camel hair had long been integrated into global value chains. The Count de Lesdain (1908, 100), who passed through Dingyuanying at the start of the twentieth century, wrote that "the Chinese buy sheep's wool, camel's hair, horses and camels for the caravans which transport their purchases to the export centres. A good number of the Chinese buyers act for European firms at Shanghai or Tianjin." By 1941, the merchant house Xiangtailong, for example, was collecting on average 5,000 kilograms of camel hair from herders in Alasha every year, and around 1,000 kilograms of sheep's wool (Li Wanlu 2007).

15. I have used this toponym to help preserve the anonymity of my interlocutors. The historical region of Khöövör is today divided up between several administrative units.

1. Situating Pastoralist Heritage

1. The fate of Inner Mongolia was ultimately sealed geopolitically. The Sino-Soviet treaty of 1945 had foreclosed the possibility of Inner Mongolia joining the MPR, with China also formally recognizing the latter's independence (Xiaoyuan Liu 2006).

2. Alasha was part of Ningxia until 1954, when it was subsumed by Gansu along with Ningxia. Upon accession to the IMAR in 1956, Alasha Banner (C. *qi*; M. *khoshuu*) became part of Bayannuur League (C. *meng*; M. *aimag*), along with Ejine Banner to the west. In 1961 Alasha was divided into two banners (Right and Left).

3. This close relationship was a result of their seventeenth-century alliance against the Zunghars, an Oirad Mongol group based in what is today northern Xinjiang (Perdue 2005).

4. From the mid-eighteenth century the Qing had forbidden Han Chinese from moving beyond the Great Wall (C. *chu kou*), as a policy of exclusion (C. *fengjin*) was implemented throughout Mongolian regions (Bulag 2002a). This policy was designed to preserve the martial prowess and pastoral identity of the Mongols (Bello 2016), but as the nineteenth century wore on was not strictly enforced.

5. Following the large-scale migration of Han Chinese farmers into Inner Mongolia from the late Qing, Chinese counties were established to govern them, reducing the territory of the Mongolian banners.

6. In this respect Inner Mongolia differed from the Soviet Union, where nomadism was not held to be a defining national characteristic of any of the Central Asian peoples (Thomas 2018).

7. *Hui* today refers to the Hui nationality (C. Huizu), one of China's fifty-six nationalities, who are Chinese-speaking Muslims. In the past the term referred

more broadly to Muslims, including Turkic Muslims in Xinjiang. In Mongolian the Muslim Mongols have often been referred to as *Mongol Khoton*, and in Chinese, *Meng Hui*. Older members of the community, in particular, will often use simply *Khoton* to distinguish themselves from surrounding Mongols, whom they refer to as *Mongol*. However, the use of this ethnonym in the public sphere was regularly disparaged, since it is the Mongolian equivalent of the Chinese *Hui*, referring to the nationality from which the Muslim Mongols were keen to distinguish themselves. Instead, the unwieldy term "members of the Mongol nationality who believe in Islam" (M. *Islam shütlegtei Mongol ündesten*) was preferred.

8. A useful review of the various theories as to the origins of the Muslim Mongols is provided by the Hui anthropologist Mingjun Ding (2006). According to a story, which I heard from several Muslim Mongols, the ancestors of the Muslim Mongols were five grape sellers from Xinjiang who were unable to return home from Alasha after they lost their money, whereupon they married local Mongol women and settled in the banner. Some more educated Muslim Mongols, such as the local scholar An Mönkh (2005), dismiss this as the stuff of legend, saying that Muslim Mongols were already in Alasha when traders from Xinjiang arrived, but acknowledge that some Uyghur traders were incorporated into the Muslim Mongols until as recently as the 1950s. When I interviewed him in 2013, Mönkh said that although elder generations of Muslim Mongols described their ancestors as Uyghur and Kazaks, this was not the whole story. He was eager to stress that some of the ancestors of the Muslim Mongols in Alasha were Muslim Mongols from Xinjiang. He reasoned that since Islam arrived in China on the back of Chinggis Khan's Eurasian conquests, it is highly likely that some of the khan's own *minzu* became Muslim. He said that the ancestors of the Alasha Muslim Mongols would not originally have been able to integrate into the banner had they not had some Mongols among their number.

9. The name Dingyuanying is a reference to the wars against the Zunghars.

10. Even while I lived in the region, Alasha lacked any real passenger railway. Travelers alighted at the station at Yinchuan in Ningxia and then took a small bus across the mountains to Bayanhot. A railway line connecting Bayanhot to Yinchuan is scheduled to open in 2026.

11. Agriculture was possible in the easternmost part of Alasha, where water could be brought from the Yellow River. In 1927, despite the opposition of the banner prince, Dengkou County (C. *xian*) was carved out of this part of Alasha's territory (Bayar 2002, 248), where Belgian missionaries had established farming communities of Han converts (Taveirne 2004).

12. While party leaders were pleased with the early success of their United Front policies in co-opting Alasha's elites, they were less certain of their influence among herders living in remote "nests of sand" (C. *sha wo*), where the influence of "feudalism" was hard to dispel. Well into the 1950s, herders still avoided grazing their animals on pastures that had been controlled by nobles and monasteries

prior to 1949 (IMAR EG 2009, 46). CCP cadres lamented that the socialist consciousness (C. *shehuizhuyi yishi*) of ordinary herders was still weak (Shi Jifa 2001, 95).

13. The fact that the powerful Tumed Mongols from near Hohhot are considered western (M. *baruun*) Mongols in Inner Mongolia speaks to the political marginalization of Alasha in the IMAR, since the Tumed area could only really be considered western if one ignores Alasha.

14. The most powerful Mongol cadre in the history of the Inner Mongolia Autonomous Region was Yun Ze, or Ulanhu ("Red Son" in Mongolian), as he was more commonly known. Born into a community of Sinicized Tumed Mongols in the area around Hohhot, Ulanhu played a key role in extending the authority of the CCP over Inner Mongolia in the face of competing political movements for Inner Mongolian autonomy (Xiaoyuan Liu 2006; Bulag 2002b). He became the first chairman of the Inner Mongolia Autonomous Region in 1947. Ulanhu also established a political dynasty in Inner Mongolia. His son, Bükh, served as chairman of Inner Mongolia from 1982 to 1993, and Bükh's daughter, Bu Xiaolin, was chairwoman of Inner Mongolia from 2016 to 2021.

15. The Inner Mongolian People's Party had in fact been dissolved in 1947, with its members becoming part of the CCP.

16. Some scholars have referred to this as a genocide (Haiying Yang 2017), though others have recently suggested it should be conceptualized instead as a politicide, designed not to destroy the Mongols as a people or culture but rather to render them unable to exercise political leadership in their autonomous region (Cheng et al. 2023).

17. Of the 25,000 who arrived in Alasha during this period, 16,000 settled there permanently (ALBG 2000, 46). Others were later resettled in Bayannuur League.

18. In 1981, the regional branch of the party published a plan for the development of the IMAR, which suggested that it had no intention of halting the migration of Han Chinese settlers into the region. In response, angry Mongol university students organized a strike and later marched on the center of Hohhot with eight demands, which included an end to Chinese migration into Inner Mongolia and a return to Ulanhu's "livestock first" policy in the region. Eventually, after being rejected by the central government in Beijing, the protesters backed down, and numerous Mongol officials were purged. However, in 1984 a report by the Chinese Academy of Social Sciences criticized the party's development plan, arguing that unrestricted Han Chinese migration into the IMAR would have severe ecological consequences in terms of desertification. Mongol officials managed to persuade their Han colleagues to order farmers living in those areas most unsuited to agriculture either to become herders or to return to their native villages (Jankowiak 1988, 287). In 1986 the IMAR party announced a policy of "reading the sutra of the grass and the trees, promoting pastoralism" (C. *nian cao mu jing, xing*

xumu ye; Liu Xiaowang and Wulunsai 2017, 101). The IMAR party secretary responsible for this was Zhang Shuguang, an ally of Hu Yaobang, general secretary of the CCP, whose policies toward minority regions were relatively lenient. His downfall in 1987 brought an end to his ally's pro-pastoralist policy in the IMAR. (I thank Uradyn Bulag for this observation.)

19. Ejine Banner was historically distinct from Alasha, established in 1753 by the Qing to incorporate a group of Torghut Mongol pilgrims from Kalmykia in tsarist Russia who had originally traveled to Tibet but been caught up in the turmoil of the Zunghar wars and thus had to submit to the Qing (Perdue 2005).

20. In 1985 the government of Alasha League created a two-thousand-meter track especially for racing camels on the outskirts of Bayanhot, and in the same year drew up camel racing regulations modeled on those for horse racing (ALBG 2000, 921).

21. The notion of camel culture that emerged in early twenty-first-century Alasha took its cue from concepts circulating elsewhere in Inner Mongolia. In 2002, for example, *Mongolians and the Horse* (Manlai and Wanchog 2002), edited by academics at the Inner Mongolia Agricultural University in Hohhot, was published on the 840th anniversary of Chinggis Khan's birth. It argues that the origins of horse cultures across the world are to be found among the ancestors of today's Mongol nationality. While this encyclopedia used the notion of horse culture to celebrate the world historical status of the Mongols, the Alasha camel culture designation initially carved out a space of *local* distinctiveness before being scaled up with narratives of the Silk Road.

22. Ejine Banner was assigned camel racing, Alasha Right Banner the craft of camel tack, and Alasha Left Banner camel veneration rituals. This specialization notwithstanding, all of these practices have been sponsored to varying degrees across Alasha League.

23. While I was not permitted to visit Ejine, friends from that banner who now lived in Bayanhot occasionally grumbled at the way they had been subsumed into an Alasha cultural identity. Some of the work of amateur scholars from Ejine reveals attempts to push back against this subsumption: in 2015, for example, a Mongolian-language book titled *The Camel Culture of Poplar Country* was published (Chuluu 2013). Ejine Banner has used its poplar forests, whose autumn leaves attract tourists from all over China, as a form of branding.

24. This website, Alasha Culture Net (C. Alashan Wenhua Wang; www.alswh .com), now appears to be defunct.

25. The notion that camel caravans are characteristic of China's Inner Asian frontier hybridity is also found in the work of American scholar and traveler Owen Lattimore (1928, 528), who wrote that "the men of the caravans themselves represent the people of the march country, adjacent to the Great Wall, in which there has always been a mingling of influences, between the nomads and the settled Chinese. They are borderers, men of no-man's-land."

26. This was a period of feverish museum construction across Inner Mongolia, as different parts of the region jostled to promote their particular local brand. In 2019, for example, Ulaanchab Municipality near Hohhot constructed the China Potato Capital Potato Museum (Klein 2020).

27. A report of this investigation was published in *Forum for Progress* (C. Qianjin luntan), the newspaper of the Chinese Peasants' and Workers' Democratic Party (C. Zhongguo Nonggong Minzhudang). This party is one of the eight officially recognized parties in the PRC, and thus a member of the CPPCC.

28. In a manner characteristic of the rescaling described in this chapter, media reports claim that the Gobi Red Camel Herding System is characteristic of the Urad tribe (C. Wulate *buluo*), while no mention is made of the Mongol nationality (Zhang Linhu 2020).

2. The Politics of Livestock Rituals

1. This item of clothing is favored by Xi Jinping and has become popular among Chinese officials, since it supposedly conveys a sense of frugality and efficiency (Gewirtz 2015).

2. This story was also documented by the American scholar and traveler Owen Lattimore when he passed along a caravan route through Alasha in the 1920s (1928, 140–41).

3. Others, however, suggested that *yellow* referred to the absence of grass along these routes, worn away by the comings and goings of travelers.

4. *Ovoo*s are found across the Mongolian cultural region and are related to similar Tibetan cairns known as *lab tse*. They are often found at high points and are the site of various rituals dedicated to the spirits of the land (Charleux and Smith 2021).

5. These ritual dances, an important part of Tibetan Buddhism, were listed as part of Alasha's intangible cultural heritage in 2008 (Huqun 2010).

6. Here Mönkh relied on a rather different understanding of culture from that of intangible cultural heritage. This was the version of culture that predominated in the early socialist period, typified by the Ulaan Möchir, the performance troupes sent to rural areas of Inner Mongolia to convey socialist messages through Mongolian songs, dances, and skits, "in order to enrich the herdsmen's monotonic [*sic*] life," in the words of a recent Chinese newspaper article (Siqi Chen 2021).

7. As Hürelbaatar Ujeed notes, "In Inner Mongolia's countryside, Buddhism is commonly viewed as part of traditional Mongolian culture, especially by younger generations" (2015, 282).

8. Culture stations constitute the most basic level of the state's cultural bureaucracy. In Alasha, they were established in 1981 and were initially responsible for organizing film screenings and providing reading material for herders (ALBG

2000, 863), though, as I show in this chapter, their role has changed in light of the current emphasis on cultural heritage.

9. Wolves had historically acted as a significant check on the growth of herds in Alasha. They were thus anathema to the post-1949 productivist state. In 1951 the banner government organized wolf-hunting teams in the various *bag*, and in one year alone six hundred wolves (and over forty buzzards) were killed (Shi Jifa 2001, 188). By 1957, wolves had been almost totally exterminated from the banner.

10. In Alasha, camels are occasionally consecrated in this way, though this was not the case in Khöövör, and this kind of consecration was not listed as part of Alasha's intangible cultural heritage. Crucially, camels that have been consecrated cannot be ridden, meaning that consecration would conflict with another element of camel culture.

11. The Mongolian *baigal* is not an exact equivalent of the English *nature*. It includes "animals, mountains, trees, grass weather and so forth as active subjects which have their own ways of being that affect humans, just as humans have ways of life that affect them" (Humphrey and Sneath 1999, 3). However, Baigal's usage of the term appeared to be much closer to *nature* as the passive object of human conservation.

12. As Eva Pils (2012) notes, the term *minjian shehui* evokes a long-standing distinction in China between officials (C. *guan*) and the people (C. *min*), rather than liberal notions of rights-bearing citizens.

13. In 2013 a confidential internal document (Document No. 9) circulated within the CCP, warning of seven dangerous Western ideas, one of which was the promotion of civil society (Froissart 2017).

3. Rural Sociality of Camel Husbandry

1. The abbreviated Chinese name was used even by Mongolian speakers.

2. These herds ranged in size from half a dozen to around sixty.

3. In some cases, donkeys were occasionally used for transportation. For example, Sarna, Batbagana's wife, sometimes rode one of these animals if her tasks took her away from the household, since she could not ride a motorbike. Donkeys were also sold to Han Chinese traders, catering to the intense demand from consumers in China for donkey meat and medicinal products made from donkey hide, demand that has seen donkey populations plummet across the world (Sulek 2022). Local Mongols regarded herding donkeys as rather embarrassing, and these animals were rarely mentioned. They were deemed to be dirty (M. *buzar*) and scorned as Han Chinese animals. On one occasion, after corralling six donkeys for sale, Batbagana made sure that we removed all the donkey dung from the pen, since it was dirty and could not be used for fuel, as camel dung was.

4. The consolidation of schools over the border in Mongolia has similarly led to women being absent from pastoral households for some of the year (Ahearn

2018). Following reforms in 2020, Mongolian-medium education has been significantly reduced in Inner Mongolian schools (Atwood 2020).

5. Across the border in Mongolia, the geographer Orhon Myadar (2021) has recently emphasized how during the Qing period a panoply of restrictions existed on the movement of Mongol herders and their access to pastureland. In Inner Mongolia, the divide-and-rule banner system implemented by the Qing forbade Mongol herders from moving outside the territory of their particular banner, resulting in numerous disputes among banners, which were arbitrated by the Lifanyuan (Ministry Ruling the Outer Provinces) (Yi Wang 2021, 37).

6. State ethnographers noted that in the deserts of what is now Alasha Right Banner, some herding families had acquired the right to rent and sell certain pastures on the edges of small lakes. Access to these pastures had originally been contingent upon duties at Buddhist temples but gradually took on the character of private property (IMAR EG 2009, 43).

7. Scholars disagree as to whether this was largely initiated by the peasants or imposed on them (Justin Lin 1988; Schmalzer 2016, 212).

8. This resulted in a dramatic increase in the number of herding households across Alasha. Some Mongol officials argue that if overstocking has become a problem in Alasha, it is because of this expansion of the herding population attendant upon Han Chinese settlement.

9. In some Tibetan regions of China, the sheep population declined as a result of decollectivization, since these animals were deemed hard to herd (Gaerrang 2019).

10. Similar arrangements were in place in other pastoral regions of China (Banks 2001; Wenjun Li and Lynn Huntsinger 2011).

11. A *mu* is a Chinese unit of land measurement equivalent to 666.67 square meters.

12. Much literature has focused on the challenges that rural-to-urban migrants in China face in obtaining urban registration (C. *hukou*) and the precariousness that results from this, and has thus tended to assume the desirability of having an urban *hukou* (e.g., Deng and Gustafsson 2014). However, some scholars have suggested that benefits associated with rural *hukou*, including the right to agricultural land and compensation for land requisition, have come to be regarded as increasingly valuable in recent decades (Chuanbo Chen and Cindy Fan 2016). In Alasha, many seemed to consider rural *hukou* more valuable than urban ones, since they came with an entitlement to payments for ecosystem services and apparently posed no barrier to the purchase of property in the city.

13. In Alasha, grass-livestock balance was also referred to as "limiting livestock according to grass" (C. *yicao dingxu*).

14. In 2013 Mönkhbayar said that one hundred meters of fencing cost around ¥300.

15. Similar rules have been described more recently in other pastoral areas of China (Banks 2001, 732).

16. It is rare for households to have spare motorbikes. Motorbikes became common in Alasha in the 1990s and were the main mode of transport for herding. However, when herders needed to travel over particularly sandy ground, they sometimes preferred to use camels. In the desert to the south of Khöövör, some herders also apparently used camels to round up their cattle, which were said to be scared of motorbikes. There was a gendered aspect to the use of motorbikes. Some older women, including Sarna, do not use them; if a task took her some distance from the household, she occasionally rode a donkey.

17. The Mongolian term *tsai* (tea) is used in Alasha to refer to various kinds of celebratory gathering, normally on a smaller scale than *nair*, and often for recently introduced celebrations, such as that held to mark a family moving into a new apartment in the city (M. *shin geriin tsai*).

18. Activities that are seen to produce red hot sociality in China include temple fairs and drinking games (Chau 2006) and gambling (Steinmüller 2011).

19. Analogous distinctions are made between different generations of Han settlers in Xinjiang (Joniak-Lüthi 2016; Byler 2021) and in Yunnan (Hansen 2005).

4. Techno-Pastoralism and Animal Labor

1. This publication was founded in 2009 in the province of Guizhou, in China's southwest, a region known for its remoteness and backwardness (Yu Luo et al. 2019). This journal has played an important role in promoting the concept of *yuanshengtai*.

2. Based on their research in Inner Asia in the 1990s, the anthropologists Caroline Humphrey and David Sneath (1999, 300) also argued that urbanization was not incompatible with mobile pastoralism. They sought to distinguish "urbanism (rural-urban integration)" from rural sedentarization.

3. The remaking of camel husbandry as heritage in Alasha has involved a particular emphasis on this object. At the Bayanhot Camel Naadam, for example, a giant fiberglass replica of a *buil* was placed next to the stands; the rebuilt *ovoo* at Bull Camel Mountain is crowned by an outsize replica *buil*; and just before I left the field I was given a *buil* made by Batbagana's nephew, who was an officially recognized cultural transmitter of the craft of camel tack. Even as herders lamented the fact that fewer and fewer camels were fitted with nose pegs, an index of their increasingly wild condition, these objects had achieved a new prominence thanks to the culture of display involved in heritage.

4. Scholars have argued that Mongols' ascription of personhood and subjectivity to all domestic animals is rooted in an animist cosmology (e.g., Fijn 2011; Stépanoff et al. 2017). In the case of the camel in Alasha, however, such ascription can be dependent on the presence of the *buil*. I came to appreciate this after hearing one herder bemoan the fact that the statues of camels erected in Bayanhot did

not have nose pegs, since camels without nose pegs "had no soul" (M. *sünsgüi*). This man's comment thus shows how herders in Alasha have come to distinguish between meat camels, objects that can be readily commodified, and the dwindling number of camels with nose pegs, which are still able to work with humans.

5. This is one of the reasons given for the taboo on camel slaughter, which I discuss in chapter 5.

6. Judd Kinzley (2018) has recently written of the transformation of Xinjiang from imperial frontier to national borderland, a process bound up with the extraction of natural resources and the attendant development of transportation infrastructure. Seen in this light, the nationalization of Alasha's salt deposits, once the property of the banner prince, was central to the shift from imperial frontier to national borderland. In the case of Alasha, however, there was a lag in the development of infrastructure, which meant that camels continued to be used to transport salt for several decades after 1949.

7. Before collectivization, herders were paid in cash for caravan work, known as a "foot fee" (C. *jiao fei*).

8. The new ritual paraphernalia of the socialist state could also be incorporated into the established rituals of the caravans. One former caravaneer, also a lama, recounts that when he first started working on the caravans, which must have been in the late 1950s, it was common for a Buddhist icon to be placed in one of the sacks carried by the last camel to protect the caravan. During the Cultural Revolution, this was replaced by a copy of Mao's Little Red Book (Mandoula 2019, 62).

9. To which Zhou Enlai is said to have modestly replied, "I'm merely a small donkey."

10. China today celebrates a panoply of spirits that are said to be subelements of the Spirit of the Chinese Nation (C. Zhonghua Minzu Jingshen). Many of these refer to achievements of the early socialist period, including "the spirit of the Long March" and "the spirit of the Revolutionary Base Area in the Taihang Mountains" (China International Publishing Group, "Getting to Know China through Keywords," china.org.cn/english/china_key_words/node_8020115 .html).

5. Commodifying Camels

1. For Alasha Mongols, it was the serving of boiled sheep's back and tail (M. *uuts*) that was the pinnacle of special occasions. Indeed, during my time in Alasha, I only ever encountered roasted whole sheep once, served during a banquet at this hotel. In Mongolia, roasting is generally reserved for game rather than the meat of livestock (Ruhlmann 2019). Serving whole animals is also exotic from the perspective of Han Chinese food cultures, which tend to involve meat being cut into smaller pieces in the kitchen and added to dishes before being served (Dunlop 2023).

2. Announcements from the Ministry of Agriculture in relation to the Payments for Ecosystem Services introduced nationally in 2011 include reference to "fine breed subsidies" (C. *pinzhong youliang buzhi*) as part of this policy (Nongye Bu 2011), but camel herders in Alasha had not received any.

3. Directly translated, 8337 referred to eight "establishs" (C. *jianshe*), three "exertions" (C. *zhuoli*), three "pay-more-attention-tos" (C. *geng jia zhuyi*), and seven "key works" (C. *zhongdian gongzuo*).

4. In 1985, the hair produced by one camel had the same value as the cashmere produced by eight goats (Zhou and Zhao 1985); by 2013, even after the price of cashmere had decreased significantly from its high point in the 1990s, the hair from one camel was slightly less valuable than the cashmere produced by two goats. In 2013 the price of cashmere in Bayantal was ¥320–40 per kilogram. Each goat produces on average 0.3 kilogram of cashmere. That year the price of camel hair was ¥50 per kilogram. Batbagan's camels produced around 2–3 kilograms of camel hair each. The following year the price fell to ¥40 per kilogram, and camel herders were complaining that few traders were visiting them to buy the product.

5. Demand for beef, seen as healthy, has increased significantly in recent years, in step with China's rising prosperity. In 2017, 7.94 million tons were consumed, and the country increasingly relies on imports to satisfy consumer demand (Chen Wang 2019).

6. We can compare this to the consumption of dogs in Tibetan regions, which began in 1960 with the formation of communes, having previously been unthinkable to Tibetans (Yeh 2013b, 85–86).

7. From the 1950s, the Production and Construction Corps was tasked with securing control over frontier areas by establishing military-agricultural settlements. In western Inner Mongolia its presence was linked to the perceived threat of Soviet invasion. The corps was disbanded in Inner Mongolia in the 1970s but continues to play a significant role in Xinjiang (Zhu and Blachford 2015).

8. See High (2013) for a discussion of this taboo in the context of Mongolia.

9. Recognizing the importance of lawfulness, I suggest, can help us understand the character of protests in 2020 against reforms to Mongolian-language education in the IMAR, which frequently made reference to constitutional provisions guaranteeing rights to minority-language education in China (Atwood 2020). It echoes the observations of other scholars of politics in China, who have drawn attention, for instance, to forms of "rightful resistance" (O'Brien 1996) that proclaim loyalty to the established principles and legitimating myths of the state.

6. Dairy Frontiers

1. According to Emilia Sulek (2019), in Tibetan areas, refraining from milking and thus leaving more for the calves is regarded as morally virtuous. Milking is an

arduous physical task and often leads to repetitive strain problems for women in Mongolian regions (Ahearn 2021).

2. This compares to somewhere between twenty-two and forty liters for a Holstein cow, and six to seven liters for a dromedary (Smits et al. 2023).

3. Qi Ruona, pers. comm.

4. *I Love Inventing* episodes can be found at http://tv.cctv.com/lm/wafm/.

5. Various versions of the machine were available, at different price points. The most expensive model, which included a fridge as well as built-in speakers that played music to soothe the camel, sold for ¥6,800. The state offers a range of subsidies of at least 50 percent, according to Tömör.

6. In recent years Chinese companies have also apparently attempted to source camel milk powder from Rajasthan in India (Ilse Köhler-Rollefson, pers. comm.).

Conclusion

1. If this were indeed a wild camel, cross-breeding would have been illegal, given this extremely rare animal's protected status. Wild camels are genetically distinct from domestic camels. Only around one thousand individuals survive in the wild, in northwest China and Mongolia. Apparently such hybridization practices were not unknown: one scientist at the Camel Research Institute told me that there were plans to institute genetic testing for race camels to screen for such hybrids and ensure fair competition.

References

52 Hezi Shiyanshi. 2021. "'Xie Dajiao' chehuo beihou: Alashan luotuo weisha sanyang er bu juanyang? Jiu bu pa hui diu?" (The background to 'Big foot' Xie's car crash: why are Alasha's camels free range? Don't they get lost?). *Bajiahao.* August 12. https://baijiahao.baidu.com/s?id=17078580735 96700859.

Abramson, Marc S. 2003. "Deep Eyes and High Noses: Physiognomy and the Depiction of Barbarians in Tang." In *Political Frontiers, Ethnic Boundaries and Human Geographies in Chinese History,* edited by Nicola di Cosmo and Don J. Wyatt, 119–59. London: RoutledgeCurzon.

Adams, Vincanne, Michelle Murphy, and Adele E. Clarke. 2009. "Anticipation: Technoscience, Life, Affect, Temporality." *Subjectivity* 28:246–65.

Agrawal, Arun. 2005. *Environmentality: Technologies of Government and the Making of Subjects.* Durham, NC: Duke University Press.

Ahearn, Ariell. 2018. "Winters without Women: Social Change, Split Households, and Gendered Labour in Rural Mongolia." *Gender, Place, and Culture* 25 (3):399–415.

———. 2021. "Milk and Human-Livestock Relations in Contemporary Mongolia." In *Socialist and Post-Socialist Mongolia: Nation, Identity and Culture,* edited by Simon Wickhamsmith and Philip P. Marzluf, 239–56. Abingdon: Routledge.

Alashan Meng Luotuo Kexue Yuanjiusuo (Alasha League Camel Science Institute). 1991. "Alashan shuangfengtuo ben pinzhong xuanyu shiyan baogao" (Alasha Bactrian camel selective breeding report). *Zhongguo xumu zazhi* (China livestock magazine) 27 (2):28–30.

Alashan Youqi Rong Meiti Zhongxin (Alasha Right Banner Fusion Media Center). 2020. "Alashan youqi: 'Tuo' qi xiaokang meng" (Alasha right banner: Realizing the dream of moderate prosperity through camels). Alashan Meng

Xingzheng Gongshu (Alasha League Administrative Office), December 3. https://www.als.gov.cn/art/2020/12/3/art_5_343471.html.

ALBG (Alasha Left Banner Gazetteer Editorial Committee). 2000. *Alashan zuoqi zhi* (Alasha left banner gazetteer). Hohhot: Neimenggu Jiaoyu Chubanshe (Inner Mongolia Publishing House).

An Mönkh (Mengke) 2005. *Alashanii Islam Shütlegt Mongolchuud* (The Muslim Mongols of Alasha). Hohhot: Neimenggu Renmin Chubanshe (Inner Mongolia People's Publishing House).

———. 2009. *Mengguzu Musilin* (The Muslim Mongols). Beijing: Zhongguo Wenlian Chubanshe (China Federation of Literary and Art Circles Publishing House).

Anderson, David G., Jan P. L. Loovers, Sara A. Schroer, and Robert P. Wishert. 2017. "Architectures of Domestication: On Emplacing Human-Animal Relations in the North." *Journal of the Royal Anthropological Institute* 23 (2):398–416.

Anderson, Virginia D. 2004. *Creatures of Empire: How Domestic Animals Transformed Early America*. Oxford: Oxford University Press.

Angé, Olivia, and David Berliner, eds. 2021. *Ecological Nostalgias: Memory, Affect, and Creativity in Times of Ecological Upheavals*. New York: Berghahn.

Atwood, Christopher P. 1996. "Buddhism and Popular Religion in Mongolian Religion: A Reexamination of the Fire Cult." *History of Religions* 36 (2):112–39.

———. 2020. "Bilingual Education in Inner Mongolia: An Explainer." *Made in China Journal*, August 30. https://madeinchinajournal.com/2020/08/30/bilingual-education-in-inner-mongolia-an-explainer/.

Ayoub, Mohammed A., Abdul Rasheed Palakkott, Arshida Ashraf, and Rabah Iratni. 2018. "The Molecular Basis of the Anti-Diabetic Properties of Camel Milk." *Diabetes Research and Clinical Practice* 146:305–12.

Ba Xuan. 2005. "'Hetao Wenhua' de yanbian ji qi gainian he neihan" (The evolution and contents of 'Hetao Culture'). *Guangming ribao* (Brightness daily), August 24. https://news.sina.com.cn/o/2005-08-24/04596765819s.shtml.

Baioud, Gegentuul. 2022. "Mongolian Language Rights and Linguistic Nationalism in China." Paper presented at the Cambridge Mongolia Forum, December 16.

———. 2023. "From Diversity to Homogeneity: Vacillating Signifieds in Propaganda Texts in Inner Mongolia." *Inner Asia* 25:39–48.

Baioud, Gegentuul, and Cholmon Khuanuud. 2022. "Linguistic Purism as Resistance to Colonization." *Journal of Sociolinguistics* 26 (3):315–34.

Banks, Tony. 2001. "Property Rights and the Environment in Pastoral China." *Development and Change* 32 (4):717–40.

———. 2003. "Property Rights Reform in Rangeland China: Dilemmas on the Road to the Household Ranch." *World Development* 31 (12):2129–42.

Baranovitch, Nimrod. 2016a. "Ecological Degradation and Endangered Ethnicities: China's Minority Environmental Discourses as Manifested in Popular Songs." *Journal of Asian Studies* 75 (1):181–205.

———. 2016b. "The 2011 Protests in Inner Mongolia: An Ethno-Environmental Perspective." *China Quarterly* 225:213–33.

———. 2021. "The Ethnic Ecocritical Animal: Animal Protagonists and Ethnic Environmentalism in Contemporary Sino-Mongolian Art and Literature." *Modern Asian Studies* 55 (3):1–49.

Barnett, Robert, and Hildegard Diemberger. 2008. "Editorial Introduction." *Inner Asia* 10 (1):1–4.

Barua, Maan. 2016. "Lively Commodities and Encounter Value." *Environment and Planning D: Society and Space* 34 (4):725–44.

———. 2017. "Nonhuman Labour, Encounter Value, Spectacular Accumulation: The Geographies of a Lively Commodity." *Transactions of the Institute of British Geographers* 42 (2):274–88.

Bassi, Marco. 2017. "Pastoralists are Peoples: Key Issues in Advocacy and the Emergence of Pastoralists' Rights." *Nomadic Peoples* 21 (1):4–33.

Batuchulu. 2017. "Guanyu kaituo xin de lüyou xianlu de jianyi" (Suggestion regarding the creation of new tourism routes). In Batuchulu and Siqinbielige, *Silu tuoling*, 93–95.

Batuchulu and Siqinbielige, eds. 2017. *Silu tuoling* (The Silk Road camel bell). Bayanhot: *Alashan Meng Zhengxie Luotuo Wenhua Yanjiu Cujinhui* (Alasha League CPPCC Committee for the Promotion of Camel Culture Research) and *Alashan Meng Zhengxie Wenshi Xuexi Weiyuanhui* (Alasha League CPPCC Committee for the Study of Literature and History).

Bayar, Nasan. 2002. "History and Its Televising: Events and Narratives of the Hoshuud Mongols in Modern China." *Inner Asia* 4:241–76.

———. 2014a. "A Discourse of Civilization/Culture and Nation/Ethnicity from the Perspective of Inner Mongolia, China." *Asian Ethnicity* 15 (4):439–57.

———. 2014b. "Nation-Building, Ethnicity and Natural Resources: The Perspective of an Inner Mongolian Coal Truck Driver across the China-Mongolia Border." *Inner Asia* 16:377–91.

Bayindai. 2007. "Gongzuo zongjie nianbao" (Annual work report). Accessed March 30, 2021. http://www.china-camel.com/index.php?s=/articles/654.html.

BBC. 2013. "China Officials Seize 213 Bear Paws." *BBC News*, June 18. https://www.bbc.co.uk/news/world-asia-china-22949409.

———. 2015. "China Inner Mongolia Attack Due to Border Dispute, Police Say." *BBC News*, December 7. https://www.bbc.co.uk/news/world-asia-china-35024043.

Beckert, Sven, Ulbe Bosma, Mindi Schneider, and Eric Vanhaute. 2021.

"Commodity Frontiers and the Transformation of the Global Countryside: A Research Agenda." *Journal of Global History* 16 (3):435–50.

Beeson, Mark. 2010. "The Coming of Environmental Authoritarianism." *Environmental Politics* 19 (2):276–94.

Bello, David A. 2016. *Across Forest, Steppe, and Mountain: Environment, Identity, and Empire in Qing China's Borderlands.* Cambridge: Cambridge University Press.

Bessire, Lucas. 2021. *Running Out: In Search of Water on the High Plains.* Princeton, NJ: Princeton University Press.

Biermann, Christine, and Robert M. Anderson. 2017. "Conservation, Biopolitics, and the Governance of Life and Death." *Geography Compass* 11 (10):1–13.

Billé, Franck. 2009. "Cooking the Mongols / Feeding the Han: Dietary and Ethnic Intersections in Inner Mongolia." *Inner Asia* 11 (2):205–30.

Bindi, Letizia, ed. 2022. *Grazing Communities: Pastoralism on the Move and Biocultural Heritage Frictions.* New York: Berghahn.

Blakie, Piers M., and Joshua S. S. Muldavin. 2004. "Upstream, Downstream, China, India: The Politics of Environment in the Himalayan Region." *Annals of the Association of American Geographers* 94 (3):520–48.

Blumenfield, Tani, and Helaine Silverman, eds. 2013. *Cultural Heritage Politics in China.* New York: Springer.

Borchigud, Wurlig. 1996. "Transgressing Ethnic and National Boundaries: Contemporary 'Inner Mongolian' Identities in China." In *Negotiating Ethnicities in China and Taiwan,* edited by Melissa J. Brown, 160–82. Berkeley: University of California Institute for East Asian Studies Center for Chinese Studies.

Borjigin, Burensain. 2004. "The Complex Structure of Ethnic Conflict in the Frontier: Through the Debates around the 'Jindandao Incident' in 1891." *Inner Asia* 6:41–60.

——. 2017. *The Agricultural Mongols: Land Reclamation and the Formation of Mongolian Village Society in Modern China.* Translated by Thomas White. Yokohama: Shumpusha.

Boullenois, Camille. 2020. "Poverty Alleviation in China: The Rise of State-Sponsored Corporate Paternalism." *China Perspectives* 3:47–56.

Braester, Yomi. 2016. "Traces of the Future: Beijing's Politics of Emergence." In *Ghost Protocol: Development and Displacement in Global China,* edited by Carlos Rojas and Ralph A. Litzinger, 15–35. Durham: Duke University Press.

Braun, Bruce P. 2014. "A New Urban Dispositif? Governing Life in an Age of Climate Change." *Environment and Planning D: Society and Space* 32:49–64.

Bristley, Joseph. 2020. "Scale and Number: Framing an Ideology of Pastoral Plenty in Rural Mongolia." *Social Analysis* 64 (1):63–79.

Brosius, J. Peter. 1997. "Endangered Forest, Endangered People: Environmentalist Representations of Indigenous Knowledge." *Human Ecology* 25 (1):47–69.

Brown, Kerry. 2006. *The Purge of the Inner Mongolian People's Party in the Chinese*

Cultural Revolution, 1967–69: A Function of Language, Power, and Violence. Folkestone: Global Oriental.

———. 2018. "The Anti-Corruption Struggle in Xi Jinping's China: An Alternative Political Narrative." *Asian Affairs* 49 (1):1–10.

Bulag, Uradyn E. 2000. "From Inequality to Difference: Colonial Contradictions of Class and Ethnicity in 'Socialist' China." *Cultural Studies* 3–4:531–61.

———. 2002a. "From Yeke-Juu League to Ordos Municipality: Settler Colonialism and Alter/Native Urbanization in Inner Mongolia." *Provincial China* 7 (2):196–234.

———. 2002b. *The Mongols at China's Edge: History and the Politics of National Unity.* Lanham, MD: Rowman and Littlefield.

———. 2004a. "Editorial Introduction: Hybridity and Nomadology in Inner Asia." *Inner Asia* 6:1–4.

———. 2004b. "Inner Mongolia: The Dialectics of Colonization and Ethnicity-Building." In *Governing China's Multiethnic Frontiers*, edited by Morris Rossabi, 84–116. Seattle: University of Washington Press.

———. 2007. "From Empire to Nation: The Demise of Buddhism in Inner Mongolia." In *The Mongolia-Tibet Interface: Opening New Research Terrains in Inner Asia*, edited by Uradyn E. Bulag and Hildegard G. M. Diemberger, 19–57. Leiden: Brill.

———. 2008. "Contesting the Words that Wound: Ethnicity and the Politics of Sentiment in China." *Inner Asia* 10 (1):87–111.

———. 2010. *Collaborative Nationalism: The Politics of Friendship on China's Mongolian Frontier.* Lanham, MD: Rowman and Littlefield.

———. 2017. "Clashes of Administrative Nationalisms: Banners and Leagues vs. Counties and Provinces in Inner Mongolia." In *Managing Frontiers in Qing China: The Lifanyuan and Libu Revisited*, edited by Dittmar Schorkowitz and Ning Chia, 349–88. Leiden: Brill.

———. 2020. "Dying for the Mother Tongue: Why Have People in Inner Mongolia Recently Taken Their Lives?" *Index on Censorship* 49 (4):49–51.

———. 2021. "Minority Nationalities as Frankenstein's Monsters? Reshaping 'the Chinese Nation' and China's Quest to Become a 'Normal Country.'" *China Journal* 86:46–67.

Bulag, Uradyn E., and Hildegard G. M. Diemberger, eds. 2007. *The Mongolia-Tibet Interface: Opening New Research Terrains in Inner Asia.* Leiden: Brill.

Bum, Tsering. 2018. "Translating Ecological Migration Policy: A Conjunctural Analysis of Tibetan Pastoralist Resettlement in China." *Critical Asian Studies* 50 (4):518–36.

Burger, Pamela A., Elena Ciani, and Bernard Faye. 2019. "Old World Camels in a Modern World: A Balancing Act between Conservation and Genetic Improvement." *Animal Genetics* 50 (6):598–612.

Byler, D. 2021. *Terror Capitalism: Uyghur Dispossession and Masculinity in a Chinese City*. Durham: Duke University Press.

Cassidy, Rebecca. 2009. "The Horse, the Kyrgyz Horse, and the 'Kyrgyz Horse.'" *Anthropology Today* 25 (1):12–15.

Chabros, Krystyna. 1992. *Beckoning Fortune: A Study of the Mongol Dalalya Ritual*. Wiesbaden: Harrassowitz.

Chao, Emily. 1996. "Hegemony, Agency, and Re-presenting the Past: The Invention of Dongba Culture among the Naxi of Southwest China." In *Negotiating Ethnicities in China and Taiwa*, edited by Melissa J. Brown, 208–39. Berkeley: University of California Institute for East Asian Studies Center for Chinese Studies.

Charleux, Isabelle. 2002. "Padmasambhava's Travel to the North: The Pilgrimage to the Monastery of the Caves and the Old Schools of Tibetan Buddhism in Mongolia." *Central Asiatic Journal* 46 (2):168–232.

Charleux, Isabelle, and Marissa J. Smith. 2021. "Points of Transition: Ovoo and the Ritual Remaking of Religious, Ecological, and Historical Politics in Inner Asia." *Études mongoles et sibériennes centrasiatiques et tibétaines* 52:5–10.

Chau, Adam Y. 2006. *Miraculous Response: Doing Popular Religion in Contemporary China*. Palo Alto, CA: Stanford University Press.

———, ed. 2011. *Religion in Contemporary China: Revitalization and Innovation*. Abingdon: Routledge.

Chen, Jie. 2015. "Death of the Desert." *China Dialogue*, July 14. https://chinadialogue.net/en/pollution/8015-death-of-the-desert/.

Chen, Chuanbo, and C. Cindy Fan. 2016. "China's Hukou Puzzle: Why Don't Rural Migrants Want Urban Hukou?" *China Review* 16 (3):9–39.

Chen, Nancy N. 2010. "Feeding the Nation: Chinese Biotechnology and Genetically Modified Foods." In *Asian Biotech: Ethics and Communities of Fate*, edited by Charis Thompson and Kaushik Sunder Rajan, 81–94. Durham: Duke University Press.

———. 2020. "Making Memories: Chinese Foodscapes, Medicinal Foods, and Generational Eating." *Memory Studies* 13 (5):820–32.

Chen, Siqi. 2021. "Wulanmuqi Art Troupe Brings Colorful Entertainment for Herdsmen." *Shenzhen Daily*, March 26. http://www.szdaily.com/content/2021-03/26/content_24077153.htm.

Cheng, T. J., Uradyn E. Bulag, and Mark Selden. 2023. *A Chinese Rebel beyond the Great Wall: The Cultural Revolution and Ethnic Pogrom in Inner Mongolia*. Chicago: University of Chicago Press.

China Daily. 2006. "Glass of Milk a Day, Makes Premier Happy." March 26. http://www.chinadaily.com.cn/china/2006-04/26/content_577182.htm.

Chinese National Committee for Man and the Biosphere. 2008. *Ren yu shengwuquan* (Man and the biosphere).

Chio, Jenny. 2014. *A Landscape of Travel: The Work of Tourism in Rural Ethnic China*. Seattle: University of Washington Press.

Choy, Tim. 2011. *Ecologies of Comparison: An Ethnography of Endangerment in Hong Kong*. Durham: Duke University Press.

Chuluu. 2013. *Torait nutagiin temeen soyol* (The camel culture of poplar country). Alasha League CPPCC.

Christmas, Sakura. 2017. "An Imperial Sheep Chase." *China Dialogue*, April 25. https://chinadialogue.net/en/nature/9743-an-imperial-sheep-chase/.

———. 2019. "Japanese Imperialism and Environmental Disease on a Soy Frontier." *Journal of Asian Studies* 78 (4):809–36.

Chun, Lin. 2019. "Mass Line." In *Afterlives of Communism: Political Concepts from Mao to Xi,* edited by Christian Sorace, Ivan Franceschini, and Nicholas Loubere, 121–26. Acton: Australia National University and Verso.

Clarke-Sather, Afton. 2020. "'But We Are the Most Backward': Hierarchical Categorization of Modernity in Contemporary Chinese National Identity." *Political Geography* 83:1–10

Cliff, Tom. 2016. *Oil and Water: Being Han in Xinjiang*. Chicago: University of Chicago Press.

Conklin, Beth A., and Laura R. Graham. 1995. "The Shifting Middle Ground: Amazonian Indians and Eco-Politics." *American Anthropologist* 97 (4):695–710.

Cons, Jason, and Michael Eilenberg. 2019. "Introduction: On the New Politics of Margins in Asia." In *Frontier Assemblages: The Emergent Politics of Resource Frontiers in Asia*, edited by Jason Cons and Michael Eilenberg, 1–18. Hoboken, NJ: Wiley.

Conte, Thomas J., and Bryan Tilt. 2014. "The Effects of China's Grassland Contract Policy on Pastoralists' Attitudes to Cooperation in an Inner Mongolia." *Human Ecology* 42:836–46.

Cormack, Zoe. 2016. "The Promotion of Pastoralist Heritage and Alternative 'Visions' for the Future of Northern Kenya." *Journal of Eastern African Studies* 10 (3):548–67.

Crosby, Alfred W. 1972. *The Columbian Exchange: Biological and Cultural Consequences of 1492*. Westport, CT: Greenwood.

Cui Hong. 2002. "'Luotuo zhi xiang': Huangjing ehua Alashan luotuo zai kuqi" (Environmental degradation in camel country: Alasha's camels are weeping). *Beijing chenbao* (Beijing morning news), June 18. http://news.sina.com.cn /c/2002-06-18/0447608323.html.

Cusworth, George, Jamie Lorimer, Jeremy Brice, and Tara Garnett. 2022. "Green Rebranding: Regenerative Agriculture, Future-Pasts, and the Naturalization of Livestock." *Transactions of the Institute of British Geographers* 47 (4):1009–27.

Dalintai, Naren Gauwa, Li Yanbo, J. Enkhee, and Liu Shurun. 2012. "The New *Otor*: Risk Management in a Desert Grassland." In *Restoring Community Connections to the Land: Building Resilience through Community-Based Rangeland*

Management in China and Mongolia, edited by María Fernández-Giménez, Xiaoyi Wang, B. Batkhishig, Julia A. Klein, and Robin S. Reid, 93–112. Wallingford: CABI.

Dalintai and Zheng Yisheng. 2010. *Muqu yu shichang: Mumin jingjixue* (Pastoral areas and the market: Herder economics). Beijing: Shehui Kexue Wenxian Chubanshe (Social Sciences Academic Press).

Davis, Diana K. 2016. "Deserts and Drylands before the Age of Desertification." In *The End of Desertification?*, edited by Roy H. Behnke and Michael Mortimer, 203–23. Berlin: Springer.

de la Cadena, Marisol. 2010. "Indigenous Cosmopolitics in the Andes: Conceptual Reflections beyond 'Politics.'" *Cultural Anthropology* 25:334–70.

Dean, Kenneth. 2003. "Local Communal Religion in Contemporary South-East China." *China Journal* 174:338–58.

Delcore, Henry D. 2004. "Symbolic Politics or Generification? The Ambivalent Implications of Tree Ordinations in the Thai Environmental Movement." *Journal of Political Ecology* 11:1–30.

DeMare, Brian. 2019. *Land Wars: The Story of China's Agrarian Revolution*. Palo Alto, CA: Stanford University Press.

Deng, Quheng, and Bjorn Gustafsson. 2014. "The *Hukou* Converters—China's Lesser Known Rural to Urban Migrants." *Journal of Contemporary China* 23 (88):657–79.

Denton, Kirk A. 2012. "Yan'an as a Site of Memory in Socialist and Postsocialist China." In *Places of Memory in Modern China: History, Politics, Identity*, edited by Mark Andre Matten, 233–81. Leiden: Brill.

D'Evelyn, Charlotte. 2018. "Grasping Intangible Heritage and Reimagining Inner Mongolia: Folk-Artist Albums and a New Logic for Musical Representation in China." *Journal of Folklore Research* 55 (1):21–48.

Ding Mingjun. 2006. *Zhongguo bianyuan musilin zuqun de renleixue kaocha* (Anthropological investigations into Muslim ethnic groups at the margins of China). Yinchuan: Ningxia Renmin Chubanshe (Ningxia People's Publishing House).

Ding, Pingjun. 2008. *Gazing at the Cradle of the Dust Storm: A Photo Story of Humans and the Environment in Alxa*. Beijing: Academy Press.

Dirlik, Arif. 2006. "Timespace, Social Space, and the Question of Chinese Culture." *Monumenta Serica* 54 (1):417–33.

Driessen, Miriam. 2018. "Rural Voids." *Public Culture* 30 (1):61–84.

DuBois, Thomas, and Alicia Gao. 2017. "Big Meat: The Rise and Impact of Mega-Farming in China's Beef, Sheep and Dairy Industries." *Asia-Pacific Journal: Japan Focus* 15 (17):1–20.

Dumont, Aurore. 2021. "Turning Indigenous Sacred Sites into Intangible Heritage: Authority Figures and Ritual Appropriation in Inner Mongolia." *China Perspectives* 3:19–28.

Dunlop, Fuschia. 2023. *Invitation to a Banquet: The Story of Chinese Food.* London: Penguin.

Dwyer, Mark J., and Kirill Istomin. 2008. "Theories of Nomadic Movement: A New Theoretical Approach for Understanding the Movement Decisions of Nenets and Komi Reindeer Herders." *Human Ecology* 36:521–33.

Dzenovska, Dace. 2020. "Emptiness: Capitalism without People in the Latvian Countryside." *American Ethnologist* 47 (1):10–26.

Economist. 2019. "As China Puts on Weight, Type-2 Diabetes Is Soaring." December 12.

Eilenberg, Michael. 2014. "Frontier Constellations: Agrarian Expansion and Sovereignty on the Indonesian-Malaysian Border." *Journal of Peasant Studies* 41 (2):157–82.

Elliott, Mark. 2015. "The Case of the Missing Indigene: Debate over a 'Second-Generaton' Ethnic Policy." *China Journal* 73:186–213.

Elverskog, Johan. 2006. *Our Great Qing: The Mongols, Buddhism and the State in Late Imperial China.* Honolulu: University of Hawaii Press.

Empson, Rebecca. 2011. *Harnessing Fortune: Personhood, Memory, and Place in Mongolia.* Oxford: Oxford University Press.

———. 2012. "The Dangers of Excess: Accumulating and Dispersing Fortune in Mongolia." *Social Analysis* 56 (1):1–16.

Evans, Harriet, and Michael Rowlands. 2021. "Grassroots Values: Issues, Questions and Perspectives on Local Heritage." In *Grassroots Values and Local Cultural Heritage in China,* edited by Harriet Evans and Michael Rowlands, 1–16. Lanham: Lexington.

Evans-Pritchard, Edward. 1940. *The Nuer: A Description of the Modes of Livelihood and Political Institutions of a Nilotic People.* Oxford: Clarendon Press.

Fairhead, James, Melissa Leach, and Ian Scoones. 2012. "Green Grabbing: A New Appropriation of Nature." *Journal of Peasant Studies* 39 (2):237–61.

FAO (Commission on Genetic Resources for Food and Agriculture, Food and Agriculture Organization of the United Nations). 2007. *Global Plan of Action for Animal Genetic Resources and the Interlaken Declaration.* Rome: FAO.

Ferguson, James. 1985. "The Bovine Mystique: Power, Property, and Livestock in Rural Lesotho." *Man* 20 (4):647–74.

———. 2011. "Toward a Left Art of Government: From 'Foucauldian Critique' to Foucauldian Politics." *History of the Human Sciences* 24 (4):61–68.

Ferry, Elizabeth E., and Mandana E. Limbert, eds. 2008. *Timely Assets: The Politics of Resources and Their Temporalities.* Santa Fe, NM: School for Advanced Research.

Ficek, Rosa E. 2019. "Cattle, Capital, Colonization: Tracking Creatures of the Anthropocene In and Out of Human Projects." *Current Anthropology* 60 (S20):S260–71.

Fijn, Natasha. 2011. *Living with Herds: Human-Animal Coexistence in Mongolia.* Cambridge: Cambridge University Press.

Finnegan, Diarmid A. 2008. "The Spatial Turn: Geographical Approaches in the History of Science." *Journal of the History of Biology* 41:369–88.

Fischer, John R. 2015. *Cattle Colonialism: An Environmental History of the Conquest of California and Hawai'i.* Chapel Hill: University of North Carolina Press.

Fiskesjö, Magnus. 2006. "Rescuing the Empire: Chinese Nation-Building in the Twentieth Century." *European Journal of East Asian Studies* 5 (1):15–44.

———. 2011. "The Animal Other: China's Barbarians and Their Renaming in the Twentieth Century." *Social Text* 29 (4):57–79.

———. 2017. "China's Animal Neighbours." In *The Art of Neighbouring: Making Relations across China's Borders*, edited by Martin Saxer and Juan Zhang, 223–36. Amsterdam: Amsterdam University Press.

Foster, John B. 2017. "The Earth-System Crisis and Ecological Civilization: A Marxian View." *International Critical Thought* 7 (4):439–58.

Franceschini, Ivan, and Nicholas Loubere. 2022. *Global China as Method.* Cambridge: Cambridge University Press.

Frank, Mark E. 2018. "Hacking the Yak: The Chinese Effort to Improve a Tibetan Animal in the Early Twentieth Century." *East Asian Science, Technology, and Medicine* 48:17–48.

Franklin, Sarah. 2007. *Dolly Mixtures: The Remaking of Genealogy.* Durham: Duke University Press.

Fraser, Richard. 2020. "Cultural Heritage, Ethnic Tourism, and Minority-State Relations amongst the Orochen in North-East China." *International Journal of Heritage Studies* 26 (2):178–200.

Froissart, Chloé. 2017. "Changing Patterns of Chinese Civil Society: Comparing the Hu-Wen and Xi Jinping Eras." In *Routledge Handbook of the Chinese Communist Party*, edited by Willy Wo-Lap Lam, 352–71. Abingdon: Routledge.

Fu, Li. 2016. "The Politics of Everyday Subsistence Strategies and Hidden Resistance among Herders in Inner Mongolia." *China Journal* 76:63–77.

Gaerrrang (Kabzung). 2015. "Development as Entangled Knot: The Case of the Slaughter Renunciation Movement in Tibet, China." *Journal of Asian Studies* 74 (4):927–51.

———. 2019. "The Case of the Disappearance of Tibetan Sheep from the Village of Charo in the Eastern Tibetan Plateau: Tibetan Pastoralists' Decisions, Economic Calculations, and Religious Beliefs." *Études Mongoles et Sibériennes, Centrasiatiques et Tibétaines* 50:1–18.

Gao, Bingzhong 2014. "How Does Superstition Become Intangible Cultural Heritage in Postsocialist China?" *positions: asia critique* 22 (3):551–72.

Gare Arran. 2012. "China and the Struggle for Ecological Civilization." *Capitalism Nature Socialism* 23 (4):10–26.

Gewirtz, Julian B. 2015. "Why Is This Xi Jinping's Favorite Item of Clothing?" *New Yorker*, May 12.

Gilley, Bruce. 2012. "Authoritarian Environmentalism and China's Response to Climate Change." *Environmental Politics* 21 (2):287–307.

Gilroy, Paul. 2004. *After Empire: Melancholia or Convivial Culture?* London: Routledge.

Gladney, Dru C. 1990. "The Ethnogenesis of the Uighur." *Central Asian Survey* 9 (1):1–28.

———. 1994. "Representing Nationality in China: Reconfiguring Majority/Minority Identities." *Journal of Asian Studies* 53 (1):92–123.

Gongbuzeren, Minghao Zhuang, and Wenjun Li. 2016. "Market-Based Grazing Land Transfers and Customary Institutions in the Management of Rangelands: Two Case Studies on the Qinghai-Tibetan Plateau." *Land Use Policy* 57 (30):287–95.

Gongbuzeren, Lynn Huntsinger, and Wenjun Li. 2018. "Rebuilding Pastoral Socio-Ecological Resilience on the Qinghai-Tibetan Plateau in Response to Changes in Policy, Economics, and Climate." *Ecology and Society* 23 (2):21.

Gongbuzeren, Wenjun Li, and Yupei Lai. 2021. "The Role of Community Cooperative Institutions in Building Rural-Urban Linkages under Urbanization of Pastoral Regions in China." *Frontiers in Sustainable Food Systems* 5:1–9.

Goodman, David. 2002. "The Politics of the West: Equality, Nation-Building, and Colonisation." *Provincial China* 7 (2):127–50.

Goossaert, Vincent, and David A. Palmer. 2010. *The Religious Question in Modern China*. Chicago: University of Chicago Press.

Govindrajan, Radikha. 2018. *Animal Intimacies: Interspecies Relatedness in India's Central Himalayas*. Chicago: University of Chicago Press.

Grant, Andrew. 2017. "'Don't Discriminate against Minority Nationalities': Practising Tibetan Ethnicity on Social Media." *Asian Ethnicity* 18 (3):371–86.

———. 2018. "China's Double Body: Infrastructure Routes and the Mapping of China's Nation-State and Civilization-State." *Eurasian Geography and Economics* 59 (3–4):378–407.

Greenhalgh, Susan. 2020. "Governing through Science: The Anthropology of Science and Technology in Contemporary China." In *Can Science and Technology Save China?*, edited by Susan Greenhalgh and Li Zhang, 1–24. Ithaca, NY: Cornell University Press.

Griffiths, Michael B., and Jesper Zeuthen. 2014. "Bittersweet China: New Discourses of Hardship and Social Organization." *Journal of Current Chinese Affairs* 43 (4):143–74.

Gu, Yi. 2020. *Chinese Ways of Seeing and Open-Air Painting*. Cambridge, MA: Harvard University Asia Centre.

Guojia Linye he Caoyuan Ju (National Forest and Grassland Administration). 2021. "Guanyu jin yi bu guifan caoyuan weilan jianshe zhidao yijian"

(Guidance and suggestions on further regularizing the erection of fencing on the grasslands). January 21. http://lcj.nmg.gov.cn/xxgk/tzgg_7157/202102 /t20210223_971948.html.

Guowuyuan (State Council). 2000. "Guowuyuan guanyu jinzhi caiji he xiaoshou facai zhizhi lan wa gancao he mahuangcao youguan wenti de tongzhi" (State Council notice regarding the ban on the collection and sale of *facai* and the prevention of indiscriminate digging of licorice root and ephedra). June 14. http://www.gov.cn/gongbao/content/2000/content_60307.htm.

Gupta, Akhil, and James Ferguson. 1997. "Discipline and Practice: The 'Field' as Site, Method, and Location in Anthropology." In *Anthropological Locations: Boundaries and Grounds of a Fieldsite,* edited by Akhil Gupta and James Ferguson, 1–46. Berkeley: University of California Press.

———. 2002. "Spatializing States: Toward an Ethnography of Neoliberal Governmentality." *American Ethnologist* 29 (4):981–1002.

Gyal, Huatse. 2019. "'I Am Concerned with the Future of My Children': The Project Economy and Shifting Views of Education in a Tibetan Pastoral Community." *Critical Asian Studies* 51 (1):12–30.

Han, Enze. 2011. "The Dog That Hasn't Barked: Assimilation and Resistance in Inner Mongolia, China." *Asian Ethnicity* 12 (1):55–75.

Han Niantong, ed. 2011a. *Caoyuan de luoji 1: Jingti xin mingyi xia de nonggeng kuangzhang* (The logic of the grasslands, vol. 1, Guarding against agricultural expansion under a new name). Beijing: Beijing Kexue Jishu Chubanshe (Beijing Science and Technology Publishing House).

———. 2011b. *Caoyuan de luoji 2: Shunying yu shidu: Youmu wenming de weilai jiazhi* (The logic of the grasslands, vol. 2, Adapted and appropriate: The future value of nomadic civilization). Beijing: Beijing Kexue Jishu Chubanshe (Beijing Science and Technology Publishing House).

———. 2011c. *Caoyuan de luoji 3: Tanxun linglei shichang zhidu* (The logic of the grasslands, vol. 3, In search of an alternative market system). Beijing: Beijing Kexue Jishu Chubanshe (Beijing Science and Technology Publishing House).

———. 2011d. *Caoyuan de luoji 4: Guojia shengtai xiangmu you lai yu mumin neisheng dongli* (The logic of the grasslands, vol. 4, China's ecological projects depend on the motivation of herders themselves). Beijing: Beijing Kexue Jishu Chubanshe (Beijing Science and Technology Publishing House).

Hann, Chris M. 1991. "Ethnic Games in Xinjiang: Anthropological Approaches." In *Cultural Change and Continuity in Central Asia*, edited by Shirin Akiner, 228–46. London: Routledge.

Hansen, Mette H. 2005. *Frontier People: Han Settlers in Minority Areas of China*. Vancouver: UBC Press.

———. 2008. "Organizing the Old: Senior Authority and the Political Significance of a Rural Chinese 'Non-Governmental Organization.'" *Modern Asian Studies* 42 (5):1057–78.

Haraway, Donna J. 2008. *When Species Meet*. Minneapolis: University of Minnesota Press.

Hardin, Garrett. 1968. "The Tragedy of the Commons." *Science* 162 (3859):1243–48.

Harrell, Stevan. 1995. "Introduction: Civilizing Projects and the Reaction to Them." In *Cultural Encounters on China's Ethnic Frontiers*, edited by Stevan Harrell, 3–36. Seattle: University of Washington Press.

———. 2002. *Ways of Being Ethnic in Southwest China*. Seattle: University of Washington Press.

———. 2007. "L'état, c'est nous, or we have met the oppressor and he is us: The Predicament of Minority Cadres in the PRC." In *The Chinese State at the Borders*, edited by Diana Lary, 221–39. Vancouver: UBC Press.

———. 2013. "China's Tangled Web of Heritage." In *Cultural Heritage Politics in China*, edited by Helaine Silverman and Tami Blumenfield, 285–94. New York: Springer.

Harrington, Anne, Nikolas Rose, and Ilina Singh. 2006. "Editor's Introduction." *BioSocieties* 1:1–5.

Harris, Rachel, and Aziz Isa. 2019. "Islam by Smartphone: Reading the Uyghur Islamic Revival on WeChat." *Central Asian Survey* 38 (1):61–80.

Hathaway, Michael. 2010. "The Emergence of Indigeneity: Public Intellectuals and an Indigenous Space in Southwest China." *Cultural Anthropology* 25 (2):301–33.

———. 2022. *What a Mushroom Lives For: Matsutake and the Worlds They Make*. Princeton, NJ: Princeton University Press.

He Jialong. 2020. *Alashan youqi meng han jiaowang jiaoliu jiaorong yanjiu* (Research on Mongol-Han contact, exchange, and mingling in Alasha Right Banner). Master's thesis, Xibei Minzu Daxue (Northwest University for Nationalities).

Heatherington, Tracy. 2010. *Wild Sardinia: Indigeneity and the Global Dreamtimes of Environmentalism*. Seattle: University of Washington Press.

Hecht, Gabrielle. 2009. *The Radiance of France: Nuclear Power and National Identity after World War II*. Cambridge, MA: MIT Press.

Heilmann, Sebastian. 2008. "From Local Experiments to National Policy: The Origins of China's Distinctive Policy Process." *China Journal* 59:1–30.

Hendrischke, Hans. 1999. "Provinces in Competition: Region, Identity and Cultural Construction." In *The Political Economy of China's Provinces: Comparative and Competitive Advantage*, edited by Hans Hendrischke and Feng Chongyi, 1–30. London: Routledge.

Herskovits, Melville J. 1926. "The Cattle Complex in East Africa." *American Anthropologist* 28 (1):230–72.

Herzfeld, Michael. 2015. "The Village in the World and the World in the Village: Reflections on Ethnographic Epistemology." *Critique of Anthropology* 35 (3):338–43.

―――. 2021. *Subversive Archaism: Troubling Traditionalists and the Politics of National Heritage*. Durham: Duke University Press.

High, Mette. 2013. "Cosmologies of Freedom and Buddhist Self-Transformation in the Mongolian Gold Rush." *Journal of the Royal Anthropological Institute* 19 (4):753–70.

Hoshino, Masahiro. 2019. "Preferential Policies for China's Ethnic Minorities at a Crossroads." *Journal of Contemporary East Asia Studies* 8 (1):1–13.

Hou, Lingling, Fang Xia, Qihui Chen, Jikun Huang, Yong He, Nathan Rose, and Scott Rozelle. 2021. "Grassland Ecological Compensation Policy in China Improves Grassland Quality and Increases Herders' Income." *Nature Communications* 12 (4683).

Hu Angang and Hu Lianhe. 2011. "Di'er dai minzu zhengce: Cujin minzu jiaorong yiti he fanrong yiti" (The second-generation nationality policies: Promoting the mingling of nationalities and their mutual flourishing). *Xinjiang shifan daxue xuebao* (Journal of Xinjiang Normal University) 32 (5):1–12.

Humphrey, Caroline. 1997. "Exemplars and Rules: Aspects of the Discourse of Moralities in Mongolia." In *The Ethnography of Moralities*, edited by Signe Howell, 25–49. London: Routledge.

―――. 2015. "Is Zomia a Useful Idea for Inner Asia?" *Mongolian Journal of Anthropology, Archaeology and Ethnology* 8 (1):92–107.

―――. 2020. "'Fast' and 'Slow': Abstract Thinking and 'Real Experience' in Two Mongolian Non-Pastoral Modes of Travel." *Inner Asia* 22:6–27.

Humphrey, Caroline, and David Sneath. 1999. *The End of Nomadism? Society, State and the Environment in Inner Asia*. Durham: Duke University Press.

Humphrey, Caroline, and Hürelbaatar Ujeed. 2013. *A Monastery in Time: The Making of Mongolian Buddhism*. Chicago: University of Chicago.

Huqun. 2010. *Shamo dayi* (The beauty of the desert). Hohhot: Neimenggu Wenhua Chubanshe (Inner Mongolia Cultural Publishing House).

Ichinkhorloo, Byambabaatar, and Emily T. Yeh. 2016. "Ephemeral 'Communities': Spatiality and Politics in Rangeland Interventions in Mongolia." *Journal of Peasant Studies* 43 (5):1010–34.

IMAR EG (Inner Mongolia Autonomous Region Editorial Group). 2009. *Mengguzu shehui lishi diaocha* (Research on the society and history of the Mongol nationality). Beijing: Minzu Chubanshe (Nationalities Publishing House).

Ingold, Tim. 1980. *Hunters, Pastoralists and Ranchers: Reindeer Economies and their Transformations*. Cambridge: Cambridge University Press.

―――. 2000. "From Trust to Domination: An Alternative History of Human-Animal Relations." In *The Perception of the Environment: Essays on Livelihood, Dwelling and Skill*, edited by Tim Ingold, 661–76. London: Routledge.

Inouye, Abraham. 2019. "Peoples Republic of China—Dairy and Products Semi-annual: Higher Profits Support Increased Fluid Milk Production." GAIN Report no. CH19042. July 17.

Jacobs, Andrew. 2015. "China Fences in Its Nomads, and an Ancient Life Withers." *New York Times*, July 11.

Jagchid, Sechin. 1999. *The Last Mongol Prince: The Life and Times of Demchugdongrob, 1902–1966*. Bellingham: Center for East Asia Studies, Western Washington University.

Jankowiak, William. 1988. "The Last Hurrah? Political Protest in Inner Mongolia." *Australian Journal of Chinese Affairs* 19–20:269–88.

———. 2013. "Urban Mongols: The Flourishing of Multiple Identities in a Vibrant Ethnic Community." *Chinese Sociological Review* 45 (3):53–73.

Ji Qingling. 2020. "Jihuo dangjian yinqing, cu nongmumin zengshou zhifu" (Promote party building, encourage herders and farmers to increase their income). *Shijian: Dang de jiaoyu ban* (Practice: Party education edition) 11:37.

Jiang, Hong. 2006. "Poaching State Politics in Socialist China: Uxin Ju's Grassland Campaign, 1958–1966." *Geographical Review* 96 (4):633–56.

Jiang, Wei, and Yifan Wang. 2019. "Inner Mongolia Sees World-First Camel Embryo Transfer." *China Daily*, February 19. http://www.chinadaily.com.cn/a/201902/19/WS5c6bcdb1a3106c65c34ea295.html.

Jiang Rong. 2004. *Lang tuteng* (Wolf totem). Wuhan: Changjiang Wenyi Chubanshe(Yangtze River Literary and Art Publishing House).

Jiang Z. Z., Yin Y., and Chai H. H. 2002. "Kuqi de luotuo" (The weeping camel). *Xinhua*. Accessed May 25, 2018. http://news.xinhuanet.com/zhengfu/2002-07/10/.

Jiao Yang. 2021. "Jing-Xin gaosu: Huangsha gebi zhong de luse piaodai" (The Jing-Xin highway: A green ribbon across the yellow sands of the Gobi). *Keji ribao* (Science and technology daily), July 9. http://www.news.cn/politics/2021-09/07/c_1127834536.htm.

Jirimutu and Chen Gangliang. 2014. *Luotuo chanpin yu shengwu jishu* (Camel products and biotechnology). Beijing: Zhongguo Qing Gongye Chubanshe (China Light Industry Publishing House).

Jirimutu, Chen Gangliang, Li Jianmei, Yu Siriguleng, Ming Liang, and Li Yi. 2014. *Shenqi de luotuo yu tangniaobing* (The mysterious camel and diabetes). Beijing: Zhongguo Qing Gongye Chubanshe (China Light Industry Publishing House).

Jones, Lee, and Jinghan Zeng. 2019. "Understanding China's 'Belt and Road Initiative': Beyond 'Grand Strategy' to a State Transformation Analysis." *Third World Quarterly* 40 (8):1415–1439.

Joniak-Lüthi, Agnieszka. 2016. "Blurring Boundaries and Negotiating Subjectivities: The Uyghurized Han of Southern Xinjiang." *Ethnic and Racial Studies* 39 (12):2187–2204.

Joniak-Lüthi, Agnieszka, and Uradyn E. Bulag. 2016. "Introduction: Spatial Transformations in China's Northwestern Borderlands." *Inner Asia* 18:1–14.

Kabzung and Emily T. Yeh. 2016. "Slaughter Renunciation in Tibetan Pastoral

Areas: Buddhism, Neoliberalism, and the Ironies of Alternative Development." In *Ghost Protocol: Development and Displacement in Global China*, edited by C. Rojas and R. A. Litzinger, 109–30. Durham: Duke University Press.

Kabzińska-Stawartz, Iwona. 1991. *Games of Mongolian Shepherds*. Warsaw: Institute of the History of Material Culture, Polish Academy of Sciences.

Kaiman, Jonathan. 2014. "Chinese Authorities Offer Cash to Promote Interethnic Marriages." *The Guardian*, September 2.

Kama, Kärg. 2020. "Resource-Making Controversies: Knowledge, Anticipatory Politics and Economization of Unconventional Fossil Fuels." *Progress in Human Geography* 44 (2):333–56.

Kaufmann, Lena. 2021. *Rural-Urban Migration and Agro-Technological Change in Post-Reform China*. Amsterdam: Amsterdam University Press.

Kexue Piyao (Dispelling Myth through Science). 2021. "Xurigan: Caoyuan shang zou chu de kexue jubo" (Shorgan: The eminent scientist who emerged from the grasslands). *Haokan Shipin*, February 19. https://haokan.baidu.com/v?pd=wisenatural&vid=10999576328076573126.

Khan, Almaz. 1996. "Who Are the Mongols? State, Ethnicity, and the Politics of Representation in the PRC." In *Negotiating Ethnicities in China and Taiwan*, edited by Melissa J. Brown, 125–59. Berkeley: University of California Institute for East Asian Studies Center for Chinese Studies.

Kinzley, Judd C. 2018. *Natural Resources and the New Frontier: Constructing Modern China's Borderlands*. Chicago: University of Chicago Press.

Kipnis, Andrew B. 2012. "Constructing Commonality: Standardization and Modernization in Chinese Nation-Building." *Journal of Asian Studies* 71 (3):731–55.

Kirksey, S. Eben, and Stefan Helmreich. 2010. "The Emergence of Multispecies Ethnography." *Cultural Anthropology* 25 (4):545–76.

Klein, Jacob A. 2009. "Creating Ethical Food Consumers? Promoting Organic Foods in Urban Southwest China." *Social Anthropology* 17 (1):74–89.

———. 2013. "'There Is No Such Thing as Dian Cuisine!' Food and Local Identity in Urban Southwest China." *Food and History* 11 (1):203–25.

———. 2020. "Ambivalent Regionalism and the Promotion of a New National Staple Food: Reimagining Potatoes in Inner Mongolia and Yunnan." *Global Food History* 6 (2):143–63.

Klinger, Julie M. 2017. *Rare Earth Frontiers: From Terrestrial Subsoils to Lunar Landscapes*. Ithaca, NY: Cornell University Press.

Klinghoffer, Arthur J. 1976. "Sino-Soviet Relations and the Politics of Oil." *Asian Survey* 16 (6):540–52.

Köhler-Rollefson, Ilse. 2008. "Community-Based Conservation of the Alashan Camel Breed in Inner Mongolia." *Drynet* 3:5–7. https://dry-net.org/wp-content/uploads/2015/10/1LPPS_NL_3.pdf.

————. 2023. "The International Year of Camelids 2024: Opportunities and Challenges." Paper presented at the Sixth Oxford Desert Conference, March 2023.

Kolås, Åshild. 2011. "Reclaiming the Forest: Ewenki Reindeer Herding as Exception." *Human Organization* 70 (4):397–404.

————. 2014. "Degradation Discourse and Green Governmentality in the Xilinguole Grasslands of Inner Mongolia." *Development and Change* 45 (2):308–28.

Korf, Benedikt, Tobias Hagmann, and Rory Emmenegger. 2015. "Respacing African Drylands: Territorialization, Sedentarization and Indigenous Commodification in the Ethiopian Pastoral Frontier." *Journal of Peasant Studies* 42 (5):881–901.

Koster, Harold A., and Claudia Chang. 1994. Introduction to *Pastoralists at the Periphery: Herders in a Capitalist World*, edited by Claudia Chang and Harold A. Koster, 1–15. Tucson: University of Arizona Press.

Lama, Jigme Y. 2018. "Tibet and Happiness in Chinese Media Discourses." In *Chinese Discourses on Happiness*, edited by Gerda Wielander and Derek Hird, 44–63. Hong Kong: Hong Kong University Press.

Landecker, Hannah. 2010. "Living Differently in Time: Plasticity, Temporality and Cellular Biotechnologies." In *Technologized Images, Technologized Bodies*, edited by Jeanette Edwards, Penny Harvey, and Peter Wade, 211–36. New York: Berghahn.

Lang, Graeme. 2002. "Forests, Floods, and the Environmental State in China." *Organization and Environment* 15 (2):109–30.

Lattimore, Owen. 1928. *The Desert Road to Turkestan*. London: Methuen.

————. 1935. "On the Wickedness of Being Nomads." *T'ien Hsia Monthly* 1 (1):47–62.

————. 1962. *Nomads and Commissars: Mongolia Revisited*. New York: Oxford University Press.

Leblon, Anaïs. 2016. "'Is Pastoralism Dead?': Between Nostalgia, Transmission and Maintenance of the Practice of Transhumant Cattle Herding in Mali." *Nomadic Peoples* 20 (2): 216–44.

Lee, Juheon. 2020. "Promoting Majority Culture and Excluding External Ethnic Influences: China's Strategy for the UNESCO 'Intangible' Cultural Heritage List." *Social Identities: Journal for the Study of Race, Nation and Culture* 26 (1):61–76.

Leibold, James. 2007. *Reconfiguring Chinese Nationalism: How the Qing Frontier and Its Indigenes Became Chinese*. New York: Palgrave Macmillan.

————. 2014. "Xinjiang Work Forum Marks New Policy of 'Ethnic Mingling.'" *Jamestown Foundation*, June 19. https://jamestown.org/program/xinjiang -work-forum-marks-new-policy-of-ethnic-mingling/#.U6QVefmSyhE.

Lesdain, Jacques. 1908. *From Pekin to Sikkim through the Ordos, the Gobi Desert, and Tibet*. London: Methuen.

Levine, Nancy. 1999. "Cattle and the Cash Economy: Responses to Change among Tibetan Nomadic Pastoralists in Sichuan, China." *Human Organization* 58 (2):161–72.

Li, Lianjiang. 2013. "The Magnitude and Resilience of Trust in the Center: Evidence from Interviews with Petitioners in Beijing and a Local Survey in Rural China." *Modern China* 39 (1):3–36.

Li, Tania M. 2000. "Articulating Indigenous Identity in Indonesia: Resource Politics and the Tribal Slot." *Comparative Studies in Society and History* 42 (1):149–79.

Li Wanlu. 2007. "Huabie Dingyuanhou he Dingyuanying" (Saying goodbye to Dingyuanhou and Dingyuanying). In *Alashan wangshi* (The history of Alasha), vol. 3, edited by Chaogetu, 520–22. Yinchuan: Ningxia Renmin Chubanshe (Ningxia People's Publishing House).

Li Wanyu. 2007. "Alashan mengguzu jituo xisu" (The camel veneration customs of the Alasha Mongols). In *Alashan wangshi* (The history of Alasha), vol. 3, edited by Chaogetu, 369–80. Yinchuan: Ningxia Renmin Chubanshe (Ningxia People's Publishing House).

Li, Wenjun, and Lynn Huntsinger. 2011. "China's Grassland Contract Policy and Its Impacts on Herder Ability to Benefit in Inner Mongolia." *Ecology and Society* 16 (2):1.

Li Yanchun. 2004. "Alashan luotuo: Siwang gaoji" (The Alasha camel: A deadly emergency). *Teenagers* 7:32–33.

Li Ye, Tuhong Fang, and Jingguo Pan. 2019. "Gongchandang ren de luotuo jingshen" (The camel spirit of communists). *Zhongguo lingdao kexue* (China leadership science) 5:15–17.

Li, Yifei, and Judith Shapiro. 2020. *China Goes Green: Coercive Environmentalism for a Troubled Planet*. Cambridge: Polity Press.

Liang Lixia. 2006. *Alashan menggu yangjiu* (Research on the Alasha Mongols). Beijing: Minzu Chubanshe (Nationalities Press).

Liang, Zhicheng, and Luodan Xu. 2004. "Regional Specialization and Dynamic Pattern of Comparative Advantage: Evidence from China's Industries 1988–2001." *Review of Urban and Regional Development Studies* 16 (3):231–44.

Lin, Hsiao-Ting. 2007. "Nationalists, Muslim Warlords, and the 'Great Northwestern Development' in Pre-Communist China." *China and Eurasia Forum Quarterly* 5 (1):115–35.

Lin, Justin Y. 1988. "The Household Responsibility System in China's Agricultural Reform: A Theoretical and Empirical Study." *Economic Development and Cultural Change* 36 (3):S199–S224.

Lindtner, Silvia M. 2020. *Prototype Nation: China and the Contested Promise of Innovation*. Princeton, NJ: Princeton University Press.

Lipes, Joshua. 2013. "Mongolian Netizens 'Punished' for Chinese Resettlement Complaints." *Radio Free Asia*, August 12. https://www.rfa.org/english/news/china/resettlement-08122013191153.html.

Litzinger, Ralph. 2000. *Other Chinas: The Yao and the Politics of National Belonging*. Durham: Duke University Press.

Liu Keyan. 2003. "Neimenggu chutai zhichi wenhua shiye he wenhua chanye fazhan zhengce" (Inner Mongolia announces policies to support cultural activity and cultural industries). *CCTV*, October 27. https://www.cctv.com /west/20031027/101038.shtml.

Liu Shurun. 2012. *Zheli de caoyuan jingqiaoqiao* (These grasslands are peaceful and quiet). Beijing: Zhishi Chanquan Chubanshe (Intellectual Property Publishing House).

Liu Xiaowang and Wulunsai. 2017 (1986). "Fahui ameng youshi, daxing luotuo zhi ye: Luelun shamo yu luotuo" (Exploiting the strengths of Alasha League, vigorously promoting camel husbandry: A brief discussion of the desert and camels). In Batuchulu and Siqinbielige, *Silu tuoling*, 101–11.

Liu, Xiaoyuan. 2006. *Reins of Liberation: An Entangled History of Mongolian Independence, Chinese Territoriality, and Great Power Hegemony, 1911–1950*. Washington, DC: Woodrow Wilson Center.

Liu Yuelian. 2017. *Tuodao yu Alashan latuo ren de jiyi* (Caravan routes and the memories of Alasha's caravaneers). Yinchuan: Yangguang Chubanshe (Sunlight Publishing House).

Long, Nicholas J., and Henrietta L. Moore, eds. 2012. *Sociality: New Directions*. New York: Berghahn Books.

Long, Qiao. 2016. "Ethnic Mongols Protests Missile Tests, Lack of Income." *Radio Free Asia*, January 26. https://www.rfa.org/english/news/china/china -mongols-01262016161304.html.

———. 2017. "Ethnic Mongolian Herders Protest Lack of Compensation for Grazing Ban." *Radio Free Asia* March 21. https://www.rfa.org/english/news /china/ethnic-mongolian-herders-protest-lack-of-compensation-for-graz ing-ban-03212017123346.html.

———. 2020. "Ethnic Mongolian Official Dead by Suicide Amid Language Protests." *Radio Free Asia*, September 4. https://www.rfa.org/english/news /china/mongolia-language-09042020103032.html.

Lorimer, Jamie. 2017. "Probiotic Environmentalities: Rewilding with Wolves and Worms." *Theory, Culture and Society* 34 (4):27–48.

Lorimer, Jamie, and Clemens Driessen. 2016. "From 'Nazi Cows' to Cosmopolitan 'Ecological Engineers': Specifying Rewilding through a History of Heck Cattle." *Annals of the American Association of Geographers* 106 (3): 631–52.

Luo, Qiangqiang, Joel Andreas, and Yao Li. 2017. "Grapes of Wrath: Twisting Arms to Get Villagers to Cooperate with Agribusiness in China." *China Journal* 77:27–50.

Luo, Yu. 2018. "An Alternative to the 'Indigenous' in Early Twenty-First-Century China: Guizhou's Branding of *Yuanshengtai*." *Modern China* 44 (1):68–102.

Luo, Yu, Tim Oakes, and Louisa Schein. 2019. "Resourcing Remoteness and the 'Post-Alteric' Imaginary in China." *Social Anthropology* 27 (2):270–85.

Maags, Christina. 2018. "Creating a Race to the Top: Hierarchies and Competition within the Chinese ICH Transmitters Scheme." In *Chinese Heritage in the Making: Experiences, Negotiations, and Contestations*, edited by Christina Maags and Marina Svensson, 121–44. Amsterdam: Amsterdam University Press.

Maags, Christina, and Marina Svensson, eds. 2018. *Chinese Heritage in the Making: Experiences, Negotiations, and Contestations*. Amsterdam: Amsterdam University Press.

Mackerras, Colin. 1984. "Folksongs and Dances of China's Minority Nationalities: Policy, Tradition, and Professionalization." *Modern China* 10 (2):187–226.

Mair, Jonathan. 2013. "Rebirth Control: Contemporary Inner Mongolian Buddhism and the Religious Authority of the Chinese State." In *Buddhism, Modernity and the State in Asia: Forms of Engagement, edited by* John Whalen-Bridge, and Pattana Kitiarsa, 209–28. New York: Palgrave.

Mak, Veronica Sau-Wa. 2021a. *Milk Craze: Body, Science, and Hope in China*. Honolulu: University of Hawaii Press.

———. 2021b. "Technologies and Dietary Change: The Pharmaceutical Nexus and the Marketing of Anti-Aging Functional Food in a Chinese Society." *Food and Foodways* 29 (4):309–30.

Mandoula. 2019. "Alashan mengguzu tuoyun shijian jiyi yanjiu" (Research on Alasha Mongols' memories of the practice of camel caravans). *Xibu menggu luntan* 4:59–69.

Manlai and Wanchog. 2002. *Mongolchuud ba mori* (Mongolians and the horse). Chifeng: Öbör Mongoliin Shinjlekh Ukhaan Teknik Mergejiliin Khevleliin Khoroo (Inner Mongolia Science and Technology Publishing House).

Marcus, George E. 1995. "Ethnography in/of the World System: The Emergence of Multi-Sited Ethnography." *Annual Review of Anthropology* 24:95–117.

Marsden, Magnus, and Madeleine Reeves. 2019. "Marginal Hubs: On Conviviality beyond the Urban in Asia." *Modern Asian Studies* 53 (3):755–75.

Marx, Karl, and Frederick Engels. 1982. *Collected Works: Volume 38*. London: Lawrence and Wishart.

McDonald, Tom. 2016. *Social Media in Rural China: Social Networks and Moral Frameworks*. London: UCL Press.

McElwhee, Pamela D. 2012. *Forests Are Gold: Trees, People, and Environmental Rule in Vietnam*. Seattle: University of Washington Press.

Meili Alashan Youqi (Beautiful Alasha Right Banner). 2023. "Juli dazao quanguo naizhi quanqiu zuida de luotuo chanye yangban diqu" (Focusing on constructing the largest camel industry model region in the country, and even in the world). *Bajiahao*, June 6. https://baijiahao.baidu.com/s?id=1767955516035245552.

Mertha, Andrew C. 2009. "Fragmented Authoritarianism 2.0: Political Pluralization in the Policy Process." *China Quarterly* 200:995–1012.

Meserve, Ruth I. 2000. "The Expanded Role of Mongolian Domestic Livestock Classification." *Acta Orientalia Academiae Scientiarum Hungaricae* 53 (1–2):23–45.

Ming, Liang, Liyun Yuan, Li Yi, et al. 2020. "Whole-Genome Sequencing of 128 Camels across Asia Reveals Origin and Migration of Domestic Bactrian Camels." *Communications Biology* 3:1–9.

Mönkhjargal. 2006. *Alasha temeen soyol* (Alasha camel culture). Hohhot: Övör Mongoliin Soyoliin Khevleliin Khoroo (Inner Mongolia Cultural Publishing House).

Moore, Jason W. 2000. "Sugar and the Expansion of the Early Modern World-Economy: Commodity Frontiers, Ecological Transformation, and Industrialization." *Review (Fernand Braudel Center)* 23 (3):409–33.

Mullaney, Thomas S. 2011. *Coming to Terms with the Nation: Ethnic Classification in Modern China*. Berkeley: University of California Press.

Myadar, Orhon. 2021. *Mobility and Displacement: Nomadism, Identity and Post-colonial Narratives in Mongolia*. London: Routledge.

Nadasdy, Paul. 2003. *Hunters and Bureaucrats: Power, Knowledge, and Aboriginal-State Relations in the Southwest Yukon*. Vancouver: UBC Press.

———. 2007. "The Gift in the Animal: The Ontology of Hunting and Human-Animal Sociality." *American Ethnologist* 34 (1):25–43.

Nagy, Peter P., Julian A. Skidmore, and Judit Juhasz. 2022. "Intensification of Camel Farming and Milk Production with Special Emphasis on Animal Health, Welfare, and the Biotechnology of Reproduction." *Animal Frontiers* 12 (4):35–45.

Naminse, Eric Y., Jincai Zhuang, and Fangyang Zhu. 2019. "The Relationship between Entrepreneurship and Rural Poverty Alleviation." *Management Decision* 57 (9):2593–2611.

Namujilecelin, Wunimenghe, Daerjia, and Changqing Yu. 2012. "Alashan chuantong youmu de bianqian jiqi shengtai yingxian" (The transformation of traditional nomadism in Alashan and its ecological effects). In *Keji chuangxin yu jingji jiegou tiaozheng: Di qi jie neimenggu zizhiqu ziran kexue xueshu nianhui youxiu lunwen ji* (Innovating in science and technology and adjusting economic structures: Selected papers from the seventh IMAR Natural Sciences Annual Conference), 670–71. Hohhot: Neimenggu Renmin Chubanshe (Inner Mongolia People's Publishing House).

Narayanan, Yamini. 2021. "'A Pilgrimage of Camels': Dairy Capitalism, Nomadic Pastoralism, and Subnational Hindutva Statism." *Environment and Planning E: Nature and Space* 6 (2):756–75.

Neimenggu Luotuo Yanjiuyuan (Inner Mongolia Camel Research Institute). 2019. "Neimenggu luotuo yanjiuyuan yuanshi zhuanjia gongzuozhan zai alashan youqi juxing luotuo yangzhi jishu peixun hui" (Inner Mongolia Camel Research Institute expert work team hold a camel husbandry skills training event in Alasha Right Banner). https://www.sohu.com/a/329781459_766310.

Neimenggu Ribao (Inner Mongolia daily). 2019. "Bu Xiaolin jieri qijian dao Alashan weiwen diaoyan" (Bu Xiaolin makes an official investigatory visit to Alasha during the holidays). *Bajiahao.* October 5. https://baijiahao.baidu.com /s?id=1646458645956292268.

Nongye Bu (Ministry of Agriculture). 2006. "Guojiaji chuqin yichuan ziyuan baohu minglü" (National list of protected livestock genetic resources). https:// www.gov.cn/govweb/ztzl/2006-06/10/content_306243.htm.

———. 2011. "Nongyebu Caizhengbu Guanyu Yinfa '2011 Nian Caoyuan Shengtai Baohu Buzhu Jiangli Jizhi Zhengce Shixian Zhidao Yijian' de Tongzhi" (Notice from the Ministry of Agriculture and the Ministry of Finance regarding the printing and distribution of the '2011 Directive on the Implementation of the Grassland Ecology Protection Subsidy and Reward Mechanism'). http://www.moa.gov.cn/nybgb/2011/dqq/201805/t20180522_6142764.htm.

Norbu and Jüngnei. 1988. *Alasha khoos bükht temee* (The Alasha Bactrian camel). Hohhot: Öbör Mongoliin Shinjlekh Ukhaan Teknik Mergejiliin Khevleliin Khoroo (Inner Mongolia Science and Technology Publishing House).

Nustad, Knut G., and Heather Swanson. 2022. "Political Ecology and the Foucault Effect: A Need to Diversify Disciplinary Approaches to Ecological Management." *Environment and Planning E: Nature and Space* 5 (2):924–46.

Nyima, Yonten. 2014. "A Larger Herd Size as a Symbol of Wealth? The Fallacy of the Cattle Complex Theory in Tibetan Pastoralism." *Area* 46 (2):186–93.

Nyíri, Pál. 2006. "The Yellow Man's Burden: Chinese Migrants on a Civilizing Mission." *China Journal* 56:83–106.

Oakes, Tim. 1999. "Selling Guizhou: Cultural Development in an Era of Marketisation." In *The Political Economy of China's Provinces: Comparative and Competitive Advantage,* edited by Hans Hendrischke and Feng Chongyi, 31–72. London: Routledge.

———. 2005. "Land of Living Fossils: Scaling Cultural Prestige in China's Peripheries." In *Locating China: Space, Place, and Popular Culture,* edited by Jing Wang, 31–51. London: Routledge.

———. 2012. "Looking Out to Look In: The Use of the Periphery in China's Geopolitical Narratives." *Eurasian Geography and Economics* 53 (3):315–26.

———. 2013. "Heritage as Improvement: Cultural Display and Contested Governance in Rural China." *Modern China* 39 (4):380–407.

Oakes, Tim, and Louisa Schein. 2006. "Translocal China: An Introduction." In *Translocal China: Linkages, Identities, and the Reimagining of Space,* edited by Tim Oakes and Louisa Schein, 1–35. Abingdon: Routledge.

Oakes, Tim, and Zhenting Zuo. 2022. "Remoteness and Connectivity: The Variegated Geographies of the Yunnan-Guizhou Plateau." In *The Routledge*

Handbook of Highland Asia, edited by Jelle J. P. Wouters and Michael T. Heneise, 418–29. Abingdon: Routledge.

O'Brien, Kevin J. 1996. "Rightful Resistance." *World Politics* 49 (1):31–55.

Ölziit. 2017. "Alasha Tövd ayan tenkheevüriin atan temee tuslasan tokhai temdeglel" (An account of the camel caravans from Alasha which aided Tibet). In Batuchulu and Siqinbielige, *Silu tuoling*, 225–27.

Ong, Aihwa. 2010. "Introduction: An Analytics of Biotechnology and Ethics at Multiple Scales." In *Asian Biotech: Ethics and Communities of Fate*, edited by Aihwa Ong and Nancy N. Chen, 1–54. Durham: Duke University Press.

Ong, Aihwa, and Li Zhang, eds. 2008. *Privatizing China: Socialism from Afar*. Ithaca, NY: Cornell University Press.

Otede, Uchralt. 2019. "The Environmental Protest Movement in Inner Mongolia." In *Handbook of Protest and Resistance in China*, edited by Teresa Wright, 406–16. Cheltenham: Edward Elgar.

O'Toole, Fintan. 2006. "Desert Storm." *Irish Times*, June 3.

Pan, Darcy. 2022. "Storing Data on the Margins: Making State and Infrastructure in Southwest China." *Information, Communication and Society* 25 (16):2412–26.

Pan, Yihong. 2006. "Revelation of the Grassland: The Han Sent-Down Youths in Inner Mongolia in China's Cultural Revolution." *Asian Ethnicity* 7 (3):225–41.

Pan Yue. 2006. "Shehui zhuyi shengtai wenming" (Socialist ecological civilization). *Lüye* (Green Leaf) 10:10–18.

Pan Zhaodong and Liu Junbao. 2005. "Caoyuan wenhua de quyu fenbu ji qi tedian" (The regional distribution and particularities of grassland culture). *Qianyan* (Frontiers) 9:7–10.

Paprocki, Kasia. 2019. "All That Is Solid Melts into the Bay: Anticipatory Ruination on Bangladesh's Climate Frontier." In *Frontier Assemblages: The Emergent Politics of Resource Frontiers in Asia*, edited by Jason Cons and Micheal Eilenberg, 25–39. Hoboken, NJ: Wiley.

Parkes, Graham. 2005. "Thinking Rocks, Living Stones: Reflections on Chinese Lithophilia." *Diogenes* 52 (3):75–87.

Parry, Bronwyn. 2004. *Trading the Genome: Investigating the Commodification of Bio-Information*. New York: Columbia University Press.

Peluso, Nancy L., and Christian Lund. 2011. "New Frontiers of Land Control: Introduction." *Journal of Peasant Studies* 38 (4):667–81.

Perdue, Peter C. 2005. *China Marches West: The Qing Conquest of Central Eurasia*. Cambridge, MA.: Harvard University Press.

Perry, Elizabeth J. 2017. "Cultural Governance in Contemporary China: 'Re-Orienting' Party Propganda." In *To Govern China: Evolving Practices of Power*, edited by Vivienne Shue and Patricia M. Thornton, 29–55. Cambridge: Cambridge University Press.

Peutz, Nathalie. 2018. *Islands of Heritage: Conservation and Transformation in Yemen*. Palo Alto, CA: Stanford University Press.

Phillips, Tom. 2017. The $900bn Question: What Is the Belt and Road Initiative? *The Guardian,* May 12.

Pils, Eva. 2012. "Introduction: Discussing 'Civil Society' and 'Liberal Communities' in China." *China Perspectives* (Online) 2012–13:2–7.

Porcher, Jocelyne, and Jean Estebanez, eds. 2020. *Animal Labor: A New Perspective on Human-Animal Relations.* New York: Columbia University Press.

Ptackova, Jarmila. 2019. "Distributing Fish or Fishing Hooks? Examples of the Targeted Poverty Alleviation Program in Tibetan Pastoral Areas of Qinghai." *Acta Orientální.* Supplementa XI:187–209.

———. 2020. *Exile from the Grasslands: Tibetan Herders and Chinese Development Projects.* Seattle: University of Washington Press.

Qian, Fengqi. 2022. "Ancient Routes, New Dream: The Silk Roads and China's Belt and Road Initiative." *Journal of Cultural Heritage Management and Sustainable Development* 12 (1):45–57.

Radin, Joanna. 2015. "Planning for the Past: Cryopreservation at the Farm, Zoo, and Museum." In *Endangerment, Biodiversity, and Culture,* edited by Fernando Vidal and Nélia Dias, 218–40. London: Routledge.

Rasmussen, Mattias B., and Christian Lund. 2018. "Reconfiguring Frontier Spaces: The Territorialization of Resource Control." *World Development* 101:388–99.

Redford, Kent. H. 1991. "The Ecologically Noble Savage." *Cultural Survival Quarterly* 15:46–48.

Regassa, Asebe, Yetebarek Hezekiel, and Benedikt Korf. 2019. "'Civilizing' the Pastoral Frontier: Land Grabbing, Dispossession and Coercive Agrarian Development in Ethiopia." *Journal of Peasant Studies* 46 (5):935–55.

Rennie, David. 2000. "Cashmere Cull to Save Beijing from Desert." *The Telegraph* (UK), September 1. https://www.telegraph.co.uk/news/worldnews/asia/china/1353638/Cashmere-cull-to-save-Beijing-from-desert.html.

Richardson, Tanya and Giza Weszkalnys. 2014. "Resource Materialities: New Anthropological Perspectives on Natural Resource Environments." *Anthropological Quarterly* 87 (1):5–30.

Rippa, Alessandro. 2020. *Borderland Infrastructures: Trade, Development, and Control in Western China.* Amsterdam: Amsterdam University Press.

Roche, Gerald, and James Leibold. 2020. "China's Second-Generation Policies Are Already Here: What China's History of Paper Genocide Can Tell Us about the Future of its 'Minority Nationalities.'" *Made in China Journal,* September 7. https://madeinchinajournal.com/2020/09/07/chinas-second-generation-ethnic-policies-are-already-here/.

Rodenbiker, Jesse. 2021. "Making Ecology Developmental: China's Environmental Sciences and Green Modernization in Global Context." *Annals of the American Association of Geographers* 111 (7):1931–48.

Rogelja, Igor, and Konstantinos Tsimonis. 2022. *Belt and Road: The First Decade*. Newcastle: Agenda.

Rogers, Sarah. 2019. "Manufactured Modernity: Dwelling, Labour, and Enclosure in China's Poverty Resettlements." *Made in China* 3 (4):58–61.

Rogers, Sarah, Jie Li, Kevin Lo, Hua Guo, and Cong Li. 2020. "China's Rapidly Evolving Practice of Poverty Resettlement: Moving Millions to Eliminate Poverty." *Development Policy Review* 38 (5):541–54.

Rong, Ma. 2014. "Reflections on the Debate on China's Ethnic Policy: My Reform Proposals and Their Critics." *Asian Ethnicity* 15 (2):237–46.

Ruhlmann, Sandrine. 2019. *Inviting Happiness: Food Sharing in Post-Communist Mongolia*. Leiden: Brill.

Ruser, Nathan, with James Leibold, Kelsey Munro, and Tilla Hoja. 2020. *Cultural Erasure: Tracing the Destruction of Uyghur and Islamic Spaces in Xinjiang*. Canberra: Australian Strategic Policy Institute.

Sagild, Rebekka Å., and Anna L. Ahlers. 2019. "Honorary Intermediaries? The Chinese People's Political Consultative Conference in Theory and Practice." *China Perspectives* 2:9–16.

Salimjan, Guldana. 2021. "Naturalized Violence: Affective Politics of China's 'Ecological Civilization' in Xinjiang." *Human Ecology* 49:59–68.

Salmenkari, Taru. 2011. "Community Building, Civil Society and Societal Service Production in China." *Journal of Civil Society* 7 (1):101–18.

Saraf, Aditi. 2020. "Frontiers." *Oxford Research Encyclopedia of Anthropology* (online). https://doi.org/10.1093/acrefore/9780190854584.013.145.

Sayre, Nathan. 2008. "The Genesis, History, and Limits of Carrying Capacity." *Annals of the Association of American Geographers* 98 (1):120–34.

——— . 2009. "Land, Labor, Livestock and (Neo)liberalism: Understanding the Geographies of Pastoralism and Ranching." *Geoforum* 40 (5):705–6.

Schareika, Nikolaus, Christopher Brown, and Mark Moritz. 2021. "Critical Transitions from Pastoralism to Ranching in Central Africa." *Current Anthropology* 62 (1):53–76.

Schein, Louisa. 2020. "Gender and the Other." In *Routledge Handbook of Chinese Culture and Society*, edited by Kevin Latham, 260–75. London: Routledge.

Schlesinger, Jonathan. 2017. *A World Trimmed with Fur: Wild Things, Pristine Places, and the Natural Fringes of Qing Rule*. Stanford, CA: Stanford University Press.

Schmalzer, Sigrid. 2016. *Red Revolution, Green Revolution: Scientific Farming in Socialist China*. Chicago: University of Chicago Press.

——— . 2019. "Layer upon Layer: Mao-Era History and the Construction of China's Agricultural Heritage." *East Asian Science, Technology and Society: An International Journal* 13 (3):413–41.

——— . 2022. "Prometheus and the Fishpond: A Historical Account of

Agricultural Systems and Eco-Political Power in the People's Republic of China." *Made in China Journal 7 (2):124–31.*

Schneider, Mindy. 2017. "Dragon Head Enterprises and the State of Agribusiness in China." *Journal of Agrarian Change* 17 (1):3–21.

Schneider, Mindy, and Samuël Coghe. 2021. "Livestock Frontiers: Editorial Introduction." *Commodity Frontiers* 3:i–viii.

Schwenkel, Christina. 2013. "Post/Socialist Affect: Ruination and the Reconstruction of the Nation in Urban Vietnam." *Cultural Anthropology* 28 (2):252–77.

———. 2020. *Building Socialism: The Afterlife of East German Architecture in Urban Vietnam.* Durham: Duke University Press.

Scott, James C. 1985. *Weapons of the Weak: Everyday Forms of Peasant Resistance.* New Haven, CT: Yale University Press.

———. 1998. *Seeing Like a State: How Certain Schemes to Improve the Human Condition Have Failed.* New Haven, CT: Yale University Press.

———. 2009. *The Art of Not Being Governed: An Anarchist History of Upland Southeast Asia.* New Haven, CT: Yale University Press.

Selden, Mark. 1971. *The Yenan Way in Revolutionary China.* Cambridge, MA: Harvard University Press.

Shapiro, Judith. 2001. *Mao's War against Nature: Politics and the Environment in Revolutionary China.* Cambridge: Cambridge University Press.

Shapiro, Judith, and John-Andrew McNeish. 2021. Introduction to *Our Extractive Age: Expressions of Violence and Resistance,* edited by Judith Shapiro and John-Andrew McNeish, 1–16. London: Routledge.

Shen, Grace Yen. 2013. *Unearthing the Nation: Modern Geology and Nationalism in Republican China.* Chicago: University of Chicago Press.

Shepherd, Robert. 2006. "UNESCO and the Politics of Cultural Heritage in Tibet." *Journal of Contemporary Asia* 36 (2):243–57.

Shi Jifa. 2001. *Zai shenmi de Alashan* (In mysterious Alasha). Hohhot: Neimenggu Renmin Chubanshe (Inner Mongolia People's Publishing House).

Shi Shuangzhu. 2011. "Caoyuan wenhua de siwei tezheng ji qi xiandai bianqian" (The distinctive thought of grassland culture and its modern transformation). *Zhongguo jingji shi luntan* (China economic history forum), May 11. http://economy.guoxue.com/?p=9089.

Shi Youtian, ed. 1998. *Alashan meng gonglu jiaotong zhi* (Alasha league road transportation gazetteer). Beijing: Renmin Jiaotong Chubanshe (People's Transportation Publishing House).

———. 2007. "Alashan de yanchan yu luotuo yunshu ye" (The Alasha salt industry and camel transportation). In *Alashan wangshi* (The history of Alasha), vol. 3, edited by Chaogetu, 396–431. Yinchuan: Ningxia Renmin Chubanshe (Ningxia People's Publishing House).

Sigley, Gary. 2020. *China's Route Heritage: Mobility Narratives, Modernity and the Ancient Tea Horse Road.* Abingdon: Routledge.

Smil, Vaclav. 2003. *China's Past, China's Future: Energy, Food, Environment*. London: Routledge.

Smits, Marcel, Han Joosten, Bernard Faye, and Pamela A. Burger. 2023. "The Flourishing Camel Milk Market and Concerns about Animal Welfare and Legislation." *Animals (Basel)* 13 (10):47.

Sneath, David. 1993. "Social Relations, Networks, and Social Organisation in Post-Socialist Rural Mongolia." *Nomadic Peoples* 33:193–207.

———. 1994. "The Impact of the Cultural Revolution in China on the Mongolians of Inner Mongolia." *Modern Asian Studies* 28 (2):409–30.

———. 2000. *Changing Inner Mongolia: Pastoral Mongolian Society and the Chinese State*. Oxford: Oxford University Press.

———. 2003. "Land Use, the Environment, and Development in Post-Socialist Mongolia." *Oxford Development Studies* 31 (4):441–59.

———. 2008. "Competing Factions and Elite Power: Political Conflict in Inner Mongolia." In *Conflict and Social Order in Tibet and Inner Asia*, edited by Fernanda Pirie and Toni Huber, 85–112. Leiden: Brill.

———. 2014. "Nationalizing Civilizational Resources: Sacred Mountains and Cosmopolitical Ritual in Mongolia." *Asian Ethnicity* 15 (4):458–72.

Sodikoff, Genese M., ed. 2012. *The Anthropology of Extinction: Essays on Culture and Species Death*. Bloomington: Indiana University Press.

Song Chenghuan. 2020. "Hasakesidan shoupi luotuo naifen yundi Lanzhou xinqu" (The first batch of camel milk powder from Kazakhstan arrives in Lanzhou's New District). *Zhongguo xinwen wang* (China news website), June 15. http://ydyl.china.com.cn/2020-06/15/content_76163486.htm.

Songster, E. Elena. 2018. *Panda Nation: The Construction and Conservation of China's Modern Icon*. Oxford: Oxford University Press.

Sorace, Christian. 2021. "The Chinese Communist Party's Nervous System: Affective Governance from Mao to Xi." *China Quarterly* 248:290–51.

Sorge, Antonio, and Jonathan Padwe. 2015. "The Abandoned Village? Introduction to the Special Issue." *Critique of Anthropology* 35 (3):235–47.

Stammler-Gossman, Anna. 2010. "'Political' Animals of Sakha Yakutia." In *Good to Eat, Good to Live With: Nomads and Animals in Northern Eurasia and Africa*, edited by Florian Stammler and Hiroki Takakura, 153–78. Sendai: Center for Northeast Asian Studies, Tohuku University.

Steinmüller, Hans. 2011. "The Moving Boundaries of Social Heat: Gambling in Rural China." *Journal of the Royal Anthropological Institute* 17 (2):263–80.

Stépanoff, Charles, and Charlotte Marchina, Camille Fossier, and Nicholas Bureau. 2017. "Animal Autonomy and Intermittent Coexistences: North Asian Modes of Herding." *Current Anthropology* 58 (1):57–81.

Stone, Glenn D. 2018. "Agriculture as Spectacle." *Journal of Political Ecology* 25 (1):656–85.

Straub, Christopher T., James A. Counts, Diep M. N. Nguyen, et al. 2018.

"Biotechnology of Extremely Thermophilic Archaea." *Fems Microbiology Reviews* 42 (5):543–78.

Sturgeon, Janet C. 2007. "Pathways of 'Indigenous Knowledge' in Yunnan, China." *Alternatives: Global, Local, Political* 32 (1):129–53.

Sulek, Emilia R. 2019. *Trading Caterpillar Fungus in Tibet: When Economic Boom Hits Rural Area.* Amsterdam: Amsterdam University Press.

———. 2022. "Donkey Selfies: Chinese Roads in Kyrgyzstan." *Roadsides* 8:17–22.

Svendsen, Mette N. 2021. "Pigs, People, and Politics: The Redrawing of Denmark's Biological, Political, Geographical, and Genomic 'Borders.'" *BioSocieties* 18:714–32.

Svendsen, Mette N., and Lene Koch. 2013. "Potentializing the Piglet in Experimental Neonatal Research." *Current Anthropology* 54 (S7):S118–28.

Svensson, Marina, and Christina Maags. 2018. "Mapping the Chinese Heritage Regime: Ruptures, Governmentality, and Agency." In *Chinese Heritage in the Making: Experiences, Negotiations and Contestations,* edited by Marina Svensson and Christina Maags, 11–40. Amsterdam: Amsterdam University Press.

Swancutt, Katherine. 2016. "The Art of Capture: Hidden Jokes and the Reinvention of Animistic Ontologies in Southwest China." *Social Analysis* 60 (1):74–91.

Swanson, Heather A., Marianne E. Lien, and Gro Ween, eds. 2018. *Domestication Gone Wild: Politics and Practices of Multispecies Relations.* Durham: Duke University Press.

Tamminen, Sakari. 2019. *Biogenetic Paradoxes of the Nation: Finncattle, Apples, and Other Genetic-Resource Puzzles.* Durham: Duke University Press.

Tan, Gillian G. 2018. *Pastures of Change: Contemporary Adaptations and Transformations among Nomadic Pastoralists of Eastern Tibet.* Cham: Springer.

Tang Jinwang. 2013. "Alashan wenhua mingren tanfang: Nashun—Alashan zhi mei" (An interview with an important figure in Alasha culture: Nasun—the beauty of Alasha). Alasha wenhua wang (Alasha culture net). http://www.alswh.com/Article_Show.asp?ArticleID=4991.

Tang Rongyao. 2009. "Alashan luotuo: Youyang tuoling he beizhuang lishi hou de yuandun" (The Alasha camel: Disappearing in the wake of melodious camel bells and tragic histories). Alasha wenhua wang (Alasha culture net). http://www.alswh.com/Article_Print.asp?ArticleID=5379.

Tang, Rufei, and Michael C. Gavin. 2015. "Degradation and Re-emergence of the Commons: The Impacts of Government Policies on Traditional Resource Management Institutions in China." *Environmental Science and Policy* 52:89–98.

Tarasova, Zoia. 2020. *Human Anxieties, Bovine Solutions: Political Subtexts of Native Cattle Conservation in North-Eastern Siberia.* PhD diss., University of Cambridge.

Taveirne, Patrick. 2004. *Han-Mongol Encounters and Missionary Endeavours: A History of the Scheut in Ordos (Hetao), 1874–1911.* Leuven: Leuven University Press.

Teets, Jessica C. 2013. "Let Many Civil Societies Bloom: The Rise of Consultative Authoritarianism in China." *China Quarterly* 213:19–38.

Thomas, Alun. 2018. *Nomads and Soviet Rule: Central Asia under Lenin and Stalin*. New York: I. B. Tauris.

Thrift, Eric. 2014. "'Pure Milk': Dairy Production and the Discourse of Purity in Mongolia." *Asian Ethnicity* 15 (4):492–513.

———. 2016. "Pastoralism beyond Livestock." Eric Thrift website, January 13. http://mcdrc.org/ericdthrift/research/pastoralism-beyond-livestock/.

Tiezzi, Shannon. 2013. "The Mass Line Campaign in the 21st Century." *The Diplomat*, December 27.

Tighe, Justin. 2005. *Constructing Suiyuan: The Politics of Northwestern Territory and Development in Early Twentieth-Century China*. Leiden: Brill.

Tracy, Megan. 2013. "Pasteurizing China's Grasslands and Sealing in *Terroir*." *American Anthropologist* 115 (3):437–51.

———. 2016. "Multimodality, Transparency, and Food Safety in China." *PoLAR: Political and Legal Anthropology Review* 39 (S1):34–53.

———. 2018. "(Re)making Quality in China's Dairy Industry." *Asian Anthropology* 7 (4):237–53.

Tsang, Steve. 2009. "Consultative Leninism: China's New Political Framework." *Journal of Contemporary China* 18 (62): 865–80.

Tsetsenbilig and Tsagatai. 2013. *Alasha mongolchuudiin tseer yos* (The taboos and customs of the Alasha Mongols). Hohhot: Neimenggu Wenhua Chubanshe (Inner Mongolia Cultural Publishing House)

Tsing, Anna Lowenhaupt. 2003. "Natural Resources and Capitalist Frontiers." *Economic and Political Weekly* 38 (48):5100–5106.

Turnbull, Jonathon, and Maan Barua. 2023. "Living Waste, Living on Waste." *Transactions of the Institute of British Geographers* 48 (8):474–90.

Ujeed, Hürelbaatar. n.d. "Creating A Supra-Ethnic Identity and Regional Identities in the Inner Mongolian Autonomous Region, China." Unpublished paper.

———. 2015. "The Social and Cultural Practices of Buddhism: The Local Context of Inner Mongolia in the First Half of the Twentieth Century." In *Buddhism in Mongolian History, Culture, and Society*, edited by Vesna A. Wallace, 280–91. Oxford: Oxford University Press.

Upton, Caroline. 2005. "Institutions in a Pastoral Society: Processes of Formation and Transformation in Postsocialist Mongolia." *Comparative Studies of South Asia, Africa, and the Middle East* 25 (3):584–99.

———. 2014. "The New Politics of Pastoralism: Identity, Justice, and Global Activism." *Geoforum* 54:207–16.

Vandergeest, Peter, and Nancy L. Peluso. 1995. "Territorialization and State Power in Thailand." *Theory and Society* 24:385–426.

Vasantkumar, Chris. 2012. "Han at *Minzu*'s Edges: What Critical Han Studies Can Learn From China's 'Little Tibet.'" In *Critical Han Studies*, edited by

Thomas S. Mullaney, James Leibold, and Stéphane Gros, 234–56. Berkeley: University of California Press.

Vidal, Fernando, and Nélia Dias. 2016. "Introduction: The Endangerment Sensibility." In *Endangerment, Biodiversity and Culture*, edited by Fernando Vidal and Nélia Dias, 1–38. Abingdon: Routledge.

Vitebsky, Piers. 2005. *The Reindeer People: Living with Animals and Spirits in Siberia*. London: Harper Perennial.

von Schnitzler, Antina. 2013. "Traveling Technologies: Infrastructure, Ethical Regimes, and the Materiality of Politics in South Africa." *Cultural Anthropology* 28 (4):670–93.

Voyles, Traci. 2015. *Wastelanding: Legacies of Uranium Mining in Navajo Country*. Minneapolis: University of Minnesota Press.

Vreeland, Herbert H. 1953. *Mongol Community and Kinship Structure*. New Haven, CT: Human Relations Area Files.

Wahlberg, Ayo. 2012. "China as an 'Emerging Biotech Power.'" *Third World Quarterly* 33 (4):623–36.

Waldron, Scott, Colin Brown, and Adam M. Komarek. 2014. "The Chinese Cashmere Industry: A Global Value Chain Analysis." *Development Policy Review* 32 (5):589–610.

Wallace, Vesna A. 2012. "Mongolian Livestock Rituals: Appropriations, Adaptations, Transformations." In *Understanding Religious Ritual: Theoretical Approaches and Innovations*, edited by John P. Hoffman, 168–85. Abingdon: Routledge.

Wang, Chen. 2019. "Chinese Consumers Ignore Calls to Eat Less Beef." *China Dialogue*, April 3. https://chinadialogue.net/en/business/11166-chinese -consumers-ignore-calls-to-eat-less-beef/.

Wang Qiucai. 2016. "Alashan tuodao yu sichou zhi lu" (Alasha's caravan routes and the silk road). *Qianjin luntan (Forum for progress)* 1:60–61.

Wang Xiaochun. 2021. "Alashan Youqi: Yi qun luotuo yi ge chanye zhifu yi fang" (Alasha Right Banner: A herd of camels, an industry, a region gets rich). *Neimenggu Xinhua wang* (Inner Mongolia New China website). http://www .nmg.xinhuanet.com/xwzx/xxfb/2021-08/23/c_1127787455.htm.

Wang, Xiaowei. 2020. *Blockchain Chicken Farm and Other Stories of Tech in China's Countryside*. New York: Fararr, Straus and Giroux.

Wang, Xinxin, and Kevin Lo. 2022. "Pastoralism and Conservation: The Politics and Notions of Environmental Justice under the Grazing Ban Policy in Inner Mongolia." *Political Geography* 99:1–11.

Wang, Yi. 2021. *Transforming Inner Mongolia: Commerce, Migration, and Colonization on the Qing Frontier*. Lanham, MD: Rowman and Littlefield.

Wang, Yuting. 2018. "The Making of China's 'Good Muslims': From Middleman Minority to Cultural Ambassadors." *China Review* 18 (4):131–54.

Wang, Zuoyue. 2014. "The Cold War and the Reshaping of Transnational Science in China." In *Science and Technology in the Global Cold War*, edited by Naomi Oreskes and John Krige, 343–70. Cambridge, MA: MIT Press.

Weiner, Benno. 2020. "The Aporia of Re-remembering: Amdo's 'Early Liberation Period' in the Qinghai *Wenshi Ziliao*." In *Conflicting Memories: Tibetan History under Mao Retold*, edited by Robert Barnett, Benno Weiner, and Françoise Robin, 41–77. Leiden: Brill.

Weis, Tony. 2013. *The Ecological Hoofprint: The Global Burden of Industrial Livestock*. London: Zed.

Weisiger, Marsha L. 2011. *Dreaming of Sheep in Navajo Country*. Seattle: University of Washington Press.

Weszkalnys, Giza. 2016. "A Doubtful Hope: Resource Affect in a Future Oil Economy." *Journal of the Royal Anthropological Institute* 22 (S1):127–46.

White, Thomas. 2021. "Pastoralism after Culture: Environmental Governance and Human-Animal Estrangement at China's Ecological Frontier." *Journal of the Royal Anthropological Institute* 27:30–48.

———. 2023. "Sparks from the Friction of Terrain: Transport Animals, Borderlands, and the Territorial Imagination in China." *Environment and Planning D: Society and Space 41 (3):433–50.*

White, Thomas, and Natasha Fijn. 2020. "Introduction: Resituating Domestication in Inner Asia." *Inner Asia* 22:162–82.

Williams, Dee M. 2000. "Representations of Nature on the Mongolian Steppe: An Investigation of Scientific Knowledge Construction." *American Anthropologist* 102 (3):503–19.

———. 2002. *Beyond Great Walls: Environment, Identity, and Development on China's Grasslands*. Stanford, CA: Stanford University Press.

Winter, Tim. 2019. *Geocultural Power: China's Quest to Revive the Silk Roads for the Twenty-First Century*. Chicago: University of Chicago Press.

Woodworth, Max D. 2017. "Disposable Ordos: The Making of an Energy Resource Frontier in Western China." *Geoforum* 78:133–40.

Worster, Donald. *1994. Nature's Economy: A History of Ecological Ideas. Cambridge: Cambridge University Press.*

Wu Ning. 2015. "Alashan mengguzu yu luotuo de hudong ji qi shengtai yishi" (The interaction between Alasha Mongols and their camels and its ecological significance). *Zhongyan minzu daxue xuebao* (*Zhexue shehui kexue ban*) (Journal of Minzu University of China [Philosophy and social sciences edition]) 42 (3):70–74.

———. 2018. "Shenghuo shijian yu fei wuzhi yichan: Yi Alashan mengguzu yangtuo xisu 'fei yi' xiangmu wei ge an" (Living practice and intangible cultural heritage: A case study of Mongolian camel raising custom in Alasha). *Zhongyan Minzu Daxue Xuebao* (*Zhexue shehui kexue ban*) (Journal of Minzu University of China [Philosophy and social sciences edition]) 5 (45):130–35.

———. 2019. "Goujian shengtai wenming de bentu shiyu: Jiyu Alashan muqu ren-tuo guanxi de sikao" (A local perspective on the construction of ecological civilization: Reflecting on the relationship between humans and camels in Alasha's pastoral regions). *Qinghai Minzu Daxue Xuebao (Shehui kexue ban)* (Journal of Qinghai Nationalities University [Social sciences edition]). 1:74–81.

Wu, Sarina. 2020. "To Share or Not to Share: Contested Heritage in Inner Mongolia, China: A Case of Overtone Singing (*Khoomei*)." *International Journal of Heritage Studies* 26 (3):267–80.

Wu, Xu. 2014. "The Farmhouse Joy (*Nongjiale*) Movement in China's Ethnic Minority Villages." *Asia Pacific Journal of Anthropology* 15 (2):158–77.

Wu Yihang and Sheng Lianxiang. 2016. "Alashan luotuo chongbai ji jisi xisu" (Alasha camel worship and veneration customs). *Cai zhi* (Ability and wisdom) 11:218–20.

Wulanfu. 1990. *Wulanfu lun muqu gongzuo* (Ulanhu on policies toward pastoral regions). Hohhot: *Neimenggu Renmin Chubanshe* (Inner Mongolian People's Publishing House).

Wunimenghe. 2015. "Youmu wenhua de chuancheng yu fazhan: Lun luotuo yu caoyuan shengtai de guanxi" (The continuation and development of nomadic culture: On the relationship between camels and the grassland ecology). *Yuanshengtai minzu wenhua xuekan* (Journal of original ecological national culture) 7 (3):3–9.

Wuricaihu. 2017. "Gebi mutuo wenhua de shengtai jiazhi" (The ecological value of Gobi camel herding culture). In Batuchulu and Siqinbielige, *Silu tuoling*, 174–80.

Xinhua. 2012. "Mijing Alashan" (The hidden land of Alasha). *Xinhua*, April 10. http://www.nmg.xinhuanet.com/nmgwq/als/lylibrary/2012-04/10/c_111757872.htm.

Yan, Hairong. 2003. "Spectralization of the Rural: Reinterpreting the Labor Mobility of Rural Young Women in Post-Mao China." *American Ethnologist* 30 (4):578–96.

Yan, Hairong, and Yiyuan Chen. 2013. "Debating the Rural Cooperative Movement in China, the Past and the Present." *Journal of Peasant Studies* 40 (6):955–81.

Yan, Yunxiang. 2012. "Food Safety and Social Risk in Contemporary China." *Journal of Asian Studies* 71 (3):705–29.

———. 2017. "The Ethics and Politics of Patient-Physician Mistrust in Contemporary China." *Developing World Bioethics* 18 (1):7–15.

Yang, Haiying. 2017. "The Truth about the Mongolian Genocide during the Cultural Revolution." *Asian Studies* 6:1–75.

Yang, Jie. 2014. "The Politics of Affect and Emotion: Imagination, Potentiality and Anticipation in East Asia." In *The Political Economy of Affect and Emotion in East Asia*, edited by Jie Yang, 2–28. Abingdon: Routledge.

Yang, Yimin. 2020. "Dairying Transformed Mongolia." *Nature Ecology and Evolution* 4:288–89.

Ye Qianji. 1988. *Shengtai nongye: Nongye de weilai* (Ecological agriculture: The future of agriculture). Chongqing: Chongqing Chubanshe.

Yeh, Emily T. 2009. "Greening Western China: A Critical View." *Geoforum* 40 (5):884–94.

———. 2013a. "The Politics of Conservation in Contemporary Rural China." *Journal of Peasant Studies* 40:1165–88.

———. 2013b. *Taming Tibet: Landscape Transformation and the Gift of Chinese Development*. Ithaca, NY: Cornell University Press.

———. 2014a. "Reverse Environmentalism: Contemporary Articulations of Tibetan Culture, Buddhism, and Environmental Protection." In *Religion and Ecological Sustainability in China*, edited by James Miller, Dan Smyer Yu, and Peter van der Veer, 194–219. London: Routledge.

———. 2014b. "Tibet in China's Environmental Movement." In *On the Fringes of the Harmonious Society: Tibetans and Uyghurs in Socialist China*, edited by Trine Brox and Ildikó Bellér-Hann, 235–62. Copenhagen: NIAS.

———. 2022. "The Cultural Politics of New Tibetan Entrepreneurship in Contemporary China: Valorisation and the Question of Neoliberalism." *Transactions of the Institute of British Geographers* 47 (1):139–52.

Yeh, Emily T., and Gaerrang. 2011. "Tibetan Pastoralism in Neoliberalizing China: Continuity and Change in Gouli." *Area* 43 (2):165–72.

Yeh, Emily T., and Mark Henderson. 2008. "Interpreting Urbanization in Tibet: Administrative Scales and Discourses of Modernization." *Journal of the International Association of Tibetan Studies* 4:1–44.

Yeh, Emily T., and Kunga T. Lama. 2013. "Following the Caterpillar Fungus: Nature, Commodity Chains, and the Place of Tibet in China's Uneven Geographies." *Social and Cultural Geography* 3:318–40.

Yeh, Emily T., and Elizabeth Wharton. 2016. "Going West and Going Out: Discourses, Migrants, and Models in Chinese Development." *Eurasian Geography and Economics* 57 (3):286–315.

Yiletu. 2019. "Alashan youqi fazhan luotuo chanye daidong tuopin jingyan diaocha yu sikao" (Inquiring into and reflecting on the experience of poverty alleviation through the development of the camel industry in Alasha Right Banner). Meili Alashan Youqi (Beautiful Alasha Right Banner), December 5. https://baijiahao.baidu.com/s?id=1652065219067644413.

Yu Yuan and Li Xiancheng. 2021. "Yu Yuexian cu si 'luotuo zhi xiang' beihou: Bu shou yueshu de shamo zhi chuan, ruhe yu feiben de qiche gongcun" (The camel country context to Yu Yuexian's sudden death: How can the unrestrained ships of the desert co-exist with fast-moving cars). *Jimu xinwen* (Far-sighted news), August 8. https://www.163.com/dy/article/GH269LQS 053469LG.html.

Yu, Fei. 2019. "New Yak Breed Brings Herders Renewed Hope." *China Daily*, July 8. https://www.chinadaily.com.cn/a/201907/08/WS5d229d05a3105895c2e 7c2d4.html.

Yuan Pei. 2014 "Nongyebu Xiuding *guojiaji chuqin ziyuan baohu minglü*" (The Bureau of Agriculture's revised 'list of national livestock protected genetic resources'). *Zhongguo xumuye zazhi* (The Chinese journal of animal husbandry) 6:10–11.

Zee, Jerry. 2019. "Groundwork in the Margins: Symbiotic Governance in a Chinese Dust-Shed." In *Frontier Assemblages: The Emergent Politics of Resource Frontiers in Asia*, edited by Jason Cons and Michael Eilenberg. Oxford: Wiley.

———. 2020. "Machine Sky: Social and Terrestrial Engineering in a Chinese Weather System." *American Anthropologist* 122 (1):9–20.

Zhang, Amy. 2020. "The Black Soldier Fly: An Indigenous Innovation for Waste Management in Guangzhou." In *Can Science and Technology Save China?*, edited by Susan Greenhalgh and Li Zhang, 89–99. Ithaca, NY: Cornell University Press.

Zhang Linhu. 2020. "Luotuo 'dagong,' mumin 'tang zhuan'! Zhege Gebi tan shang fa 'tuo cai'" (Camels go to work while herders have a lie-down! In this Gobi region, they've struck 'camel gold'). *Zhongguo xinwenwang* (China news), June 26. https://www.chinanews.com.cn/sh/2020/06-26/9222489 .shtml.

Zhang Peiye, Dalai, Shouyi Tian, Lei Ning, Huanle Li, and Guochen Yang. 1991. "Shuangfengtuo xuanyu he pinzhong qun jianli de yanjiu" (Research on the establishment of selective breeding and a breeding herd for the bactrian camel). *Neimenggu xumu kexue* (Inner Mongolia animal husbandry science) 2:18–21.

Zhang, Wei, Xiaolin Xu, Hui Zhang, and Qiang Chen. 2016. "Online Participation Chaos: A Case Study of Chinese-Government Initiated E-Polity Square." *International Journal of Public Administration* 39 (14):1195–1202.

Zhang, Xia. 2020. "'The People's Commune Is Good': Precarious Labor, Migrant Masculinity, and Post-Socialist Nostalgia in Contemporary China." *Critical Asian Studies* 52 (4):530–49.

Zhongguo Xinwen Wang (China news net). 2023. "Neimenggu alu keerqin caoyuan youmu xitong bei lianheguo liangnong zuzhi shouyu quanqiu zhongyao nongye wenhua yichan di" (Inner Mongolia Ar Khorchin Grassland Nomadic System is declared a site of globally important agricultural heritage by UNESCO). May 24. https://baijiahao.baidu.com/s?id=1766784162231571866.

Zhou Jianguo. 2015. "'Luotuo jingshen' ying shi hao ganbu de biyao pinzhi" ('Camel spirit' should be a necessary quality in good cadres). *Zhongguo Gongchandang Xinwen Wang* (CCP News website), June 18. http://cpc.people.com .cn/pinglun/n/2015/0618/c241220-7176863.html.

Zhou Wanyou, and Tianzuo Zhao. 1985. "Liyong huangmo, fazhan luotuo"

(Utilize the desert, develop camels). *Xinjiang nongye kexue* (Xinjiang agricultural sciences) 4:46–47.

Zhou, Wei. 2010. "Riding Roughshod in Inner Mongolia." *China Dialogue*, November 23. https://chinadialogue.net/en/nature/3958-riding-roughshod -in-inner-mongolia/.

Zhou, Yongming. 2013. "Branding Tengchong: Globalization, Road Building, and Spatial Reconfigurations in Yunnan, Southwest China." In *Cultural Heritage Politics in China*, edited by Tani Blumenfield and Helaine Silverman, 247–59. New York: Springer.

Zhu, Yuchao, and Dongyan Blachford. 2015. "'Old Bottle, New Wine'? Xinjiang *Bingtuan* and China's Ethnic Frontier Governance." *Journal of Contemporary China* 25 (97):25–40.

Zinda, John A. 2019. "Managing the Anthropocene: the Labour of Environmental Regeneration". *Made in China Journal* 3 (4):62– 67.

Zinda, John A., and Jun He. 2020. "Ecological Civilization in the Mountains: How Walnuts Boomed and Busted in Southwest China." *Journal of Peasant Studies* 47 (5):1052–76.

Index

Page numbers in *italics* refer to illustrations.

dispossession at, 138, 165; extractive, 126–41; imperial, 110, 189n6; livestock, 16, 21, 165; pastoral, 20, 23, 98; 124; resource, 18, 124, 129, 137, 144; scientific, 144, 148–51, 171–74; wildness of, 20, 158, 165. *See also* remoteness

Gansu, *23*, 29, 128, 133, 134, 161, 181n2; Minqin County in, 36, 82, 96, 113
gelding ritual, 91–92
gender, 91, 92, 145, 188n16
genetic resources, 85, 119, 123–24, 137, 141, 169, 172, 175; conservation zones, 12, *81*, 86; FAO action plan for, 123; as narrative resources, 174; origins of concept, 16. *See also* conservation
goats, 77, 82, 87, 136; cashmere, 2, 4, 39, 41, 82, 89, 126, 190n4; as cause of desertification, 3, 5, 15; fortune-beckoning ritual for, 62; in vitro fertilization of, 150; lack of comparative advantage in, 156–57; market price for meat of, 175; milking of, 145; mode of herding, 80, 83, 85, *87*, 88, 90, 92, 94; obscuring of, 63; sale of, to comply with grazing ban, 5, 139, 162, 175–78, *177*; stocking limits applied to, 42, 63, 84, 86. *See also* sheep; *tavan khoshuu mal*
governmentality, 104–5
grassland culture, 44–47
grassland degradation, discourse of, 3, 4, 7, 10, 130, 169
grass-livestock balance, 84–85
grazing ban (*jinmu*), 11, 18, 51, *81*, 118, 160, 162, 168, 169, 175–76, *177*, 180n8; as cause of urbanization, 100, 118; criticism of, 43; and extraction of resources, 130; green grabbing via, 142; herder choice, 84–85

Han Chinese, 22, 47, 64, 95, 122, 124, 127, 131, 133, 134, 136, 140, 177, 180n7; consumers, 136–37, 140, 162; farmers, 23, 31, 32, 36, 34, 51, 78, 181n5; foodways, 95, 96, 189n1; intellectuals, 6, 48, 64, 66, 101, 116, 170; migration from Minqin County (Gansu), 32, 113, 128; officials, 7, 19, 31, 44, 56; pastoralists, 89, 94–98, 160, 167, 176, 187n8; Qing-era restrictions on migration of, 129, 181n4; scientists, 9–10, 37, 43, 165, 173; settler colonization of Inner Mongolia, 11, 31–37, 45, 51, 82, 94, 124, 128, 183n18; tourists, 121, 139, 141; traders, 139, 186n3
heritage: agricultural systems, 40–41, 51, 169, 170, 177; and BRI, 49; camel husbandry as, 6, 29, 42, 53–76, 97, 107, 119, 169, 176, 188n3; Chinese media coverage of, 24, *25*, 74; competition with Mongolia, 12, 180–81n13; conflicts of authority over, 53–76; culinary, 121; folk songs as, 178; and issue framing, 12, 42, 51, 63, 75, 170; as local knowledge, 42–43; and memories of early socialist period, 100, 109–10, 120, 119; negative evaluations of, 42, 71, 74; as politics, 12–13, 29, 39–44, 51, 97; publications on, 17, 111, 112, 116; as rescaling, 41, 51, 53–76; rituals as, 53–76, 185n5; state promotion of, 13, 22, 28, 41, 52, 71–76; and state-society relations, 53–76; and taming of camels, 109, 120; and tourism, 41, 51, 71–75; transmitters of, 28, 54–55, 60, 68, 169. *See also* camel culture; camel nose peg; camel tack; intangible cultural heritage

Hohhot, 3, 6, 22, 24, 38, 122, 132, 170; universities in, 17, 22, 127, 148, 150

horses: conservation of, 11; decline in numbers of, 77, 82; as draft animals, 111; high regard of Mongols for, 13, 108–9, 184n21; mode of herding, 88, 90, 94; racing of, 42, 176; *See also* cattle; goats; sheep

household responsibility system, 82, 101

Hui, 32, 47, 60, 98, 130, 134, 173; as camel traders, 127, 136, 139; definition of, 181–82n7; migration of, 32, 97; pastoralists, 52, 93

hukou, 187n12

Humphrey, Caroline, 118–19, 188n2

hybridity, 14, 15, 47–48, 95

indigeneity, 9, 76

indigenous innovation, 18, 106, 151–54, 171

intangible cultural heritage, 12, 28, 29, 40, 53–54, 58, 63, 109, 111, 169

Iran, 172–73

Islam, 22, 59, 181–82n7, 182n8. *See also* Muslim Mongols

issue framing, 12, 169

Japan, 2, 3, 4, 30, 33, 115, 150, 155

Jindandao Incident, 31

jinmu. See grazing ban

Khalkha, 32, 46, 128. *See also* Mongolia, independent country of

Khoshuud, 30, 32, 46, 128

Kinzley, Judd, 189n6

labor, 43, 68, 81, 144; animal, 108–9, 111, 115–17; cooperation in, 83, 90–91, 97, 109, 114; interspecies, 100, 109; reduction of, 105–7, 114, 118, 120, 152, 157, 159, 178; shortages, 86, 100, 118, 119, 159; socialist

reordering of, 111, 113. *See also* pastoralism

language, 25, 26, 58, 78, 93, 98, 147, 178; in cities, 164, 180n7; and *minzu* classification, 31, 32, 47; policies toward Mongolian, 14, 48, 170, 178, 190n9

Lattimore, Owen, 184n25, 185n2

law, 136–38, 190n9

Li, Yifei, 7

Liu, Shurun, 10

livestock improvement, 16, 35, 38, 99, 106, 172. *See also* breeding

Lorimer, Jamie, 103

Man and the Biosphere initiative, 9, 109. *See also* UNESCO

market reforms, 4, 5, 119, 129

materiality, 11, 97

mining, 71, 74, 76, 121, 133, 164; boom in Inner Mongolia, 5, 130–31; environmental damage caused by, 56, 138; ethnic dimension of, 131, 133; relationship with local state, 55, 66–67, 76, 131, 164; small-scale, 23, 131, 137, 138, 140

minjian, 8, 58, 67, 70

Minqin County. *See under* Gansu

minzu, 52, 58, 59, 95–96; blending of, 47; building, 31–33; classification, 31, 95; second-generation policies, 48, 170; translation of, 180n10; *Zhonghua minzu* (Chinese nation), 47, 48, 49, 189n10

Minzu Games, 38

mobility: of camels, 5, 11, 90, 93–94, 87, 97, 102, 170–71, 176; coordination during socialist period, 81; ecological benefits of, 4, 101; as heritage, 41; modernity of, 41, 98–107; states' fear of, 158. *See also otor*; techno-pastoralism

state environmentalism, 1, 12, 22, 29, 42, 54, 62, 63, 65, 75, 105, 118, 161, 164–65, 170; as contested project, 5–10, 39–44, 51, 101–4, 167–70; positive assessments of, 6; scholarly critiques of, 7. *See also* authoritarian environmentalism; coercive environmentalism; payments for ecosystem services

stocking limits, 5, 12, 62, 100, 123, 157, 168, 178; exemption of camel from, 42, 75, 101, 123

strange stones (*qishi*), 131–35, 136, 137

Swanson, Heather, 10

tavan khoshuu mal (five kinds of livestock), 13, 56, 62, *63*, 108, 176. *See also* cattle; goats; horses; sheep

technology, 2, 35, 100, 105, 120, 123, 143, 144, 174; and hygiene, 163; innovation, 18, 106, 151–54, 171; science and, 6, 17–18, 146, 150, 165, 171–72; and spatial hierarchies in China, 150; surveillance, 17; transfer of, 106, 153. *See also* biotechnology; science; techno-pastoralism; technopolitics; WeChat

techno-pastoralism, 41, 107, 115, 120, 159, 172

technopolitics, 18, 107

temporality, 19, 72, 110, 111, 144, 151; conjoining of primitivity and futurity in camel, 171; politics of time, 107. *See also* anticipation

Tengger Desert, 41

Tibet, 3, 66, 95, 135, 158; Buddhist connections with, 57–59, 67, 76; comparison with pastoralists in, 122, 124, 157, 159; PLA use of Alasha camels in, 117

time. *See* temporality

tourism, 29, 49–52, 55, 59, 93, 133, 135, 139, 140, 172; and commodification of heritage, 41–44, 71–76; and food, 121–22, 125, 141

traditional ecological knowledge, 29, 42, 105, 169

tuimu huancao. See Removing Livestock and Restoring Grassland policy

Ulaan Bukh Desert, 77, 142, 153, 162

Ulaan Möchir, 185n6

Ulanhu, 34–35, 37, 80, 106, 111, 149, 170, 183n14

UNESCO, 40–41, 109, 180–81n13. *See also* Man and the Biosphere initiative

urbanization, 5, 7, 16, 22, 100, 114, 118, 162; conflation with modernity, 156, 162; effects on nonhumans, 119; and herding, 97, 100, 105–7, 109, 118; hollowing out of rural areas, 118, 162; toxicities of, 125. *See also* Bayanhot; Beijing; Hohhot

uuts (boiled sheep's back and tail), 55–56, 60, 69, 70, 73, 93, 189n1

Voyles, Traci, 20

WeChat, 85, 152; bridging rural-urban divide, 122, 141; and marketing of camel products, 125, 139–40, 162–63; as method, 26; and *minzu* identity, 26–27, 123, 127; performance of environmental subjectivity on, 124. *See also* digital care

wild camels, 175, 191n1

wolves, 11, 62, 186n9

Wuhai, 71–72, 161–63

Culture, Place, and Nature

Studies in Anthropology
and Environment

China's Camel Country: Livestock and Nation-Building at a Pastoral Frontier, by Thomas White

Sustaining Natures: An Environmental Anthropology Reader, edited by Sarah R. Osterhoudt and K. Sivaramakrishnan

Fukushima Futures: Survival Stories in a Repeatedly Ruined Seascape, by Satsuki Takahashi

The Camphor Tree and the Elephant: Religion and Ecological Change in Maritime Southeast Asia, by Faizah Zakaria

Turning Land into Capital: Development and Dispossession in the Mekong Region, edited by Philip Hirsch, Kevin Woods, Natalia Scurrah, and Michael B. Dwyer

Spawning Modern Fish: Transnational Comparison in the Making of Japanese Salmon, by Heather Anne Swanson

Upland Geopolitics: Postwar Laos and the Global Land Rush, by Michael B. Dwyer

Misreading the Bengal Delta: Climate Change, Development, and Livelihoods in Coastal Bangladesh, by Camelia Dewan

Ordering the Myriad Things: From Traditional Knowledge to Scientific Botany in China, by Nicholas K. Menzies

Timber and Forestry in Qing China: Sustaining the Market, by Meng Zhang

Consuming Ivory: Mercantile Legacies of East Africa and New England, by Alexandra C. Kelly

Mapping Water in Dominica: Enslavement and Environment under Colonialism, by Mark W. Hauser

Nature Protests: The End of Ecology in Slovakia, by Edward Snajdr
Forest Guardians, Forest Destroyers: The Politics of Environmental Knowledge in Northern Thailand, by Tim Forsyth and Andrew Walker
Being and Place among the Tlingit, by Thomas F. Thornton
Tropics and the Traveling Gaze: India, Landscape, and Science, 1800–1856, by David Arnold
Ecological Nationalisms: Nature, Livelihood, and Identities in South Asia, edited by Gunnel Cederlöf and K. Sivaramakrishnan
From Enslavement to Environmentalism: Politics on a Southern African Frontier, by David McDermott Hughes
Border Landscapes: The Politics of Akha Land Use in China and Thailand, by Janet C. Sturgeon
Property and Politics in Sabah, Malaysia: Native Struggles over Land Rights, by Amity A. Doolittle
The Earth's Blanket: Traditional Teachings for Sustainable Living, by Nancy Turner
The Kuhls of Kangra: Community-Managed Irrigation in the Western Himalaya, by Mark Baker

www.ingramcontent.com/pod-product-compliance
Lightning Source LLC
Chambersburg PA
CBHW020242290326
41929CB00045B/1492